97

Highway 61

Also by William McKeen

Rock and Roll Is Here to Stay: An Anthology

Highway 61

A Father-and-Son Journey through the Middle of America

William McKeen

Photographs by Graham McKeen

W. W. Norton & Company New York London

For information about permission to reproduce selections from this book, write to
Permissions, W. W. Norton & Company, Inc., 500 Fifth Avenue, New York, NY 10110

Manufacturing by Quebecor Fairfield
Book design by Chris Welch
Production manager: Julia Druskin

LIBRARY OF CONGRESS CATALOGING-IN-PUBLICATION DATA
McKeen, William, 1954–
Highway 61 : a father-and-son journey through the middle of America / by William McKeen.
p. cm.
ISBN 0-393-04164-6 (hardcover)
1. United States—Description and travel. 2. United States Highway 61. 3. United States—
History, Local. 4. McKeen, William, 1954– —Journeys—United States. 5. McKeen, William,
1954– —Family. 6. McKeen, Graham. 7. Fathers and sons—United States. I. Title.
E169.04 .M379 2003
977'.034—dc21

2002015985

W. W. Norton & Company, Inc., 500 Fifth Avenue, New York, N.Y. 10110
www.wwnorton.com

W. W. Norton & Company Ltd., Castle House, 75/76 Wells Street, London W1T 3QT

1 2 3 4 5 6 7 8 9 0

For Nicole, my love

Oh God said to Abraham, "Kill me a son"
Abe says, "Man, you must be puttin' me on"
God say, "No." Abe say, "What?"
God say, "You can do what you want Abe, but
The next time you see me comin' you better run"
Well Abe says, "Where do you want this killin' done?"
God says, "Out on Highway 61."

—Bob Dylan, "Highway 61 Revisited"

As I was walking that ribbon of highway
I saw above me that endless skyway:
I saw below me that golden valley:
This land was made for you and me

—Woody Guthrie, "This Land Is Your Land"

Acknowledgments

This book is based on a trip with my son, Graham, in the summer of 2001. Some of the on-the-road observations were supplemented with after-the-fact interviews. Three minor names were changed to protect privacy.

Graham was a superb driver and traveling companion. We didn't share one cross moment during our long drive, and I thank him for spending his summer with me. I also thank the rest of my family for enduring a chaotic few months—Sarah, Mary, Savannah and Nicole and my mother.

Most of the people I want to thank are identified in this book, but I particularly want to honor our hosts—Margaret Hatch in Apple Valley, Minnesota; Terry and Kim Quinn in Bettendorf, Iowa; Ron Cobb in St. Louis; Blake Fontenay in Memphis; Sherry Alexander in New Orleans; and Toby and Lucia Howe in Pensacola. Several people helped by making travel suggestions, copy editing, reading excerpts or helping with research: Pamela Benner, Andrea Billups, Greg Borchard, Kristin Carter, Lisa Duke, Mike Foley, John Freeman, Wayne Garcia, John Griffith, Cynthia Johnson, Kurt Kent, Jon Roosenraad, Renee Schwartz, and Eirit Zakaim.

Two people deserve the preponderance of thanks: my agent and friend, David Hendin, and the brilliant editor Amy Cherry, who took a steamer trunk and turned it into a valise.

Highway 61

Somewhere on Highway 61

We come from the North, crossing the Pigeon River at the drive-through U.S. Customs station.

"Did you hide the stash?" I ask.

"Sure," Graham says. "I stuck it inside a candle."

We pull up by the sign that says WAIT UNTIL YOU ARE SIGNALED TO MOVE FORWARD. Even though there are no other cars, we wait obediently, twenty yards back from the booth. Finally, a customs inspector sticks his head out his window and waves us forward.

"Sorry," Graham says when we pull up to the booth. "I couldn't see you because of the glare."

"That's . . . *OK*." The customs inspector is dark haired, slim, with a thick Nixon-like stubble. He speaks slowly, as if we're dim-bulb children. "Where you fellows from?"

"Gainesville, Florida," Graham says.

The inspector raises his eyebrows. "Those dealer plates?" He nods toward the monitor in his booth that displays a camera's rear view of our bug-spattered Explorer.

"No," Graham says. "Actually, they're University of Florida plates."

"I *thought* they looked different," the inspector says. He sounds like Mr. Rogers. "This your car?" he asks Graham.

"Yes," Graham says. "Well, actually it's my dad's." He leans back to give the inspector a good view of me. "That's him right there." The inspector nods toward me and I smile.

"How long you been in Canada?" We're his only customers and he's in no hurry.

"Just two days," Graham says.

"Not even that." I lean across my son. "We crossed over yesterday noon at Sault Ste. Marie."

For some reason I'm paranoid, even though there is no stash—that's just one of our little jokes. Hell, there isn't even any beer.

The inspector seems puzzled. Does the discrepancy in our memories make him suspicious? "What was your purpose in Canada?"

"We just drove around Lake Superior."

His look: *Why would you want to do that?*

"And what is your destination?"

"New Orleans," Graham says. "We're taking this highway all the way down." He looks past the inspection station, down into Minnesota.

Again the look. The inspector turns toward us, showing his face for the first time. "For what purpose?" he finally asks.

"My dad's writing about it," Graham says.

I smile at the inspector, leaning down to see him across the front seat.

Eye contact, finally. "Start this way," the inspector says. " 'It's bumpy.' "

We smile at him, a pair of grinning dunces.

"Have a safe trip," he says.

"**W**here are we now?" Graham asks.

I look over the two-page Minnesota spread in the road atlas. "Somewhere on Highway 61, along the north shore." I point out the narrow sliver of land north of Lake Superior.

Graham's eighteen and needs a shave. He's taller than I am, and his bright little-boy eyes are heavy lidded with lack of sleep and too much beer. He's a college student and he does what college students do.

"Are we anywhere near a *town?*" he asks. "I could use a Red Bull or something. And I'm sure you have to pee."

My legendary bladder, size of a dime. "As always," I say, glancing at the atlas. "Yeah, in a few more miles there ought to be a convenience store."

Minnesota flashes by outside my window. I live in Florida and I didn't pack a coat—it's late May, for crying out loud. But it's been in the high twenties at night and in the sixties during the day—cold for me. Graham lent me his bright yellow windbreaker this morning. "Weather wimp," he said, pulling it from his backpack.

I wonder if he remembers all my drives up from Florida. As a divorced father, I used to steal weekends and take spring breaks, semester breaks, any time my university cancelled classes, and make fifteen-hour-straight madman drives to be with my kids in Indiana. I never knew how to pack and spent lots of spring breaks bitching about the cold. Graham started calling me "weather wimp" when he was in single digits.

When I think of him—something I do often, since we live so far apart—it's the little boy I see. He couldn't say his *R*'s until he was eight. "Hey, Daddy . . . it's just me, *Gwayham*"—a voice on the phone every afternoon. I'd get his daily rundown of what happened in school; the latest on the Cubs; and his annotated updates on Big-10 basketball.

We still talk on the phone, just not as often. College students have so many social obligations and he's a hard guy to catch. His standard greeting now: "Hey, what's up?" He comes off as a prematurely world-weary dude, heavy sighs a major part of his vocabulary. He sleeps *a lot*, but to hear him talk it's never enough. When he was a little boy, he used to get up before anyone else, pour some Sugar Pops and sit in front of the television to see what happened in the world of baseball after he went to bed. I'd hear him padding around the living room. "Don't worry," he'd call back to my room when he heard me stirring. "It's just me, *Gwayham*."

He earned a D average his first semester in college but redeemed himself in the spring semester with a flurry of Bs.

I'm bringing him on this trip not because of some father-son bonding thing, but because I think he's the child that needs me most right now. My daughters are fine, but Graham doesn't have a clue what he wants to do with his life and so I figured he might as well drive my car. At least I'll get him off his ass for the summer.

And there's something in it for me too. I'm forty-six and he's eighteen, and this may be my last chance to look at him and see the little boy.

Road Warrior

We'd hit the road three days before. "What's the date?" I asked my son as we pulled out of his mother's driveway.

Graham pondered a moment. "Memorial Day, isn't it?"

"Two forty-six in the afternoon; we're finally getting started. Do you want to be Dr. Duke or Dr. Gonzo?"

No hesitation: "Gonzo."

"OK."

Another fantasy. We're not Hunter Thompson characters, just a relatively normal father and son taking a trip together. I'm a college professor, and my son's a college student. We're leaving his hometown, Bloomington, Indiana, for points north. There's no agenda and Graham likes it that way. Last year, we spent a week together in the Florida Keys, waking each day without a plan. Every few minutes, while driving down the Overseas Highway, sandwiched between iridescent blue-green water, he'd exclaim, "Damn! This is beautiful." When I'd suggest a stop—for fishing, swimming or eating—he'd shrug, "Sure, Dad—we're free spirits."

The Keys trip gave us the guiding principle for this summer's trip down Highway 61. *Free spirits*. Start up in Canada, where Highway 61 begins, and free fall to New Orleans, stopping whenever we want and doing whatever we feel.

A good, simple idea when we cooked it up, but a year later so many things have changed.

Sometime during the year, I seemed to have lost my little boy. It wasn't just his going to college (though not *off* to college; he stayed in his hometown and went to Indiana University . . . *my* hometown and *my* college), but that was part of it. He just seemed distant. He moved out of his mother's house, and freedom had affected him. No one told him when to get up and when to go to bed. No one rifled through his drawers—as his mother, my ex-wife, was wont to do—looking for marijuana. No one stood over him to make sure he did his homework.

I'd always had a good, close relationship with my kids, despite the distance between doorways (853 miles), so I experienced withdrawal when Graham moved into a dorm. He couldn't place long-distance calls, so I talked to him only when I managed to catch him.

We talked every day when Graham was in elementary school. We connected long-distance on baseball, then fishing, then music. Growing up, we were buddies. He had wavy hair like mine, but his was a prettier shade of honey brown. When he had to start wearing glasses, he picked a pair matching my tortoise-shells. He also had my frame: short legged, stocky, a little on the husky side. When people told me we looked alike I always said, "He's just like me—only better."

When Graham was eight, I introduced him to my friend Sam in Florida during spring break.

"I met a miniature Bill McKeen today," Sam told his wife.

And so he was—a *mini-me*.

When he was seven, he nominated me for father-of-the-year, a high-water mark of my early fatherhood. "I nominate my father, William McKeen," he wrote in the hometown paper back in Indiana. "He does a lot for me. He plays pool, soccer, basketball, baseball, Frisbee, air hockey and racketball with me. He buys me a lot of toys and goes swimming with me. He takes me to Disney World, Busch Gardens, Boardwalk & Baseball and takes me to baseball games. He takes me to restaurants. He sleeps with me when we are at a hotel."

We paired off in hotels—girls in one bed, Graham and I in the other. His childhood nomination defined a Good-Time Daddy, a long-distance divorced father, taking his kids places, missing the difficult day-to-day parenting the mother does. I wasn't there for the math homework or the history homework, but I felt I was *there* as much as I could be—for a father who lived 853 miles away.

But now I'm *here*—in the passenger seat and Graham is at the wheel. Last week, I was in the Keys with my fiancée, Nicole, a half-Cuban, half-Italian Key West girl, planning our wedding. It'll be a family affair. Nicole's daughter, Savannah, will be flower girl, and my daughters, Sarah and Mary Grace, will be bridesmaids. Graham, of course, will be best man.

After the long weekend in Key West, I spent a few days at work in Gainesville, then hit the road the Sunday of Memorial Day weekend for the long haul to Indiana. It's a trip I've made over three hundred times—sometimes in my sleep—but for the first time, I'm leaving behind a life: my wife-to-be and her four-year-old daughter, soon to be my four-year-old daughter.

I've been making the Florida-Indiana run for sixteen years. It used to be easy; now it's a struggle. This time, the fifteen-hour drive seems like thirty. I attempt napping in a parking lot outside Atlanta. I buy a liter of Diet Pepsi and stop at nearly every exit in Tennessee—I know them all—and when I hit Kentucky, I feel I'm almost home. Five hours later, sacked out in my old room at my mother's house, for the first time all day I'm not sleepy. I stay awake until two, catching up on six months' worth of *People* magazines.

Graham and his sisters have a family reunion (mother's side) out of town every Memorial Day weekend, so I plan to sleep late. After the family reunion, Graham might want to wait a day before hitting the road; we'll miss holiday traffic too. They'll be home around noon, he said on the phone a few days before.

Graham calls around eleven. "We're back. When are we leaving?"

"I thought you might want to rest up from your weekend," I say. "Let's start tomorrow. You guys have fun?"

"Let's leave now. I'm trapped in this house with three women."

"All right. I'm ready when you are."

I'd seen Sarah only a few weeks before. Most of the year, she's at the University of Florida, where I teach. Mary is fourteen, and seeing her is more of a rarity. Somehow—though she has never known a time when her mother and I lived together—we have become very close. In a lot of ways, I think, I am closer to her than to Sarah and Graham. Maybe it's because we were both parental afterthoughts.

Graham's in the front yard when I come up the road. He hugs me and tosses an athletic bag, a backpack and some fishing equipment in the Explorer and flashes something that looks like a loose-leaf notebook.

"Some required listening, *professor*," he says, turning pages of homemade discs in plastic sleeves. "I've been doing research."

I want to spend some time with the girls, but Graham paces the kitchen like a leashed tiger. Sarah has to work and Mary has a school report to finish, so we leave in the early afternoon.

I ceremoniously hand Graham my keys. "Here you go, my man," I say.

He hugs his mother and sisters good-bye and we pull out of the driveway on a hot Indiana Memorial Day.

Provisions

The cooler in the back of the Explorer is stocked with fruit juice, string cheese and vegetables. My mother also packed us a cardboard box from Sam's Club: Captain's Wafers (enough to feed a squadron), sour-cream-and-onion potato chips, two bags of Chips Ahoy!. For clothes, I'd brought mostly rock 'n' roll T-shirts, a couple pairs of jeans and sneakers. I wore my comfortable maroon-and-gray bowling shoes. I brought most essential hygiene products but had somehow forgotten a comb.

I also brought maps, books and a crate of CDs: Bob Dylan, Professor Longhair, Muddy Waters, Toots & the Maytals, Robert Johnson, Tony Bennett, Sunnyland Slim, Miles Davis, Little Richard. Right before leaving Florida, I took a box into Graham's room—really more of a museum of his life with me than an actual, honest-to-God lived-in *room*—and packed some pictures: Graham at nine, rounding third, booking it for home; Graham probably around twelve, holding up a fish we'd caught off the pier at Cedar Key; the two of us, arms locked, in front of the house we rented at Crescent Beach (Sarah must've taken that one). I packed a few old baseball cards, some battered spring-training tickets and his tattered paperback guide to fishing. I also packed the yellowed newspaper that featured my father-of-the-year nomination. I wanted his childhood relics with me.

We have a pretty significant drive before we even get to Highway 61. Anything other than the interstate between Indiana and Florida is bonus to Graham. He was born in Kentucky, but we moved when he was two months old, when I got a job at the University of Oklahoma. Just as I was leaving Oklahoma after four years for my new job at the University of Florida, his mother and I separated, found out we were pregnant, went ahead with the separation, tried to reconcile, separated again, then got divorced. She moved to Indiana with the children, and I stayed in Florida with my job.

On the Indianapolis bypass, slowed by construction, I ask, "Do you remember much about Oklahoma?"

"A few things. I remember that creek near our house. And there was a park across the street, right?"

"Right. Anything else?"

He blinks into the distance, tapping his hand on the steering wheel. "Ah, just flashes here and there. That's about it."

He reaches over and punches me in the arm. "Slugbug!" One of the legacies of a long-ago girlfriend who taught my kids to play. Every time we see a Volkswagen Beetle, it's a race to call it first, then land a punch. Amazingly, no one has gotten seriously hurt over the years.

Graham's travel has been limited. Even Northern Indiana will be new territory. Then we have the wonders of Michigan and Canada—where I've never been. I can't wait to get him to Minnesota, I tell him. My father used to take me there in the summer, and I want to share that with Graham.

I shut up. I can't start gushing all my plans. We'll let things run their course.

The Land Where "Cool" Was Born

Fairmount, Indiana, is a postcard-perfect small town with beautiful old houses and lawns like putting greens. Its distinction is as the birthplace of James Dean, prototype movie rebel. He was a shooting star—three movies, dead and gone, all within eighteen months. *Live fast, die young, leave a good-looking corpse.* I once saw a photo of his Porsche Spyder after the crash, and I doubt the corpse was good looking.

His appeal hit a generation before mine. When I finally saw *Rebel Without a Cause* on TV, I could appreciate his prettiness and what his scene chewing and brooding did for the young people of the 1950s, but it didn't do much for me—though I could certainly understand his attraction to Natalie Wood. As I look back on the movies of that time, Marlon Brando seems a little more natural, and Paul Newman was a more mass-market-friendly antihero. Still, I'm proud James Dean came from my home state because we need help on the *good* side, since we gave the world the Rev. Jim Jones, Charles Manson, John Dillinger and Michael Jackson.

Fairmount's also hometown to "Garfield" creator Jim Davis, CBS News correspondent Phil Jones, and Bob Sheets, director of the

You get teased a lot when you're from Indiana (mostly by people asking "What's a Hoosier?"), so I always took pride that my home state produced James Dean. His hometown of Fairmount calls itself "the land where 'cool' was born."

National Hurricane Center. "The girls around here must feel like shit," Graham says. "They don't put them in the brochures."

It's Memorial Day and Park Cemetery is busy. There are gravel lanes wide enough for cars, but most of the people are on foot. The cemetery is big and, like the rest of the town, immaculate. We drive down a few rows, reading names off markers, smelling wet, freshly cut grass, wind blowing the biting scent of manure from the farm across the road, and the subtle aroma of flowers placed for the holiday. A small sign gives directions to a simple marker—JAMES DEAN—and nothing else.

I wonder how different things would have been without him. Bob Dylan said that seeing James Dean on screen at the Victory Theater in Hibbing was one of the things that ignited him, that made him first want to be different.

"Of course, you know he's probably not really there."

I look at Graham. "Sure he is. They didn't bury him in California."

"No, what I'm saying is . . ." he points a couple of feet to the right. "He's probably here."

"What do you mean?"

"Bodies—they shift after they're planted."

"You're kidding. Where'd you hear that?"

"In class last fall."

So we look at the neatly tended patch of grass next to James Dean's grave. I read the marker and do the math. "Wow. He would have been seventy. Can you imagine James Dean seventy?"

"I'm not sure I can imagine him twenty-five."

"Maybe he's one of those people who had to die young. I read something recently about Dylan, something written about his sixtieth birthday. The writer said he couldn't forgive Dylan for *not* dying young."

"*What?*"

"Yeah, kind of rude. And look at what we would have missed."

It's disrespectful to talk this way in front of James Dean. Maybe he would have had a grand, productive middle age like Dylan. Maybe he would have aged interestingly or become a recluse like Brando. I imagine Dean's Own salad dressing. Then again, maybe dying young spared him the hell of TV *Movies of the Week*.

Connections

This trip is all about connections. We picked Highway 61 because of His Grand Exalted Mystic Bobness and *Highway 61 Revisited*. We picked it because of the blues. We picked it because it goes places Graham has never seen. The highway connects North and South, industrial and rural, black and white, rich and poor. It parallels our greatest river and provides the narrow thread that brings together some of the disparate parts of the country.

It connects me to my past. I've been crossing this highway all of my life. I've been to some of these places with my family, with my father at the wheel. I can remember the aroma of the farm fields in Iowa, the coffee smell on my father's breath, the tinny sound of music from the car's speakers as my dad searched the stations.

When I think of my childhood, it's from the back seat, my father looking at me from the rear-view mirror, my mother teasing him about his driving. He drove fast.

My car is a faded reddish orange 1997 Ford Explorer with a "check engine" light that's been on for thirty thousand miles. I bought it used from two guys named Vinnie and Carmine in Pompano Beach when I was visiting South Florida, and it's six thousand miles overdue for an oil change.

We have to drive north, cross into Canada and pick up Highway 61 where it begins in Thunder Bay. As we drive through Michigan, we're impatient for the real trip to begin. Interstate highways are like network television—they've taken the character out of the country: Georgia looks like Indiana, which looks like Missouri. But for a few rolling hills here and there, it's all the same.

We want to make Canada by nightfall, but after a few hours of Michigan, one wrong turn and a torrential rainstorm—Graham's never driven through anything like this—we stop in Ithaca, a small town in central Michigan. We want something quaint, like the Bates Motel—only without the psychopathic innkeeper.

The Ithaca Motel opens along Main Street like a dime-store Japanese fan. Nothing's changed here since the 1950s, and it looks like the motels where we used to stay when I was a kid—six bucks a night for two double beds and a cot. This one costs forty-five dollars.

We collapse on the beds and Graham cruises the channels, lingering over a baseball game. I hope maybe we'll stay up and have a *Field of Dreams* moment, but he soon goes on, stopping on a documentary about sharks. I take my usual double dose of Tylenol PM and drift off to an Australian accent and urgent warnings of Great Whites.

Waking early is my curse. I check my watch and it's only 6:30. I look over at Graham, in the chaos of his sheets, sleeping the same way he did as a boy—sprawled, bedspread between his legs, fists clenched. He wears boxers, and his big thighs—a gift from me—are arched in runner's position, his face pressed against the pillow. He said to wake him whenever we needed to leave, but I can't bring myself to rouse him. He may look like a man but to me he's still a kid, and my boy needs his sleep.

Stories We Can Tell

The ubiquitous *they* always tell us that at the end of our lives we've spent twenty years asleep. Not me—I'm far behind the curve.

They never offer statistics about driving—about time spent in cars. Think of all of those poor-schmuck commuters stuck in traffic . . . all those soccer moms shuttling their snotty little kids between practices . . . all of those people stuck on the Disney World entrance ramp for weeks at a time. Then there's me. I think I'll end up spending half my life in cars.

Ten years ago, I'd occasionally fly home to see the kids. But it got to be too much trouble (expensive tickets, airport parking and hassles of not living in—or flying to—a city with a decent-sized airport), and I also hated giving up control. The flight schedules were never convenient. Turned out that when I drove home, I got more time with the kids than when I flew. Plus, behind the wheel, I was the boss.

Plato said that the unexamined life is not worth living. Driving gives me time to examine every second of my life. Sometimes on the highway, I drift off and shake myself awake an hour later and realize

I haven't given a thought to driving in all that time. I've been thinking of other trips.

I'd driven all day from Florida, got into my mother's house around midnight, and knocked myself out with a couple of sleeping pills. When I woke in the morning, my mother said that Graham had already called twice.

He was six and I'd come to get him and Sarah for his first full summer in Florida. Mary, just a toddler, is too young for the trip, her mother said.

They lived in an apartment then and when I pulled up, Graham was waiting outside in a blue and white striped shirt ("Parking-Lot League," it said) decorated with red stars, and his battered, ever-present Cubs hat. I got out and hugged him.

"Hey, Boy," I said. "You ready to go?"

He didn't say anything—just stood there, beaming, cheeks puffed. He was big. They grow faster when you see them only once a month. I held his shoulders and looked at him. He was so happy, I thought he might cry.

I press those moments into my mind like flowers in a book. Once, when Sarah was two, I was trying to put her down for a nap. I got in bed next to her and soon realized I was sleepier than she was. She turned to the wall, trying to do what daddy wanted, but not really in the mood. I put my hand across her back. Without spreading my fingers I covered her shoulder to shoulder. I thought, *I want to remember this the rest of my life.* Now she's a tall, charming, stunningly beautiful young woman, and every time I see her I remember that day I held her in one hand.

My memory is legendary in my family. I can remember every rest stop during family trips. I remember what song was playing when we were on I-35 in Oklahoma, driving back to Indiana from a visit to Texas ("Time Is Tight" by Booker T. and the MG's). I remember every motel, including the Alamo Court in Chattanooga—so dirty we slept on the floor because it was cleaner than the bed. I remember the obscenities scrawled on the men's room wall at the Mobil station in Cuba, Missouri. It was the first time I'd seen some of those words written down.

As the youngest, I got stuck with dog detail. There were five of us—Mom, Dad, brother Charlie, sister Suzanne and me—so we had five dogs. We never went anywhere without the dogs, and someone had to struggle with them at rest stops, usually me. At the Christmas dinner table, I remind my family of the time in Riley, Missouri, when everyone else got a hamburger and I was left outside with the dogs. I was the third kid in the family, the bottom feeder.

Graham and Sarah picked on Mary mercilessly when she was little. I tried to comfort her. "Mary, they're just doing their job," I'd say. "You're the third kid, and so it's their job to pick on you. That's what Uncle Charlie and Aunt Suzanne used to do to me." So when they'd be teasing her in the back seat, Mary would say, "Daddy?" I'd look in the mirror as she held up three fingers. "Third kid," she'd say.

Mary started making our summer trips when she turned five. Graham and Sarah fought over the shotgun seat. Mary sat in back, being teased by whichever sibling was pulling the shift with her.

I'd tell stories to pass time. Graham liked the one about the night he was born. His labor kept us up all night and when he was delivered, his ear was folded down on his cheek. *Well that's all right*, I thought. *It's no big deal . . . we can fix it.* Then the ear popped up. *All right*, I thought. *Now he's perfect.* Graham loved that story and used it when he wrote his autobiography in sixth grade.

Graham and Mary loved to hear stories about big sister Sarah when she was little. She called vegetables *beshbettles* and was obsessed with the Wicked Witch from *The Wizard of Oz*. When we took her trick or treating the first time (as Super Grover), she lagged between houses and I finally realized she thought she had to eat the candy from one house before getting any at the next.

"What a doofus," Graham would say.

"Shut up," Sarah would say. "I didn't have proper instructions."

I didn't have any stories like that about Mary. When her mother and I separated, she left Florida, five months pregnant, to go to Indiana.

Since Sarah was born on October 8 and Graham on June 8, I figured the stars would line up for Mary's arrival on March 8. That date fell during my spring break, so I drove up from Florida and planned to preside over her birth. It didn't happen. Back in Florida, still recovering from the drive, I got a call two days later that my ex-wife was in labor. I started driving around three in the afternoon and around midnight, in the mountains of southern Tennessee, I fell asleep. If it hadn't been for an otherworldly light, I would be dead.

"Look, Daddy."

Every year, right after we pass through the rolling hills south of Manchester, Tennessee, Mary sits up and begins to look for a neon sign that runs the length of a huge fireworks outlet, nudged between the east- and west-bound lanes on I-24, in a valley near Lookout Mountain.

"That's the sign that saved your life."

Graham groans, world weary even at nine. "Get over it, Mary."

The steady hum of the road stopped as my tires started spitting gravel, and then something so bright appeared, it shone through my eyelids. . . .

TENNESSEE–ALABAMA FIREWORKS

I pulled the wheel back quickly, seconds before I would have gone down a ravine—saved by a surreal, holy glow.

By that time, I knew the baby was born and that she was indeed Mary Grace. Why was I driving so fast, literally (nearly) killing myself? I pulled off on the side of the interstate and closed my eyes, sleeping for a couple of hours while eighteen-wheelers roared by inches from my head.

"That's the sign that saved your life, Daddy."

Every time we pass it, it's the same. A moment of silence. To Mary, it is a shrine.

That's Mary's story. There are so many others about the other kids, and every summer, like ritual, they want them repeated, to pass the time during the long drive.

"I love your stories," Graham says. They're stories about when we all lived together, when we were a family.

Bowling Shoes

I open my eyes—but barely—in Ithaca, as tired as I've felt in my life. *Lord*, I think, *and it's only been one day.* Across the room, in the disaster of his bed, Graham sprawls, inhaling his pillow. I pull on my jeans and let myself out. Surprised by the chill, I shove my hands in my pockets and walk a couple of blocks to downtown Ithaca's social center, a BP station. My arrival breaks up the convenience-store gabfest, as if Ithacans know I'm a stranger from some state to the south. Maybe it's the Alligator Records T-shirt. Maybe it's my hair, which looks like Jimmy Neutron's when I wake. Rifling through Graham's dopp kit in the motel bathroom, I'd realized he'd also forgotten a comb. Maybe I smell funky. I don't care. *Please gimme some coffee.*

Back at the motel I shower, then wake Graham, tugging on his toe. "*'Ey,*" I say, in a cartoon British accent. "*Le's rawk 'n' rowl.*" I think I borrowed that voice from Sam Cutler, the Rolling Stones tour manager in *Gimme Shelter.*

Graham hops out of bed, cleans up and we hit the road. When we stop for breakfast a half hour later at Bob's Big Boy in Mount Clemens, we again draw stares, probably because of my bowling shoes and Graham's maroon-and-tan bowling shirt. Maybe our waitress thinks we're some celebrity father-and-son bowling team, and she's trying to figure out where she saw us on deep cable.

US 127 wraps itself by some gorgeous lakes and cuts through woods still taking on full spring colors. Even when the highway joins I-75—a familiar road to me, since it's the last leg of my Indiana–Florida run—the blandness doesn't dim the beauty of the colorful trees and the rolling hills.

Graham's stoked, happy to finally see Michigan, but also enjoying the responsibility. He's never driven this much, and guiding the War Wagon gives him a feeling of power.

The bridge at the Straits of Mackinac draws an *oh wow!* from Graham worthy of the Keys' Overseas Highway—a slender road over an expanse of shimmering water. The boy sees the world in terms of fishing potential, and that looks good as we cross into the Upper Peninsula. A few boaters huddled in parkas dot the water. As we cross over from Sault Ste. Marie, Michigan, to Sault Ste. Marie, Ontario, it occurs to me that we have no Canadian money. Credit cards will work, but my lovely assortment of plastic is nearly maxed out. "It's great to be in Canada," I tell Graham. "Now let's leave."

We negotiate through Sault Ste. Marie and charge some gas. The liter thing throws me off, and I can't figure if we've gotten a deal or just suffered another oil company gouging. After a few ponderous stop-and-go miles through town, we latch onto the Trans-Canada Highway, which will take us to Thunder Bay, where we'll meet Highway 61. We expect this world to look different, but other than gas prices in liters, this could be Atlanta with a chill.

Outside town, as we point the War Wagon up the highway toward the north shore of Lake Superior, things change: no ugly billboards scar the roadside; litter-free countryside; low speed limits; tiny road signs. A sign up ahead: THUNDER BAY, 690 KM.

"Good God," I say. "I thought we'd get to Thunder Bay this evening."

"It's kilometers, Dad," Graham says. "Can't be that bad." He figures the conversion and comes up with a rough estimate: 420 miles.

"On to Plan B," I say, opening up the atlas to Ontario. Towns freckle the shore. They look really small, spooned into mountainous terrain. There's a national park forty miles before Marathon if we get tired. We have tents and sleeping bags.

The stream that borders Highway 17 is like a curtain of fabric, waving dark blue next to us. Signs offer night moose warnings. Then rock formations begin—pyramids and circles of rocks, all nearly the same size, all looking clean and polished, spaced a few miles apart. Smiley faces are painted on the largest, smoothest rock in the construction. A few advertise names or relationships: "Kim and Colin." The illustrations and the lettering are all remarkably professional looking.

"Even the vandals are neater here," Graham says.

A moose warning sign. Two kilometers later, another sign.

"All right already," Graham says. He points to yet another moose warning.

"It's like they only schedule the moose in these two-kilometer sections," I say. "Think of all the money these signs cost, and then they stick them every two kilometers. Why don't they just put up a sign that says, 'Assloads of Moose Next 60 Miles'?"

"You're in Canada."

"Sorry. *Next 60 Kilometers.*"

Highway 17 remains frustratingly inland from Lake Superior. The road winds through forests and hillsides, the rock sculptures among the few signs of human life. At Pancake Bay, the lake is finally fully visible, wide as an ocean but not as angry.

When we come to the Chippewa River I regret the bowling shoes. We cross a bridge and look down at rapids with tourists hopping around on rocks.

"We're free spirits, right?" Graham says.

He parks near the river and we bound up a trail, but when we get to the river bend, it's too slippery for my tractionless shoes. From a bank overlooking the river I watch my son, in his four-wheel-drive sneakers, cross the river on the flat-rock steps. The sky is cloudless, an unearthly blue. Graham kneels on a large rock in the middle of the river, focusing his camera on the red rocks above, water rushing past him. I sit on the bank and do the *pressing-this-into-memory* thing.

After another hour, we make it to the Michipicoten River, where we finally start to head west. We've been going straight north, and now we're driving into the sunset. Graham pinches out air-guitar solos and steers the car with slight movements of his pinkies.

"That is one *superior* lake," Graham says. "I got to get me a crib up here—some log cabin."

He mouths a funk guitar solo. *"Ching-a, ching-a, ching-a. . . ."* He stops abruptly. "Did you know they have three kinds of Oh Henry! bars here in Canada? I saw them in that gas station when we crossed the border."

"I did not know that."

"Large-packed, regular and . . . something else."

"Wheat germ maybe? They seem like healthy dudes up here."

He resumes the funk guitar solo. I watch him playing air guitar, steering this hurtling machine with his little fingers, sun shining through the bug spatter on the windshield, wind stirring the hair on his forehead.

Goose and Moose

We stop in Wawa for an early supper at the Columbia Restaurant—turkey and dressing, a Thanksgiving in May. "Sign says the population is forty-six hundred," I tell Graham. "But it's so damn small. You think those are metric people?"

A four-ton statue of a Canada goose stands on a pedestal on a bluff over the highway, luring travelers. To Graham's disappointment, the town is not a guitar-playing colony named after the wah-wah pedal. *Wawa* is an Ojibway word for "wild goose." Proud Wawaians like to note that the big goose is the most photographed landmark in North America. I think of Mount Rushmore and the Statue of Liberty, but I wouldn't want to say that to any lumberjacks.

Back on the road, Graham plays some of his homemade discs—some hip-hop (Common, Jurassic 5), fairly straight rock 'n' roll (Incubus) and self-indulgent English whining (Radiohead). But the six-disc player skips with nearly every bump.

"My CDs play all right," I tell him. "Maybe yours are all scratched up. You should keep them in the cases." *My fatherly prodding.* I keep my CDs in my jewel boxes, all alphabetized. I've bought Graham and his sisters tons of CDs over the years—including expensive box sets for Christmas (everyone should own *Star Time* by James Brown, so they all got a copy)—but the kids treat them like Frisbees.

"Whoa." I'm looking out the window and don't see the moose on the road until Graham slows. "Cool," he says.

Two moose stand there, looking toward the hills off to our right.

"What do we do?" he asks, stopping. No drivers in either direction.

"Just sit. It's their road."

The moose are oblivious. The War Wagon rattles like a chain smoker's lung, so the moose *had* to hear us. Finally, they glance our way, blink and slowly walk off the road. When they get to the bank, they hustle off into the trees.

"Damn," Graham says. "I wish I would have gotten a picture. I can't believe it—*I saw some moose.*"

"What do you think of Canada so far?"

"It's *phat,*" he says. "That's *P-H.*"

"I know."

We're on fumes when we make it to Rossport, a little town at the mouth of Nipigon Bay. There's a cluster of cabins around a large building and as we get out of the car, two couples on the balcony hoist mugs of beer our way.

The lobby is a front parlor with a mahogany staircase leading up

The cabins at the Rossport Inn, on the shores of Lake Superior, barely give you enough room to take off your pants. Graham and I took the deluxe two-room cabin at the left.

to the revelers—and probably some rooms. From the room straight ahead, we hear laughter, which stops when we come in. A large, white-bearded man in a gray cashmere sweater, a refugee from the Hemingway look-alike festival in Key West, stoops when he walks into the parlor.

"Hi," I say. "Do you have any rooms?"

"We have cabins. A cabin OK?" His voice is quiet and delicate for such a large man.

We negotiate for the largest of the cabins, so we each have a bed. The innkeeper is eager to help us get settled, but he's busy in the back room. Can we wait a couple of minutes?

"Sure," I say. I nod toward the back room. "You still serving?"

"Just drinks now."

"A beer sounds good," I say.

"Would you like a couple?"

"Oh yeah."

"What kind?" Graham asks.

The innkeeper fixes him with a look. "I'll just get you a beer," he says finally.

He goes into the back room and comes out a moment later with two icy bottles of Sleeman's Cream Ale. After one sip, I realize it is the best beer I have ever had. Graham reclines on a couch, looking out the large picture window over Lake Superior. He's a legal drinker in Canada, and this is one of the peak moments of his life—his first public beer; he feels like a man.

We each get another beer when we check in. If we want light or heat, the innkeeper says, we'll have to flip the circuit breaker and be sure to turn it off in the morning. "We have a good breakfast."

The cabin has a small kitchen and front room and a bedroom barely large enough for the two double beds.

"These Canadians are hearty dudes," I tell Graham. "No blankets. Just a sheet and a bedspread."

"I'll be fine," he says. "When I finish this Sleeman's, I think I'm going to sack out."

It's nearly nine, but there are still shards of light, so we walk to the dock and look across the lake, toward the islands clustered near the shore. Fireflies are thick, like stars come down to earth. The houses of the village show signs of life, but it's real life, not TV life. There's no television in our cabin, no TV at the inn, no dirty-white TV glow from the front rooms of these houses. I lived on military bases overseas when I was a child, so I wasn't weaned on television. When we returned to the states, we stayed at a hotel in New York and I was fascinated by my first television. It required regular feedings of quarters. I watched, transfixed, and when the screen went blank I'd ask Dad for another quarter.

Graham and I don't need passive entertainment tonight. The stars, the conversation, the speculation on Lake Superior fishing and the Sleeman's are enough.

When we get back to the cabin Graham collapses in bed. I read *The History of the Blues* by Francis Davis, preparing for our trip south.

When a train—horn sounding, lights piercing—appears through the bedroom window, coming within twenty yards of the cabin just past midnight, Graham doesn't stir. As the train fades, the only sounds I hear are the crickets outside and the breathing of my son across the room.

Useless and Pointless Knowledge

When I emerge from the cabin in the morning, the sun off the lake momentarily blinds me and it takes a few minutes to adjust. A couple of other cabins are occupied and one woman, built and clothed like a linebacker, is stuffing a suitcase into the back of a Jeep Cherokee with Ontario plates. "Good morning," she booms my way. I have energy for only a smile.

I pop open the back of the War Wagon and fish out an orange juice from the watery remains of ice in the cooler. I sit on the bumper and thumb through some of the books I packed. Besides *The History of the Blues*, I've got the whole roots-music series by Peter Guralnick (*Feel Like Going Home*, *Lost Highway* and *Sweet Soul Music*) and Alan Lomax's memoir *The Land Where the Blues Began*. I brought much of the Bob Dylan library in case we want to track down his Minnesota haunts. We're cheek by jowl with the Big River for much of the trip, so I packed *Life on the Mississippi* and *The Adventures of Huckleberry Finn*. I brought some travel books too. There's that Larry McMurtry book called *Roads*, about driving inter-states. As an antidote, I brought *Blue Highways* by William Least Heat-Moon. I also have *Zen and the Art of Motorcycle Maintenance*, Robert Pirsig's book about another father-and-son trip. I read it years ago but felt no desire to emulate the motorcycle teeth-in-the-wind experience. My dad was a surgeon who pronounced dead a lot of kids who'd wiped out on motorcycles, and he forbade us to ever ride one. He's been dead thirty years, but I still haven't ridden one. *Talk about your powerful personalities.*

What I remember most about the book is that wherever Pirsig goes he sees shadows of himself in an earlier life at the same places. As we near the Minnesota North Country, I think of being there forty years before—as a little boy on vacation with my family. My father was stationed in Nebraska and we came north three consecutive summers, all dreaming of the day Dad would finally retire from the service and go into private practice. *Where would we live when we grew up?* Those trips were reconnaissance missions for my father.

Then there's *On the Road.* The big news back in Bloomington is that the owner of the Indianapolis Colts dropped a couple million on the original scroll manuscript of Kerouac's book and donated it to the Lilly Library at Indiana University. Kerouac wrote the book in three weeks on a roll of newsprint. I read it when I was Graham's age. Will he discover it in this crate? Will he even look in this box?

Here's another book, an anthology called *Family Travel.* The subtitle is "The Farther You Go, the Closer You Get." *I can always hope.*

The inn serves pancakes thick as flannel blankets. We sit at a corner table and look out on the lake, eavesdropping on eight middle-aged women. Can't figure out the connection. *Family reunion?* Maybe it's some e-mail group of businesswomen in Ontario who met here because it's midway in the province.

Graham feels like hip-hop this morning and puts a homemade disc in the CD changer. He wants to educate me about his music, so for a couple of hours he plays snippets of songs. He's the professor now, trying to interest me in a rapper named Mos Def. I understand; I always wanted to get my dad to listen to Bob Dylan.

The song is full of preening sexual references and prominently features *that word*, that racial epithet (though rappers say it as *nigga*). For a moment, I'm channeling my dad. *I can't believe my kids listen to this stuff.* Dad used to stick his head into my room when *Blonde on Blonde* was playing, shake his head and say, "That guy can't sing." "I know, Dad," I'd say. "But he's a great singer."

Dad's tastes ran to Wagnerian opera. We woke to *The Flying Dutchman* overture at 6 A.M. most school days. He had speakers the size of grocery carts.

But this stuff . . . I'm not sure I get it. These are the words so many people fought to eradicate. I'm embarrassed to listen to it. It's not even *music*. Then I think: *My God, I am my dad.*

Growing up in the military—even when we were stationed in the South in the 1960s—we always went to integrated schools until we moved to Texas. When I graduated from sixth grade, my class was split into separate junior highs as we entered public schools. That fall, I was in my first all-white class, and one day a gym coach told us to "run like niggers."

Graham and his sisters grew up in a different country. They've never seen segregation. As children of the 1980s, they love black music and culture. And *that word* is a big part of the music. *Is this really what everyone was fighting for?*

After hours of rap and hip-hop, interrupted by the occasional spacey Radiohead, I make my request: "We might have to put some Bob Dylan on soon," I tell him. "We're getting close to Minnesota." I start to sing in my halting, vowelly Dylan imitation, *"If you're goin' . . . to the north country fair. . . ."*

I see a bright yellow Beetle on the road ahead. "Slugbug!" I say, landing one on his shoulder. We're still playing the game we started in 1987. I'm ahead 4,256 to 4,255, but Graham challenges my count.

I glance at the back of the Explorer, an explosion of clothes, books, compact discs, a cooler and a box of Captain's Wafers. Two days on the road, already the car is trashed.

A song bite plants itself in my head and I boom out, "Rock and roll, hoochie koo."

Graham immediately falls into place with the backing vocal, slower, the words spaced out just like they are on the record: *"Rock . . . and . . . roll, . . . hoochie . . . koo."*

"Lawdy Mama, tie my shoe . . . "

"Is that really what he says?" Graham asks.

"If it isn't, it ought to be. Rick Derringer, real name Rick Zehringer, a native of your home state, Boy."

I ask: Does it annoy him or amuse him when I stuff his head full of so much—*what did Dylan call it?*—"useless and pointless knowledge"? He smiles and shakes his head no.

Graham's musical taste is as eclectic as mine. I shift between Johnny Cash and Enya and Tony Bennett and Led Zeppelin. He seems to have inherited that from me. He tells me he's loved being a college student this year because he's been to so many concerts. He used to see concerts only when I was in Indiana. This year, on his own at college, he's seen the Roots, Phish (twice), Jurassic 5 ("I got to party with them after the show," he says) and 311, which was apparently one of the defining moments of his musical life.

"They were playing a song called 'Fuck the Bullshit.' . . . "

"A love ballad of some kind?"

"Exactly. The bass player crawled on top of the monitor and he jumped off and landed right on top of me."

"You must've been very proud."

Where the Highway Begins

There's a huge island called the Sleeping Giant out in Lake Superior—a sign we're close to Thunder Bay. Graham, ever the impatient listener, plugs Cat Stevens into the CD player. As we drive by immaculate far-spaced suburban homes in Canada, Stevens's precise, coy voice seems well suited. We're back among the mannered.

Oh very young
What will you leave us this time?

"You know when I left home? I graduated on a Saturday and we drove down to Nashville for Uncle Charlie's med school graduation. That was on a Wednesday. So we were all in a motel. It's the last time we were all together as a family, Uncle Charlie and Aunt Suzanne. . . . Dad died that fall. Anyway, I had to start work in West Palm Beach the end of that week. So I got up at five o'clock in the morning, and that's where I said good-bye to my parents—in the hallway of a motel when I was nineteen. I get in the car, turn the ignition . . . and this is the song playing on the radio."

He says nothing. My Moment must not impress him. "I'm in the mood to see a dead animal," he finally says. *So much for sentiment.*

Suddenly he's scat singing. I've spent the last forty-eight hours in his constant company, other than when he was in the bathroom. Only two beers have been consumed. No drugs have been ingested. This must be a genuine, honestly earned good mood.

We see a cross by the side of the road. "Somebody died there," I say. "Did I ever tell you about my near-fatality?"

"When was this?"

"I was seventeen. Five in the morning and I was on my way to work at the newspaper, in my dad's car. I came across an icy patch on West Third. I skidded, flipped and went into a ditch. No seat belt. I got out and stood there next to the car, and this guy comes out of his house—it's his yard I landed in—and he says, 'I already called the ambulance. I figured you was a fatality.' "

"Crazy."

"Yeah, I know. My folks came and I insisted on going to work, so they dropped me at the newspaper office. I worked the whole shift, then after deadline said to the editor, 'I had an accident this morning.' It hit me just then."

Finally, Thunder Bay, announced by a sign with the city's motto, "Superior by Nature." We'd seen only one black person in Canada—a man on the streets of Sault Ste. Marie and now, headed back down into the United States, we see only our second black Canadian—again, walking the streets of a border town.

Highway 17 makes a big loop around the city and turns west toward British Columbia. That's when we see the first Highway 61 sign. "There it is!" Graham yells. The "61" is in a crown, a colonial remnant. It points straight ahead; Highway 17 goes off to the right.

Finally, we're on 61. A few miles south of Thunder Bay we reach Minnesota. The fields look brushstroked with wheat. To our right are mountains, part of the Mesabi Range, rich in iron ore.

"We ought to listen to this Bob Dylan song called 'North Country Blues,'" I tell Graham. "It's told from the point of view of the wife of a miner. It'd make us all nice and depressed."

The northern Minnesota equivalent of the night-moose-warning sign is the "bump" sign. The road, as advertised by the finicky customs agent at Pigeon River, is a continual bump.

"I wonder what a bump has to do to earn a 'bump' sign," I ask. "Is that where a city councilman lost a tire? They put up a sign there? It's no different from any other bump." The Explorer vibrates as we hit another rough patch. "There's a bump—unlabeled. It jarred my kidneys just as much as the other one. Yet it has no sign."

Graham's thundering Led Zeppelin through the War Wagon. This is the music of my youth. The rock 'n' roll history professor in me has to lecture my son about all of the artists Led Zeppelin ripped off. Willie Dixon, the Chicago bluesman and producer, was a source. We're listening to "Boogie With Stu," a straight copy of "Ooh! My Head" by Ritchie Valens, killed in the same plane crash as Buddy Holly. And maybe *that* song was a rip-off of Little Richard's "Ooh! My Soul."

"At least they ripped off from the best," I tell him. "I think Led Zeppelin was just an amalgamation of all of their American influences, and they sort of chewed them up and spit them out."

Graham doesn't care where it came from; he just likes the music.

In the North Country Fair

Highway 61, despite the bumps and its below-the-salt status as merely a state highway this far north, is a spectacular road when it comes into America. It runs along the triangle overhanging Lake Superior, the view of the lake occasionally blocked by pines. These are the Boundary Waters, and some of the land between the United States and Canada is still in dispute. Where Minnesota, Ontario and Manitoba meet, the U.S. border takes a sudden jag north and claims an Indian reservation on the other side of the Lake of the Woods. There's no direct road to the reservation from Minnesota, and the guidebooks call the Northwest Angle the "oddball territory." The Boundary Waters Canoe Area Wilderness is a million acres without the hum of motors, no structures marring the landscape, few people to spoil nature's awesome stillness. It's freckled with lakes—*didn't Thoreau call a lake the earth's eye?*—and it's possible to canoe for days and not see evidence of other human beings. Radio waves can intrude, but packing a radio isn't required by law.

I hold up the atlas for Graham, who takes his eyes off the road for a moment to get his bearings. "Look at that," I say. "Imagine that place. *Just imagine it.*"

He nods. "Yeah, imagine the fish."

Fish. They swim through his dreams, mingled with baseball heroics and rock 'n' roll glory.

But we can't go there. It's off the road and we don't have the time or money for three or four days in the wilderness. Nice to dream, though.

The gods have smiled on us; it is another blue-sky spectacular day, despite the lingering—and unexpected—chill. We catch the edge of Grand Portage State Forest, cutting through the convenience-store towns of Hovland and Croftville. Grand Portage is where the fur trappers carried their canoes around the Pigeon River—water too rough and customs inspector too slow, no doubt—to get inland from Lake Superior. This was the capital of fur trading in North America and, for a moment, we ponder the thought of some hygienically challenged dudes in dead animal skins traipsing through the gravel parking lot of the convenience store where we've stopped. Other than this store, things probably look pretty much the way they did when Gaston and LaBeouf came over this ridge, on the way to more peaceful waters.

Finally, a reduce-speed sign. "Look for a diner," I tell Graham.

Grand Marais has a beautiful harbor and the aroma of a resort—a smell I'm used to, since I live near Disney World. At times, I wish Disney ran the world. Things would be a lot cleaner. When I think this, I fear the Green Police will show up at my door and demand I hand over my Carl Hiaasen books, obviously not worthy of being a Cool Florida Dude.

The streets have that Disney feel as we steer the War Wagon through the town, looking for a place to have lunch. Most of the people must be tourists, I tell Graham, since the town has only thirteen hundred residents and it looks like all of them are trying to park.

It's eco-tourist heaven. The Gunflint Trail starts here, a paved path that winds sixty-three miles north and west to Saganaga Lake at the Canadian border. This time of year, the trail has wildflowers, great fishing and migrating songbirds. There are also sumptuous hunting lodges with fireplaces, hot tubs, saunas and a lot of other stuff that would bankrupt me.

Grand Marais was a fur-trading center, founded in 1823 by the John Jacob Astor's American Fur Company, which later branched out into a commercial fishing outfit. The town got its name from the

French trappers, who called it Great Marsh after the soggy bottom near the big lake. The Chippewa named the lake Kitchi Gamma, which means "great water."

"Lots of 'great' stuff around here," I tell Graham, glancing through some Grand Marais propaganda in a guidebook as we park in front of Sven and Ole's Pizza Parlor. French, Indians, Scandinavians, now Yuppies. Just the latest link in the evolutionary chain. "Every new tribe has to come up with its own name. I'm surprised they haven't renamed this place Land-Roverville."

Most of the businesses are in a narrow peninsula jutting into the lake. A long pier cups the harbor, and a small lighthouse with an exposed stairway completes the rustic view. We go into the Lake Superior Trading Post on the street fronting the shore. It's like stepping into an L.L.Bean catalog—young professionals in flannel, overpriced camping equipment too expensive to actually take outside. Real outdoorsmen don't shop here do they? Looks like a bunch of academics from Midwest universities roughing it for a weekend in $80 shirts by Columbia and everything-but-running-water backpacks by Patagonia. I think about the Boundary Waters again as I look at a canoe suspended from the ceiling. Is it decoration, or would the damn thing really float? Could we glide across the glass of those lakes, getting in touch with nature, not to mention our inner father and son? What the hell, I think. Let's pull out the VISA card and let it suffer a glorious death here: *Yes, we'd like the canoe, and that Himalaya tent and a dozen flannel shirts in all of the earth tones you have . . . and some boots. . . .* We could become debt fugitives, alternating nights on the American and Canadian shores. It's a brief but vivid fantasy.

Outside, I return to reality—"Grand Merry Ass," as Graham calls it. Across the street, back toward the hills, is the Beaver House, which advertises "fishing supplies, ice and beaver flicks." A huge fish sculpture—a large-mouth bass—cuts through the corner of the building, as if stuck there by Paul Bunyan.

"That store mystifies me," I say to Graham. "You can buy porn films and live bait in one place? We ought to franchise this concept down in Florida."

"One-stop perversion centers," Graham says.

But there's no evidence of perversion inside, no ready explanation for "beaver flicks." The camping and fishing equipment is good stuff, more utilitarian and reasonably priced than the designer camp stoves in the perfectly rustic trading post across the street. Outside the Beaver House, a True Believer pulls up in a battered white pickup and nods to us as we hold the door for him. A real outdoorsman wouldn't be caught down the street at the trading post of the soccer moms. His rusted bumper has a sticker: WARNING: FISH POX.

We go to the East Bay Motel and Restaurant for lunch—a club sandwich for me, a hamburger for Graham. As an appetizer, we order the specialty of the house, rye raisin bread. The beer selection is disappointing (Miller and Anheuser-Busch, no North Country microbrews, no Sleeman's Cream Ale, no Canadian beer of any kind), and so I decide to go for coffee to add further to the buzz. It's just noon, and I anticipate a long day and no idea where and when it will end.

Even though we're at the back of the dining room, the windows offer a skybox view of the lake, and the room softly echoes with the murmurs of little-old-lady Minnesota accents. A few kids are with their parents on the deck outside the restaurant, looking at the boats out on the lake, but inside it's just little old ladies and the father-and-son bowling team.

South of Grand Marais, we skirt the edge of the big lake for a few miles in silence, and the next town has a perfect Scandinavian name: Lutsen.

Up on the hill above the highway, I see the glint of sun off something bright, and we stop on the shoulder and hike up the embankment. What we find is a series of tin sculptures, the characters from *The Wizard of Oz*.

Gerry Loh's sculptures of *Wizard of Oz* characters stand sentinel over Highway 61. Here's the Tin Man, the Scarecrow, and, of course, the Cactus. We figure the Cactus's big dance number was cut out of the original film, but we hope it will be restored on the limited-edition DVD.

"I just love to build things," says the artist, Gerald Loh, retired Cook County maintenance director. "I make highway distractions." Down state, he says, there's a chain-saw sculptor who's done a series of bears. "You'll see lots of things up and down the North Shore, made by goonballs like me."

Led Zeppelin shrieks as we blast down Highway 61 again, looking over a bluff at the lake, Earth's big-ass eyeball.

A Boy Who Loved Maps

The North Shore drive runs 150 miles from Thunder Bay to where the pointed finger of Superior divides Duluth, Minnesota, and Superior, Wisconsin. In "Song of Hiawatha," Longfellow called Superior "the shining Big-Sea-Water." For me, it's always been that huge blue arch on the maps I studied so intently as a kid, back when I wanted to be a cartographer. I used to draw maps on notebook paper and planned to assemble the sheets into a huge blue-lined globe in the living room. When I read Hardy Boys novels I'd draw maps to better visualize the action. When I give directions I speak in points of the compass, which annoys the *turn-left, turn-right* people of the world. This is the first time I've seen Superior, and I want to preserve this in my memory too.

Graham's air-drumming to "Moby Dick" while going around a bend at sixty miles per hour.

"Hey," I say. "Take it easy with the drums, will you?"

"All right. Hey, when's the last time we'll be able to see Superior?" Graham asks.

Already he's talking about endings. "I guess when we get to Duluth, that's when we lose the lake," I said. "It's like a slice of pie and that's the point. We head south from there."

The Led Zeppelin disc ends and I decide to take charge. I put on Muddy Waters. We listen to him growl "Rollin' Stone."

"This doesn't really seem like blues territory," Graham says.

"Yeah, although I suppose they have a lot to be pissed off about. There's the weather. And then, of course, when the L.L.Bean catalog is late, they commence to wailing." I grab the harmonica I keep in the glove box.

Got my new catalog . . . red flannel is out of stock.
Got my new catalog . . . red flannel is out of stock.
Don't know what I'll do . . . gonna put my Volvo up for hock. . . .

"I can't wait to get to Mississippi," Graham says, a subtle comment on my playing. I know one riff on the harmonica, the classic Muddy Waters "Mannish Boy" thump.

The Grand Marais coffee has worked through me, and I ask Graham to pull over when I see what looks like a rest stop ahead—a scattering of cars on the side of the road, an assortment of green information signs. We are drawn to the sound of rushing water—this is to the west, away from the lake—and we head off down a trail behind the parking area. As we come out of the pines at the bottom of the ravine, we see the Temperance River, white water so loud we have to shout.

"Can we stay here a while?" he yells.

"Of course! We're free spirits!"

Although the rocks are worn smooth as car fenders, we quickly scramble up the side of a cliff—with a little help from a railing. The bowling shoes slip, but except for a jolt to my knee I'm doing just as well as the L.L.Bean troops in their $250 weekend hiking boots.

The father-and-son bowling team looks out of place among the eco-tourists in goose-down vests. The farther back we get from Highway 61, the more we find as the park fans out—more cliffs, tributaries and an area called Hidden Falls. Despite my controversial footwear, we've climbed quite high, and we look down, across the highway, and see Superior.

I sit to enjoy the view while Graham continues climbing, taking pictures. He's thinking about studying photojournalism, and this is a chance to see if he likes it. He's amused by the people in their expensive roughing-it gear, but too shy to take their pictures.

Later we scramble around the cliffs for a half hour. "You ever see anything like this before?" Graham asks when we're on top of a cliff.

"Yeah," I say, out of breath. "Oddly enough, this part right here looks like Utah."

"I wish I could see Utah."

"It was cool," I said. "It was back in high school, one of those road trips I took with my mom and dad when I was the only kid left at home. I remember in Utah, this geyser—it was bubbling out of the ground . . . *steaming*. . . . I've always been fascinated by the possibility of disaster."

"I'd like to see a geyser."

We thought it was a rest stop, but it turned out to be an adventure. Graham said he'd
seen few things more beautiful than northern Minnesota's Temperance River.

"Someday, we'll go out West. Promise."

Along the Cauldron Trail, we trip over roots thick as boa constric-
tors, and dodge dive-bombing monarch butterflies. Graham runs
around and I tell him once to be careful—still the overprotective

parent, even though he's much more athletic than I am and certainly more well shod. Deafened by the water, when I look up, Graham's scaling a cliff. If he falls, he'll be crushed against the rocks. He scares the hell out of me.

The roar of the falls is so even it's like the white noise used to help insomniacs sleep. Graham comes back down to a more sane elevation and joins me for a half-mile hike back to Highway 61, then we cross the road to see where the river meets the big lake. After all of the fury across the highway, the river calms and majestically joins Lake Superior, white water darkened to royal blue.

Just Like a Woman

Back on the road, Howlin' Wolf groans through "Smokestack Lightning."

"People look at Highway 61 the wrong way," I tell Graham. "It's like the way some men look at a woman. They only see the below-the-waist part. They miss the head and heart. So when I talked about this trip to my friends, all they could think about was Mississippi and the blues. They didn't think about Minnesota. But this is Highway 61 too."

"I've never seen country like this," Graham says, glancing toward the lake again. "I'm kind of glad I came on this trip—*really freakin' glad.*"

He rarely expresses emotion. *Maybe "really freakin' glad" is as close as he'll come to "I love you."*

"Me too," I say.

Still a little chilly in northern Minnesota, and the colors are garish, rebelling against the dreariness of winter just past. We have only a slight change of seasons in north Florida but here, you appreciate spring because of the harshness of winter. There are still shades of brown and burnt orange flashing by our car windows, but the green is bright and surreal.

"I've got an idea," I tell Graham. "Here's how we can make some money off all those white middle-aged blues fans. Let's get a pickle jar. This might require actually buying a jar of pickles and consuming it. When the jar is empty, let's pick up some gravel from along the highway, store it in the pickle jar, then package it in little vials, like test tubes or something, and sell it as 'Highway 61 Gravel.' All those tax-attorney blues fans out there will love it."

"Do you think that's our target audience? Attorneys?"

I remember a concert from a couple of years before. "I saw Keb' Mo' once. There he is, the fucking personification of Robert Johnson, sort of a Disneyfied blues man. I looked around the auditorium, and there was not one black person in attendance. There were all of these gray-haired-ponytail professional types, yelling, 'Tell it! Tell it!' at Keb' Mo'. It was so ridiculous. Here was a black man playing the music that may be one of the greatest contributions of black Americans to mainstream culture, and the audience is a bunch of wannabe hip dudes who are totally clueless. They could paint their skin black and they still would be too fucking white to live."

"What the hell?" Through the trees on a bluff to our right, Graham catches a glimpse of another sculpture.

We park and crunch through gravel loud as breakfast cereal and find a huge carved bear. Can't be the one Gerry Loh mentioned, because it's in the wrong place. I'd guess this one's fourteen to fifteen feet high, a grizzly or some other ferocious, noncuddly bear, carved into a tree overlooking the highway and the lake. No sign, no artist's signature. Like Gerry Loh said—goonballs, keeping the highway travelers entertained.

"There's some weird shit here in Wisconsin . . . Minnesota, wherever the hell we are," Graham says.

Duluth

Gore Vidal titled his satire of American life *Duluth*, even though he claimed his novel took place in an imaginary city somewhere between the Great Lakes and the Mexican border. With a name like *Dull*-uth, the town is ripe for lampooning. But as we enter on Highway 61—known as London Road as it comes into town—Duluth looks great. I figure it's another unfairly maligned, butt-of-jokes town like Cleveland. Three-story homes, frame and brick, in colors so carefully arranged, I suspect there must be a rigid house-painting ordinance: blue, beige, white, hunter green, back to beige. One of the homes has two onion turrets overlooking the harbor.

"This is really beautiful," I say. "Not that I want to move to Duluth, but I wonder how much these things cost."

"Weather wimp," he says. "You couldn't stand your first winter here."

"I bet these lakefront homes are *really* cold in the winter. But look how beautiful they are." I wonder if Vidal even visited Duluth before stealing its name.

The cross streets rise to the west to meet the hills, and we head from the residential to the business part of Duluth. "Reminds me of San Francisco," Graham says, "even though I've never been there."

The national news menu is featuring a Duluth story—Bob Dylan's childhood home is up for sale on eBay, the on-line auction site. It's four blocks to our right, walking distance from downtown, advertised as a "must-have for the ultimate die-hard Dylan fan." I might describe myself that way, but with the bids starting at eighty-five thousand dollars it's a little out of my range for a souvenir. Although it's not much larger than the shack I'm trying to unload in Florida— eighteen hundred square feet—it's a two-story house, a pinkish tan color, built in 1909. The eBay ad says young Bobby Zimmerman took his first steps here and that his bedroom still features his carving in the woodwork. What the house lacks in space and new trim it makes up for with a 180-degree view of Lake Superior and rock 'n' roll history.

Downtown is a maze of clean and orderly one-way streets. The Electric Fetus has a pure 1960s name, a weird juxtaposition like Bubble Puppy (a band of the time) or Stone Balloon (a record store back home) and was started at the University of Minnesota in 1968, later branching out to Duluth and St. Cloud. The store has an old-fashioned emporium look with its Victorian lettering, but the window displays Tori Amos (*Torn Anus* in McKeen family lingo), Dave Matthews and, of course, local-boy-made-good Bob Dylan. To us the store is heaven and hell: it's everything we want in one place (CDs, DVDs, posters, rock 'n' roll paraphernalia), and us without any recreational money to speak of. I see a couple of things I'm dying for: an import CD of *The Everly Brothers Sing Great Country Hits* (with seven bonus tracks) and a three-CD Johnnie Taylor retrospective, tracing his career from the gospel days with the Soul Stirrers to his last recordings for Malaco in the 1990s. I ponder the emptiness of my life without these two recordings, but then decide that feeding and sheltering my son for the next few weeks is probably the better use of my money.

But there's a good chance *Duluth Does Dylan* would be hard to get outside this zip code. A bunch of local artists do startling reinterpretations of some of Dylan's best songs. The Black Labels, The Black-Eyed Snakes, Gild, Accidental Porn—I've never heard of any of these bands, but I don't listen to as much Duluth music as I should. The performances are all gutsy, few more so than Jamie Ness's version of "Sad-Eyed Lady of the Lowlands." He turns Dylan's twelve-minute dirge into a swing tune. I sample most of the disc at one of the store's listening stations. The cartoon cover shows the furry-headed boy from *Blonde on Blonde* sucking on a Popsicle while at the Original Coney Island, down the street from the Fetus.

Graham checks out the clothing and incense section. The patchouli oil is thick, and when I come up next to him he says, "This town's pretty cool."

As we leave, we hear a guy entering the store, calling to his friend across the street, "I'll be in the Fetus."

"Cool how they call it by its last name," Graham says, putting on a Grateful Dead voice, *"Dude . . . catch you later at the Fetus."*

We're in the fun part of downtown—a music store, a hot-dog stand and now a baseball-card store. Baseball's obsession with statistics is why Graham excels in math. When I visited after the divorce, we'd spend hours with rented Nintendo games. I got him "Major League Baseball" and taught him all about batting averages and earned-run averages—necessary to picking a dream team from the computer-generated rosters of real-life ballplayers. That led him to baseball cards, the real game and his devotion to the Cubs. The one drawback to his Florida visits was that local cable didn't carry the Cubs, so he had to make do with the Braves.

He looks over some of the card store's memorabilia—a Kirby Puckett–autographed bat catches his eye, but the store doesn't hold him like the Fetus did. Children grow up, their interests change. I miss his always wearing a Cubs hat. He went through three of them before he was twelve.

"I'm surprised this store is still going," I say, whispering so the proprietor doesn't hear. "I thought the bottom fell out of the baseball-card collecting thing long ago."

"It did," he shrugs. "Too bad; this is a nice store."

When he was ten and realized the odds were against growing up to be a major league baseball player, he shifted his ambition. He wanted Peter Gammons's job when he retired as host of ESPN's *Baseball Tonight*. I told him Gammons was a journalist—what I was— and that being a sportswriter would be a great life. Then Graham hatched a corollary to his plan: He would be a sportswriter and own a baseball-card store on the side. While he was at work, he instructed me, I could mind the shop for him. He wanted me to live near him

Outside the Muffler Clinic in Duluth, Minnesota, discarded auto parts make for an odd welcome to the city's ambitious Lakewalk. A few yards away rollerbladers and power walkers blissfully enjoy a brisk afternoon by Lake Superior.

when I retired. He said it so innocently, so perfectly, with the future all lined up before him.

We cross the elevated walkway to the redeveloped spit of land jutting into Lake Superior. Duluth does not die and go to the suburbs at five o'clock. Legions of supercilious joggers come out to trot along the Lakewalk. This former dock area has been renovated to attract crowds downtown (shops, bars, restaurants) yet still retains its steve-dorean charm. Two pasty-white crackheads on the skywalk recoil when we walk by, but calm down when they see we're not cops, just visiting geeks. (Bowling shoes are a dead giveaway.) Passing over an alley full of discarded mufflers, I see a large black man taking a public shit. When we make eye contact, it's a toss-up which of us is more embarrassed. Other than him, everyone on the Lakewalk is a catalog person—hiking boots, expensive flannel, rosy cheeks, wealth.

Canal Park—and the four-mile-long Lakewalk—is beautiful: bars with happy people, shops with souvenirs, nice motels out of our price range. Canal Park is dominated by the Aerial Lift Bridge, a distinctive landmark that caps the east end of the rectangle of fun on the water. People romp with dogs, and joggers zip by us. *More in-line skaters per capita than any other city in America.*

Being with Graham and listening to him happily jabber lifts me out of my financial funk. It's bumper-sticker wisdom—at the end of your life, do you think you'll want more time with your family or will you want more money? *I'd like more of these please . . . a lot more of these.*

It's still a little chilly for a weather wimp, but I forget that and watch Graham watching ruddy-faced Minnesotans jogging by in running clothes skimpy even by South Beach standards. The pompadour remains a popular hairstyle here, and the *Sopranos*-style matching exercise ensemble does not have the ironic overtones it might elsewhere. The lake merges with the sky in a dark blue, and boats dot the horizon. A huge barge seems stationary, but isn't, out on the lake. Two stories above the Lakewalk we see partyers at Fitger's Brewery. Sitting there, watching the view and sucking on a microbrew seems attractive, but we're determined to walk all the way down to the Duluth Armory.

The Armory, at the east end of the Lakewalk, is a four-floor greenish-colored brick structure, built in 1915 and now set for condemnation. Though it is still sturdy and rugged from a distance, building inspectors say it suffers from major structural weaknesses; trees grow through the roof, and a collection of decaying animal carcasses fester throughout its twenty thousand square feet. But I'm not here as an architectural critic or a structural engineer. This is a rock 'n' roll temple, the site of the passing of generations—a sun-also-rises, sun-also-sets moment. Two nights before he died in a 1959 plane crash, Buddy Holly played the Duluth Armory. At the front of the stage, Bob Zimmerman—not yet Dylan—was there, having driven over from Hibbing for the show. Bob squirmed his way through the crowd to look up at the young rock 'n' roll star. They locked eyes, or so Bob says—he's always been his own best mythmaker—and the torch was passed. When he won the Grammy Award for album of the year in 1998—for his meditation on death and dying, *Time Out of Mind*— Bob mentioned Buddy Holly's Armory show in his acceptance speech: "I just have some kind of feeling that he was, I don't know how or why, but I know he was with us all the time we were making this record in some kind of way."

Good Duluthers are trying to save the old building and turn it into an arts and music center. The plan is to name the center for Bob Dylan. *Rave on.*

Hibbing Detour

The Bob Vibe is too strong to ignore, so we take a side trip to the town where he grew up. His family left Duluth when he was six and moved to Hibbing, about fifty miles off Highway 61.

We make a short swing south to Cloquet before jutting north to Hibbing. It's early evening and we're losing light, but Cloquet has the only Frank Lloyd Wright gas station in America. Graham likes all of the classic boy stuff—fishing, sports, loud guitar—but he also likes art museums and interesting buildings. So he's on the hunt for a certain Phillips 66 station, but we're not sure of the address. After cruising downtown Cloquet for a while (past Grandma's Cloquet Café with its advertisements for "Hamburgers—Fries—BEER" and the Munger Tavern with "Blatz" neoned into the name), we find a Phillips station.

"That can't be it," says my driver and architecture critic.

"If Frank Lloyd Wright designed that," I say, "then we're going to dig up his carcass and heave it off the ugliest aluminum strip mall we can find."

More circling. "You know he was born on my birthday," Graham says. "I mean the other way around." His birthday is about a week away.

"Pretty cool," I say. "I get B. B. King and Lauren Bacall on my birthday—now that's an unbeatable combination."

"I don't know. B. B. King is good, but Frank is cooler."

Everywhere, Cloquet screams the names of what we want—Beer and Food. At Gordy's Hi-Hat Drive Inn: "Hamburgers, $1.19— We're almost giving them away!"

Finally, we find the station. It has a pagoda-like copper roof and a classic utilitarian look, but the bright green sign for Kelly Tires and Atlas Auto Parts detracts from the effect. There's a tower coming out of the station, screaming PHILLIPS in vertical lettering.

"It's interesting," I say slowly. "But I don't know if it's his best work."

"A Floydian slip," Graham says. Ever the good brother, he hops out of the car and stands at a traffic island to take a photograph while cars whiz by, some honking to scare him. The picture is for big sister Sarah, who's studying architecture.

We miss the character of Highway 61, but it's nice to have a straight-shot highway up to Hibbing, and we speed. Graham's a week away from nineteen, still too young to drink legally, but I promise him another night with a cold beer. His mother might not approve of my serving him beer, but I have the same attitude my father had: I'd rather you drink with me than hide it. This is why I had no interest in getting drunk in high school, when all of my friends were hiding out in the woods with their warm quarts of Stroh's.

"You know, first year of college and all, I never got sick once from drinking," Graham says.

"You are a better man than I am, Gunga Din. I could not make the same claim for my freshman year."

"At parties, people were puking all around me. But not me."

Time to plug in *The Freewheelin' Bob Dylan*. Graham says he's never heard it all the way through.

Savannah calls on the cell phone, just as Bob hits the harmonica solo on "Blowin' in the Wind." Her voice is prematurely husky: "I called to say goodnight, Daddy." She's met her biological father only once, and so I am Daddy to her.

"Thank you. You going to bed? You want to say goodnight to Graham?"

I hold the phone to his ear. "Hey, Savannah. You know where I am? I'm in Minnesota, that's 'way far away from Florida. It's only fifty degrees, kind of chilly. I'll see you in a couple weeks, OK?"

Savannah is irresistible, of course. She's beautiful, she's smart, she's funny. She's also four, the age Graham was when his mother and I broke apart. I've been trying to gauge how he feels about this whole thing—about my getting married again, about a little girl who adores him as a "big brother," about how he feels seeing a different four-year-old call me Daddy.

It's getting dark and Graham is blinking, tired of driving.

If you're traveling to the North Country Fair . . .

"Good timing, Bob, just as we exit for Hibbing." After turning on to State Road 37, it's another sixteen miles into town.

"He sounds so old."

"He was, like, twenty when he recorded this. He used to have to try to sound old. Now it comes easy."

A car is speeding out of Hibbing, coming toward us, with head-lights flickering.

"Look, son, a car on LSD."

After it's safely by, Graham sighs.

"Did you ever hear about that movie, *The Car*? It came out around the time you were born. Your mom and I saw it in a drive-in. Hell, for all I know, you were in the back seat."

"What was it about?"

"It was this car. Maybe it was supposed to be on LSD. Anyway, it just knocked down walls, came into people's houses, killed them . . . you know, the usual bad-movie kind of stuff."

"Sounds like a *really* bad movie."

"It was. It's one of those career-ruining movies. James Brolin was in it, and he was sort of on his way up. Then he made *The Car*, and I don't think he ever made another good movie again. Later, of course, he suffered the greater indignity of marrying Barbra Streisand."

"Really?"

"Afraid so. Michael Caine almost ruined it all with *The Hand*. That was about a disembodied . . ."

"*Hand*," he responds on cue.

"Yes, and it went around killing people. When I was a kid, there was a movie called *The Crawling Eye*, with Peter Breck. I actually liked him; he could've been a good actor. But then he made that junk."

Bob is singing "Down the Highway," perfect since we're busting ourselves to get to his hometown and crawl into a warm bed.

"It's funny Savannah's named her imaginary friend '*Bobdillon*,' isn't it?" I ask.

"Yeah. I wonder what kinds of things they do together. You think he sings?"

"I don't know. I never had an imaginary friend. You had Ghostie. What did you guys do?"

"Ghostie was just a scapegoat," he says. I laugh. The restored movie-theater seat in my house has yellow Magic Marker streaks that "Ghostie" made. "He wasn't very nice either," Graham says. "He only hung around a few years."

"You were so funny when you were little. You didn't talk, you just barked. We called you Dogboy."

"Did you think I was retarded?"

"No. I just figured when you had something to say you'd say it."

He smiles at the road ahead, illuminated by the headlights. "I love your stories," he says.

Bob begins "A Hard Rain's A-Gonna Fall":

Oh, where have you been, my blue-eyed son?

Hibbing is tough to figure out, and without the sun I'm disoriented. It's late when we get into town and pass a place called Zimmy's.

"I wonder if he knows about that," I say. "Remember 'Gotta Serve Somebody'? *'You may call me Bobby, you may call me Zimmy'*? You think this is an officially sanctioned Bob Dylan restaurant?"

A couple blocks away, Rudi's Pizza is open. We are the only customers. I urge Graham to gorge, so he orders a hot pizza sub with Canadian bacon, mushrooms, pepperoni, Monterey Jack cheese and mushrooms. When the counter girl, Kristen, delivers it to us at our booth, she says, "There ya *goo*," in an exaggerated Minnesota accent. "Where y'all from?" Our cover blown again, we tell her. "Oh, Florida, that's nice," and she wanders back behind the counter, exhausted from this effort at casual conversation.

Graham devours the sub, and I survey the walls of the empty dining room. Rudi's celebrates another local boy, former Boston Celtic Kevin McHale, with a framed autograph of a Rudi's napkin. There are also pictures of old Hibbing and early Greyhound buses (the business was started here). The only Dylan relic is an 8-track of the *Pat Garrett and Billy the Kid* soundtrack. There's also a framed Beavis and Butt-head poster, a black velvet landscape painting and a reverently framed photograph of Elvis.

Graham consumes the sub with dispatch, we bus our table and wave good-bye to Kristen and the cook. Some high-school-age kids across the street get rowdy whenever trucks come down Howard Street, and finally one truck honks and the kids cheer.

"La-hooooo-sers," Graham says under his breath.

I laugh. "Hey, you were in high school last year, buddy."

"I was never such a loser to stand out on a street corner, trying to get people to honk at me."

We stay at the Hibbing Park Inn. Graham likes it because it makes the third night in a row when we stay in a hotel with the city's name in it; he wants to keep the streak alive.

The woman behind the desk welcomes us graciously, curious why people would drive all the way to Hibbing from Florida. The Bob Dylan Tourist Industry obviously needs development. Graham collapses on the bed in front of ESPN, and I make a quick beer run to the lounge downstairs. No Sleeman's, but the Miller Lite tastes just fine. The beer goes quickly, and I turn off my bedside light. At the edge of sleep, I hear the murmur of baseball scores across the room.

All-Bob All the Time

I didn't particularly like Bob Dylan's voice at first, but once I heard it I couldn't forget it. It grew on me through high school and college, and years later as a professor, a publisher asked me which rock 'n' roll artist I wanted to write a book about. Without hesitation I said Dylan. I'd been a Bobhead for twenty years by then, but writing a book about him would help me learn more.

I'd done an earlier academic book on the Beatles, but that tired me of the Fab Four. The opposite happened with Bob—the more I listened, the more I heard. When interviewers called me a "Dylan expert," I demurred. The man had lived forty years in the public eye and was still a mystery, hiding in plain sight. I didn't expect to learn much about him in Hibbing that I didn't already know, but it was important to be here.

In the morning we find Bob Dylan's boyhood home, an odd-looking bluish-gray house—kind of a combination hacienda/bunker. Graham

A ghostly image of Bob Dylan—a poster made from his 1966 *Blonde on Blonde* album cover—peers from the front window of his boyhood home in Hibbing, Minnesota.

and I stand out front and Bob—a *Blonde on Blonde* vintage 1966 poster—stares out the front window.

"This is kind of weird," I say. "Think about that. Little Bobby, up there, in that second-floor room. It's late at night, he's listening to the radio in his bedroom and he turns the dial and hears WLAC in Nashville, or maybe one of those Memphis stations. Nighttime is magic."

"Because of that radio-wave thing?"

"Yeah, he heard all of this rhythm-and-blues music and that early rock 'n' roll. He said once that when he first heard Elvis, it was like busting out of jail. Imagine if he hadn't had radio. He might've just stayed here and gone into his dad's appliance business. Radio really changed the world. I mean, look around . . . there aren't any black people here, but because of the radio, Bob heard black America's music."

I'm sounding too professorial again. "I just mean that radio was subversive. It was possible to have a segregated society until radio came along. Radio didn't honor Jim Crow laws. Radio waves travel in the air. So Bob heard all of that stuff. When he tried out for his high-school talent show, they say he was banging away on the piano on stage, doing his best middle-class white boy impersonation of Little Richard. Hibbing had never seen anything like that before. So in a way, he introduced rock 'n' roll to northern Minnesota."

"Did he win the talent contest?"

"Didn't even pass the audition."

Graham takes more pictures of Bob's house. I believe that in a hundred years people will think of Bob the way they think of Mark Twain or Walt Whitman. Maybe this little house will be a national historic site.

"I wonder what growing up here was like," I say as Graham winds film. "I mean, to be Jewish in a small town where the only Jews are your relatives. I think they had a traveling rabbi who did the whole northern Minnesota circuit, so they only had services once a month. I wonder if he felt a lot of prejudice growing up. Maybe that was what gave him that great affinity for black people."

Graham looks down the street toward the massive high school. "This doesn't seem like a place where people would protest much, yet he wrote a lot of protest songs."

"If you lived in Hibbing and you bought this house . . . what would that be like?"

"I don't know if you'd be inspired and be poetic all the time. But you'd be pretty bored, because this town blows."

Time to kill until Zimmy's opens. We find a Goodwill store downstairs from the Masonic Temple. Graham likes clothes with some sort of existential message, so the mesh shorts I find with "Fergus Falls Basketball" printed on the thigh ought to be perfect, especially at $2.25. But he turns those down, as well as a bit-more-pricey ($10) Hibbing Moose Lodge jacket. Too bad it's not my size.

The town was named for Frank Hibbing—but Hibbing wasn't his real name. He was born in Germany in 1856 as Frans Von Ahlen, but after his father's death and his move to America to seek fame and fortune, he took the name of his English mother. He couldn't speak English very well, so his law career was thwarted. He made it to Duluth, where he speculated in real estate and helped cut a road through the iron-range country to the spot soon laid out as a town and named for him. He was a good, if doomed, patriarch, dying at forty. When engineers discovered that Hibbing was situated on top of iron ore, the town—then twenty thousand population—moved two miles south. Buildings, businesses, people—the whole thing moved. Because some of the miners had to commute, a Swedish immigrant named Carl Eric Wickman ferried miners for fifteen-cent rides on his truck. He joined with a Duluth businessman to run a transit service between the towns, and the company was named the Masaba Transportation Company. Within two years, the company owned 18 buses. Eight years after that, a running dog became the company logo and the business grew into the Greyhound Bus Company.

Zimmy's is a Bob-themed restaurant: all-Bob artwork, all-Bob menu (for lunch, specials include Highway 61 Pizza) and an all-Bob sound system.

Our waitress starts us off with wings and beer. There's an orange and blue Day-Glo poster of Bob with George Harrison at the Concert for Bangladesh (the same poster that hung in my room during high school). Another poster shows Bob on tour in Europe in 1978.

"I can even tell you the photographer's name: Morgan Renard."

Graham laughs. "You know too much useless information."

The manager is a petite woman in her early thirties named Linda Strobeck-Hocking. She was a Grateful Dead fan growing up in Philadelphia, so when she met Bob Hocking, an artist, it wasn't too great a leap to join him in Bob Dylan fandom. Work brought them to Hibbing. The Atrium was a successful restaurant, and when Linda became a co-owner the original plan was to turn half of the restaurant into a sports bar. Too many sports bars in the world, so they decided to make it a Dylan bar instead.

Some old-time Hibbing people thought it an embarrassment. "They don't see Bob on that grand scale," Linda says. "It was very hard for them to have that perception of him. They just saw someone successful who didn't come back to his hometown. They felt snubbed."

"Is he aware of this place?"

"Oh yeah," she says. "When we opened, we got some flak from the people who knew his mom and his dad. About four months after we opened, his mom came up from the Twin Cities and came in for lunch with her relatives and she must have spent about six hours here. She said, 'Oh, it's about time somebody did something nice for my son here in Hibbing.' She was born and raised in Hibbing, and so for her to see something positive for him made her happy. So I gave her T-shirts and menus, and her go-ahead was all it took for us. She told me, 'I'll send you some photos,' but they never came. I figured when he heard about that, he asked her not to send them. A few months later, she died."

Zimmy's draws a lot of international visitors—especially from Norway and Sweden, which produces the most hard-core Dylan fans. The week before, Zimmy's had a birthday party for Bob.

"We had the Bob Dylan Nucleus Club from Norway," Linda says. "They faxed us back in December, began making plans. Back in the sixties, they were musicians, but they said, 'Now we're all doctors and attorneys, but we still listen to Bob.' At club meetings, they play basketball and listen to Bob Dylan."

Visitors are supposed to check in at the office at Hibbing High School, but we're feeling rebellious, entering the school just as the student horde leaves for lunch. Graham says some of the kids look a little "in-breddish, fairly normal, but all white. Not even any Indians or Hispanics."

The high school looks like a castle lifted from the English country-side and set down in a Midwestern neighborhood. The mining companies spent nearly four million dollars on the school when it was built in the early 1920s. Made of red brick trimmed with Bedford stone, it's in the shape of the letter *E* and sits on ten acres. It's the best-maintained high school I've ever seen—and it hasn't been devalued by cheap interior remodeling. It's not old-fashioned, though. I look in one of the classrooms and see kids working at electric-blue iMacs.

The auditorium is straight ahead and, since we're obviously clueless, choir director Patti Stoddard shows it to us. The auditorium ceiling is hand-molded, and in the back of the molding is braided horsehair, and behind the horsehair are bronze sticks. This obsolete technique eliminates cracking. The seats are plush, the stage is huge.

"How do you keep kids from vandalizing this?" I ask. "Or do they just recognize how great it is?"

"They're proud of the school," Patti says. "Their parents were proud of the school."

The auditorium is patterned after the Capitol Theater in New York. The chandeliers are Belgian crystal and are lowered every three years for cleaning, and at the same time, all the light bulbs are replaced. It takes two hours to lower them and one to two weeks to clean them. Each chandelier cost $15,000 in 1920; now they're insured for $250,000 each.

"So that's where he lost the talent show, huh?" Graham asks when we're outside.

As the students come back from lunch, one of them tosses a spent Miller Lite can on the school's front lawn.

Back to Duluth, where we latch on to Highway 61 to resume free-falling to New Orleans. We agree to give Bob a rest.

"I guess you'd *have* to listen to radio if you lived in Hibbing," Graham says. "But so much on the radio sucks. I'd rather download. *Slugbug!*" Another yellow one.

"It was a different country then. First of all, there was no down-loading and second of all, not all radio sucked."

"I'd rather download my own."

"You still need a gatekeeper, someone who's going to say, 'You really need to hear this.' When I was a kid, you turned on the radio and there were the Beatles followed by Frank Sinatra followed by Smokey Robinson, followed by . . . Bob Dylan. I mean, there were no lines. Radio was really a magic invention, if you think about it. That was a great leap, to take the music from one place to another totally different place. Put yourself in Bob's shoes. Maybe he picked Highway 61 for that song because it went right through the middle of the town where he was born, and it went to that land he heard about on the radio. That was his connection. If he hadn't decided to write about that—hell, we wouldn't be on this trip."

"Thanks, Bob."

"Then we'd have to do something different for the summer. You'd probably be working at the theater, slinging popcorn."

Asphalt Seminar

I can't stop thinking about my father, because he loved Minnesota. When he retired from twenty years in the military and looked for a place for his private practice, he opened the atlas to M. First it was Thief River Falls. My mother ruled that out without a reconnaissance mission. Too far north. Then he looked at the Twin Cities, Rochester (the Mayo Clinic) and Red Wing. These we did visit.

My father was born into a poor family in northern Ohio and worked his way through college as a soda jerk. Eventually, he graduated from the University of Chicago. Along the way, the U.S. Army drafted him for service in the Second World War, but when they gave him aptitude tests, they sent him to medical school, not the front lines. He stayed in the service after the war—switching to the brand-new U.S. Air Force, and stayed for more than twenty years.

My dad could have had a successful practice, but he stayed in the service. I asked my mother why. "He felt he owed it to them," she said. "He wouldn't have been a doctor without the service."

Still, he didn't always speak of the air force with much reverence, usually calling it "that chicken-shit outfit." When he was invited to Lyndon Johnson's inaugural ball in 1965—a college friend was helping plan the ceremonies—we got excited about making our first trip to Washington. But when the base commander heard about it, my father was ordered not to leave. Since *he* hadn't been invited, no one would go.

We all looked forward to Dad's retirement. We'd lived in England, Germany, Nebraska, Florida and Texas by the time my father's twenty years came up. The earliest home I remember was in England—three tin Quonset huts connected by a plywood hallway. You could look up and see the sky where the corners didn't meet the ceiling. In Germany, we had an apartment off-base, and the neighborhood German kids thought it was funny to teach the little American kid the essential German profanity. We lived in an odd assortment of quarters in the United States as well. Wherever we lived, walls were beige and you couldn't change the color. My mother couldn't wait to have her own home—with color, with faucets that didn't choke rust, with appliances that didn't run on steam.

Minnesota was my father's dream. He wanted a log cabin on Lake Bemidji. When that idea faded, I began designing a dream home. (After cartography, architecture became my elementary-school passion.) My parents humored me by admiring the sketches, and they too were eventually forgotten. When my father finally left the service, we began the search for where we would start our real life. During summer break from college, my sister and brother joined us. The trip to Minnesota was one of the last gasps of that family. Soon there would be marriages and children, and things were never the same.

In the end, family pressure brought my father to Indiana, near my mother's family, and he had a successful practice in general surgery until his death five years later.

Highway 61 runs nowhere near Thief River Falls, but it does bisect the Twin Cities and becomes the main street of Red Wing. As we free-fall south, I feel my father's ghost in the back seat.

I began my career as a Road Warrior in the back seat, watching my father drive, listening to his highway seminars on history, literature and politics. A lot of what I know is what I remember my father telling me. When my brother and sister left home, I became his primary pupil. And now, it appears, I have become him, with Graham.

Where Nuts Gather

Clouds roll in, and Highway 61 lacks charm in central Minnesota. Railroad tracks parallel the highway with a wide asphalt shoulder on each side, and rollerbladers glide by.

"Good Christ, what's wrong with this state?" I ask, not expecting an answer. "Now we have rural rollerbladers. We shouldn't have to see those arrogant bastards. If we see rollerbladers in the Mississippi Delta, I'm going to puke."

"Maybe we could have rollerbladed the whole way to New Orleans," Graham says.

The state actually encourages this rollerblading. The paved rail line is the Munger Trail, and it stretches from Duluth down to Hinckley. Legislators probably thought it was a good thing to "keep Minnesota healthy." They never contemplated the fashion faux pas it would bring with it. *Spandex is a privilege, not a right.*

A high canopy of thin pines columns the highway south of Moose Lake. With so little character through this part of the drive, I contemplate switching over to I-35. We'd make much better time and avoid all of the little towns along the way—Sturgeon Lake, Willow River, Rutledge—but that would be unfaithful to our plan. And besides, Graham's having a great time, playing air guitar to Hendrix and steering the car with his little fingers. There are so few people on the road that I don't admonish him.

The Squirrel Cage Bar and Motel in Willow River has a western porch front with a lighted existential sign in mismatched letters: ARE YOU OK HERE, it says. Kierkegaard must work part time, bussing tables and putting up cryptic messages. The front door of the tavern is decorated with an illustration of a big knot hole in a tree. WHERE NUTS GATHER, it says.

Midafternoon on a Thursday in May but the place is packed. At the bar, the uniform for the men—and they are nearly all men in the Squirrel Cage customer base—is a mesh hat, pack of Newports and gray hair. Some wear flannel shirts, despite the fact that this is the warmest day we've had in Minnesota. The old-man sweat is thick as the cigarette smoke, which is worthy of an apartment fire.

The poodle-haired bartender puts a Genuine Draft in front of me, with a Happy Hour ticket.

Poodlehead doesn't move. "You have to open it," she finally says, "so I know what to charge you for the beer."

I open my ticket and show it to her. "'Half price,' it says."

"That's fifty cents."

"Ooh, I like this."

The only noise in the bar is the sound of arguing. Poodlehead presides, mostly just listening to the ranting old men. I get her attention.

"Another one, please."

"You're fast," she says, delivering the beer and another ticket. Full price this time—a buck.

The other drinkers are slower. They don't just nurse their beers; they put them in intensive care. They're too busy talking to drink.

Three in the afternoon, and it's raucous. I've been in college-town bars at eleven on a Friday night that weren't as noisy.

"Lyle, Lyle, *Lyle.* . . . Lord have mercy!" one man says in exasperation.

"You have *no* sense of humor."

Next to me a large man in a maroon Ban-Lon shirt, red suspenders and worn Wrangler jeans turns sideways on his stool, apparently trying to disengage himself from the bar. His belly, roughly the size of a small goat, pushes me to the side of my barstool and for a moment, I nearly lose my balance.

He grunts a beery apology: "I'm not bumping you, just trying to see if I know you."

"I don't think we've had the pleasure," I say, and introduce myself. He heads off to the bathroom.

We missed Hidden Talent Karaoke Night by two days. I'd like to see Red Suspenders belt out a Hank Williams tune. Maybe we could coax Poodlehead into a Judy Garland medley. I notice a big Wurlitzer in the corner and peel myself off the stool to see what they have. It's a bizarre assortment—Randy Travis, John Anderson *("We were swang-ing . . .")* and Poison, Whitesnake and other hair bands.

It's a closed society in the Squirrel Cage, and I'm not sure we could crack the inner circle of their brain trust. By the time Red Suspenders staggers out of the men's room, we're back on the highway.

The best thing about teaching is having the summer off; the worst thing about teaching is having the summer off. When the kids came for the summer, I was unemployed. I had time but no money. We lived on credit cards, one of the reasons I'm in financial purgatory— still paying for that laundry detergent I bought at Sears back in 1989. My VISA cards reflect groceries from five years ago. It'll be years before I pay off our fishing trips and Disney debts.

It's worth it, because I had a lot of intense time with the kids when they were growing up. Between summers, holidays and those crazy, long weekends, I comforted myself that I did the best I could under the circumstances.

But now I want an epiphany with Graham. I want to know: *Was it enough? Were you cheated by divorce? Was I a good father?*

I was the only child around when my father died. My sister lived in Texas with her husband and their three-year-old son. She was four months pregnant and suddenly her husband was unemployed. My brother was also married and expecting a baby, and was doing his surgical residency in Tennessee. But he'd just severed a tendon in his hand in a kitchen accident and wondered if his career was over. Having dropped out of college, I lived near my parents and spent most of my evening hours stoned and was miserably unhappy in my job as editor of a small magazine. On the day he died, we all burdened my father with our problems.

It was a Sunday and I was home for dinner and laundry. My parents and I watched *The Last Picture Show*, then my father walked me to the door.

"Cheer up," he told me as I stepped out onto the porch. "Things will get better."

"I doubt it." I turned around to look at him. The door was slowly closing. "I'll see you on Tuesday, OK?" We took music lessons together.

"Sure, Son. Take care."

I was back later that night when the paramedics brought his body down the stairs. He was fifty-three. We thought we had years to tell him how much we loved and admired him, but all we had done that day was complain.

Minnesota Prairie

The white pines along the highway were once so thick you couldn't see the sky. When the first settlers moved to this part of Minnesota in the 1860s, a sawmill opened, making Hinckley one of the biggest logging towns in the upper Midwest. Rails transported lumber to Duluth's harbor, and Hinckley's products went all over the world.

But 1894 was a dry year, and by September there had been only two inches of rain in the preceding four months. Loggers started small fires to clear out an area before moving on, but some of these cleanup fires lingered and ignited debris left behind in the camps. Two fires started on September 1 and joined when gusts of cool air flew into the fields. A tornado of fire charred the remains of the logging camps, eventually destroying six towns, leveling four hundred square miles. The fire storm lasted only six hours but was efficient in its destruction.

Those left homeless were taken to a neighboring town, but Hinckley rebuilt, claimed back its citizens and turned the fire into a tourist attraction, the Hinckley Fire Museum. No matter how good the local sweet rolls are or how many people are drawn to the Hinckley Grand Casino, the town will always be best known for burning down—unless, of course, some serial killer in the future turns out to be Hinckley-born and -raised.

The first sign for *US* Highway 61 is in Pine City, but the road makes an inglorious transition. Work crews excavate under the road, and it's mucky goo through town. Other than the mudslide road—Highway 61 is Main Street—the town is pretty, highlighted by a park with a redwood carving of a voyageur, a generic French adventurer from two hundred years before.

At Froggie's Food, Fun and Spirits, a weathered waitress with cigarette-smoke hair brings us our first round (Miller for me, Coke for

Graham), but we've hit the place at shift change. At five, she is replaced by Angie, the young, hot waitress with puckering belly button and painted-on black slacks. While Bob Seger sings "You'll Accomp'ny Me," a biker in black leather and red bandanna listens intently, closed eyes visible behind shades. When he opens his eyes and sees that I have a tape recorder on the bar, he snorts and turns his back.

Angie's fellow bartender is a big beefy guy with a Bozo-like bouffant. He nods at Graham's camera, which he's placed up on the bar. "You might want to put that away, or stick it in your pocket. Last fellow come in here with a camera was tackled before he got inside the door." He says Froggie's is the kind of place guys come to get away from their wives or ex-wives, and they don't like cameras. Graham stuffs the Pentax in his cargo shorts.

Back in the car, our clothes reek of smoke. We roll down the windows, hoping the wind will cleanse us.

"I see a lot of people smoke up here," I say. "Do you? Smoke?"

"At school, yeah, there's plenty of people who smoke. In my dorm, I'd say it was like eighty-five percent. My clothes always smelled like smoke, the whole year. I mean, yeah, I smoked some, not a lot, I guess."

"I guess I'm more against it than most people, and that's because of my dad. Not emphysema. But it clogged his arteries. He had hypertension. He smoked even after he had his first attack, which should have been a warning. When I'd get up in the morning, he was out on the back porch, standing there in his boxer shorts smoking."

Graham's mother told me she used to find packs of cigarettes in his room during high school.

"My dad was a great guy," I tell him. "But you don't know him because he smoked. You would be abnormal if you didn't try it. Everyone does. But with your asthma, I think you'd be nuts to smoke."

I stare out the window and decide to leave it there. I don't want him to think he's going to endure a lot of parenting lectures while confined in a car.

I call ahead to Margi Hatch, my friend in Minneapolis who has offered us a place to stay for the night. Margi was born in Albert Lea, Minnesota, birthplace of Eddie Cochran, writer and performer of "Summertime Blues," a great moment in early rock 'n' roll. She'd gotten married to another Minnesotan back in the 1960s, gone with him to the University of Wisconsin, where he earned a Ph.D., and ended up in Gainesville, where he was one of the stars of the history department. Margi worked at the National Public Radio station in my building and we'd known each other fifteen years. After she and her husband divorced, she became business manager for the graduate studies business. We became close friends, and my children enjoyed seeing her. Margi watched them grow up on annual visits. Three years ago, she moved back to Minnesota to be near her dying father. When she moved, it was with a genuine invitation to stay at her house if we ever visited Minnesota.

I keep losing her voice on the cell phone, so she tells me to call when we get close.

A horrible wreck detours us to the interstate for fifteen miles and we miss the highway, so I decide it's time to pull out the big gun: *Highway 61 Revisited*. The angry majesty of "Like a Rolling Stone" begins like a gunshot and we crank it up. We're two profoundly white, rhythmically impaired Indiana boys trying to sing along and keep time—much like the audience at a Bob Dylan concert. Graham and I had gone to our first Bob show together the summer before in Indiana. Graham hated Bob's voice when he was little, but that show turned him into a Bobhead.

"Is this his best album?"

"It may be his best *of a period*," I say. "He's got these *periods* of his career and each has a best or at least a top two. Of the mid-1960s rock 'n' roll period, it's a toss-up between this one and *Blonde on Blonde*."

"I think you should call him. Tell him what we're doing."

"Bob don't talk to reporters."

"You should still try."

"What would I say? 'Bob, we've been stalking you. We went to your home in Duluth, saw the Armory. Went to where you grew up, your high school. Went to the restaurant opened in your honor, that *your mom* even liked.' "

"You should try." He air-drums along with Bobby Gregg, Dylan's 1965 session drummer.

"I don't think he likes people coming to him *wanting something*," I say. "And the truth is I don't want anything from him. More great albums would be nice, but if he doesn't feel like it, I can be happy with the ones we have. Did you see him on the Oscars? He looked like Vincent Price, with that weird-ass little moustache."

"Who's Vincent Price?"

"You know, the old horror-film star? He was in the 'Thriller' video." When Graham was a little boy and that video came on TV, he used to leap into my study—he never walked; he either jumped or slid, as if into second base—and said, in the scariest voice a four-year-old could muster: "Daddy!" (Long, dramatic pause.) *"Fwiller!"* The *th*, like the *r*, was beyond his ability. That was my signal to go into the other room, so he could watch it without being scared. Those were some of my best moments as a dad—being with the kids when they were frightened.

Different Shades of Anger

North of White Bear Lake, Aerosmith comes on the radio. "You know," Graham says, "they wouldn't have existed without Led Zeppelin."

"And there wouldn't be a Led Zeppelin without Willie Dixon."

"And maybe no Willie Dixon without Robert Johnson and maybe no Robert Johnson without Charley Patton."

"I didn't think you even knew who Charley Patton was." That's the beauty of the Internet.

"People up here seem to still like hard rock a lot, judging from the radio," he says. "Maybe it's some kind of angst or something. They like Staind, Godsmack. . . . They also seem to like Ozzy Osbourne, Ozzfest, that kind of stuff."

"And farther south, you're not into that?"

"Maybe all of the cold weather just pisses people off and they need release. Maybe it's the lack of minorities as well. I don't know. This stuff doesn't have the 'soul' you hear in music from the South."

"That's interesting. So you don't think black music has angst?"

"There's anger, but it's a different kind of anger. It's a *we'll-get-through-it* anger. With hard rock, it's anger just for itself. There's nothing to be learned from it."

The highway takes us into downtown St. Paul, where it latches on to the Mississippi River. It's the biggest city we've been through, and the Volkswagen Beetles are thick. It's amazing we don't have a wreck with all of the Slugbugging going on. We want to get to Margi's house, relax and explore the Twin Cities tomorrow. But we can't help but gorge on all of the sights—including a bar advertising a "meat raffle." Graham's been to Chicago and Dallas and Miami, but he's still pretty much a country boy in the big city.

Margi's home is in a southern suburb of Minneapolis, so we take 61 nearly fifteen miles south of town, then take a hard turn to the west on State Highway 42, running along a series of southern suburbs until we get to Apple Valley. The name conjures a bucolic farm-like place, but it's just a suburban explosion of Targets, strip malls, brew pubs and chain restaurants. We stop for pizza at Old Chicago and head over to Margi's.

She gives good phone directions but waits outside her townhouse to make things easier. She hasn't seen Graham in three years and gushes about what a tall, handsome and, at this point, unshaven young man he has become.

People accuse me of being anal-retentive, but Margi's house is the most immaculate dwelling I've ever seen. She sets us down in the living room, gives us premium Minneapolis-brewed beer, puts on a jazz CD and we get caught up.

She'd moved back to Minnesota to be near her father—suffering from Alzheimer's disease—and support her mother and sister. "There was nothing to do about Dad," she says, "except bring in malted milks and play peekaboo." He died in 2000.

She's moved from Pillsbury to General Mills and dismisses talk of her job. "Sucks wads," she says. "I'm in transit for three hours and forty minutes, total, each day. The long and short of it is I'm sick and tired of the whole shebang. Minnesota is nice to your face but turns around and stabs you in the back." Visitors from Florida, old friends, are her greatest joy.

Margi can't tell us too much about the cultural life of the Twin Cities. Her job and commute drain most of her energy. Life's been too hard.

She has to leave for work at Pillsbury early the next day, and she instructs me on how to lock up the house, deal with her herd of cats and other morning chores. She puts us in the guest room on the bottom floor, and Graham and I—two bulky men—fight for space in a double bed. I edge over to the side, and he's still watching a baseball game when I fall asleep.

Dinkytown

Highway 61 veers away from St. Paul, but I can't very well bring my son to the Twin Cities and not show him around. Since we're sort of following a Bob Dylan Trail, we need to go see the University of Minnesota, where Bob started school and dropped out after one semester.

I-35 north takes us across the Mississippi, winding through Minneapolis and St. Paul. It's not hard to find the University of Minnesota and its famous bohemian neighborhood, Dinkytown. Gold-and maroon banners hang from streetlamps to tell tourists *you-are-in-Dinkytown.* How bohemian can a place with banners be?

Growing up in a college town in the Midwest, I've always been kind of snobby about the Ann Arbors, the Bloomingtons, the Urbana-Champaigns. Those are *real* college towns, built around universities— and so is Gainesville. I never saw much appeal to an NYU, the University of Chicago (Dad's alma mater), Ohio State in Columbus or Minnesota in the Twin Cities. The university doesn't *rule.* But Dinkytown must be unique because it has that small-town atmosphere, yet if you look across the river, the towers of Minneapolis loom.

Dinkytown's pretty small—just a two-block by four-block business district across from the main entrance to the university, with Fourth Street right down the middle. Critics always thought Dylan's famous kiss-off song, "Positively Fourth Street," was an assault on all of his former friends in Greenwich Village who hectored him on how to run his life. Maybe it was aimed at denizens of this other Fourth Street.

When Bob hit town in 1959, he pledged Sigma Alpha Mu, and hung out at the *Minnesota Daily.* The student newspaper still runs promotional ads featuring a baby-faced Bob with a headline: "Bob Dylan started his career here. Maybe you can too." But the bohemian life of Dinkytown was far more appealing than the straight life on campus. He gravitated toward a bunch of older students and made friends who introduced him to folk music. After playing at one coffee shop for a while, he asked the owner for a raise and was let go. One of his girlfriends, Bonnie Beecher (debate rages whether it was Bonnie or Hibbing girlfriend Echo Hellstrom who inspired "Girl from the North Country"), swiped food from her sorority's kitchen to feed Bob and drove him around town to auditions. His steadiest gig was at a St. Paul pizza parlor called the Purple Onion. He did his Woody Guthrie impersonation and was mascot to the grad-student crowd, then went off to New York, he said, to "meet Woody." *Yeah, sure.* But then he did, and he became more famous than his idol.

The streets glisten with last night's rain, and there's still a little chill. The Slugbugs proliferate around campus, but we rarely play the game while walking, for fear some innocent bystander will think we're fighting and call the cops. We walk up Fourteenth Avenue, trying to blend in, figuring we don't look too out of place, not getting that *you-a-stranger?* look we got in Hibbing and Duluth.

"The best place to go is Al's Breakfast," I tell him. "That's what all my Minnesota friends tell me."

But the line at Al's stretches out the door, despite the morning's news that Al's Breakfast is changing its long-standing "book" policy. If you wanted to eat but didn't have money, they'd let you keep a book at Al's—a long-running tab—that you'd be obligated to pay someday. Folklore has it that His Grand Exalted Mystic Bobness dined thus in his college-dropout days. History is on the side of Al's Breakfast, but our groaning bellies lead us across the street to the Dinkytowner Café. It's a two-level place and we're sent to the basement for food. The top floor is for entertainment.

The café walls are festooned with artwork, including a portrait of Bob in the corner. Our waiter is so heavily pierced I'd wager he's done time with hepatitis. Graham and I each order the Cajun Breakfast. The server arches one eyebrow with a *you-fucking-pigs* look, but I don't care. It's just what we want: crispy hashbrowns grilled with fresh green peppers, mushrooms and onions, covered with melted cheddar, and two over-easy eggs smothered in hollandaise sauce and sprinkled with Cajun spice and served with toast. We go all the way, adding andouille sausage for $2.50 more.

While we wait for this artery-clogging mess to arrive, we listen to two angry wannabe poets at the bar, smoking and coughing out *fucks* and *shits* with every breath, desperate in their attempts at being different. One is a pallid, terribly thin platinum blonde boy who looks one breath away from cadaverville. The other is huskier with a black, pubiclike beard and a Columbine overcoat too heavy for this weather. With them is a quiet young woman, hair parted down the middle in that late-1960s style I still like. She's no doubt embarrassed by the spectacle her companions are making, arguing about Art and the Nature of Human Experience, but says nothing. Still drunk from the night before, I figure. It's Friday, so if this is like other college towns, the heavy partying began last night. Graham isn't paying much attention, intent on leafing through the *City Pages*, a bulky giveaway alternative paper he picked up at the front door. I wonder if he feels on display, so obviously here with his dad. If those guys at the bar—undeniably *cool dudes* to an impressionable young college student like Graham—turn around and feast their eyes on the father-and-son bowling team, no doubt "their art" might require them to spew venomous verse in our direction. I know the performance-art type, and I suspect they are at that age when they are angry at everyone.

A mound of food arrives and we attack the hash browns and eggs, soaking both in Louisiana Red Dot. The long hours in the car have turned us into remorseless eating machines. The coffee, also devilishly hot, adds to the burn.

The two terribly troubled souls at the bar stop their howl when the King of Dinkytown walks in—not from the direction we came, but from somewhere in the bowels of the building. They genuflect toward him, but he grants his subjects no more than a curt nod.

He has a massive Afro that gives him a hirsute aura three feet in diameter. Draped fashionably down from the peak of the 'fro is a long peacock plume. His face is nearly obscured by enormous black plastic glasses, circa Buddy Holly's plane crash, and a Van Dyke beard that frames his lip and chin.

His name is Bill Grimes IV, and when I ask about Bill Grimes III I'm immediately sorry. His father, suffering from emphysema, killed himself the year before.

"He stepped down to the basement with a nine millimeter," Bill says. "He got tired of the leash—with emphysema, you've got to cart around a tank of oxygen. I wasn't glad that someone I *so totally dug* was dead, but I didn't want to see him do the hospital thing. I *understood.*"

Bill is thirty-one and talks in italics. He's a philosopher and author of the self-published *Mystified Sojourn*, a combination autobiography and philosophical treatise, centered on his decade in Dinkytown.

He grew up on the south side of Minneapolis ("our version of the ghetto") with a black father and a white mother. He went to Minnesota's Carlson School of Management and earned a degree in accounting. "But then I discovered I wasn't compatible with the corporate environment," he says, fully aware of the epic nature of the understatement. "I just can't do the *obsequious sycophant thing*. It's just not my deal."

Before the massive hair started growing, he was in the army reserves for six years, "but I wasn't going to make a career out of being a *soldier guy* either," he said.

His awakening in college and his experiences in Dinkytown led him to write the autobiography. "It starts with my last year in college," he says. "I have been obsessed with spirituality and philosophy for over a decade. It is my take on the thing. I figured I could do a better job than most of the stuff that I'd read. If I'm not being *delusional*, it's good."

He doesn't miss "the ass-kiss structure thing" and didn't stay long in his accounting job. "Most of the people in cubicles tend to be more right wing than I would generally appreciate. Throw in your basic antifemale, racist *homophobe* and that's just not my deal." For now, he works for a company called Transit Team, driving handicapped people around the Twin Cities.

"Volunteer work?" I ask.

"For what they pay me, it might as well be."

Graham likes the peacock feather dangling from the back of Bill's monster 'fro. "We don't even see that in Bloomington," he says.

Bill says, "The peacock feather is chronic. I did it as a little aesthetic sort of thing. I'm six foot three with big hair, and I try not to be too intimidating."

Turns out Bill has a nickname, Skippy Hendrix, owing to both his hair and his collection of sixteen Jimi Hendrix shirts ("I can go over two weeks without repeating myself."). "Hendrix is like a god to me," he says, "so that's OK. They say I look like the bastard love child of Jimi Hendrix."

Graham is lucky to have grown up in a college town, though Dinkytown makes his hometowns—Bloomington and Gainesville—look like backwoods settlements. Still, they are his reference points to the rest of the world, and they have skewed him a bit. Bloomington has a Tibetan temple a quarter mile from his mother's home. Celebrity Buddhists like Richard Gere, Steven Seagal and Harrison Ford often visit. Homegrown rock 'n' roll star John Mellencamp lives a mile in the other direction. The town was lovingly shown in the film *Breaking Away.* Having Indiana University around gives the community that wonderful college-town balance between the hardworking salt-of-the-earth types in their gimme caps and denim overalls and the mixture of students from Asia and Arkansas. A kid can grow up in small-town America and still have some level of sophistication.

"Pretend you're re-creating the Bob experience," I say, sipping my third Equal-charged cup of coffee. "We just came down from Hibbing. He came down from Hibbing forty years ago. Imagine being a kid—son of an appliance salesman—and you come from that place.

Now, imagine yourself set down here with peacock boy." I drain the
cup, setting it down on the table. "It has that effect of opening your
eyes to the rest of the world."

"I wonder if it was like this back then," Graham says.

"You have a great advantage, growing up in a college town," I tell
him. "I think you're readier for the world. More so than a kid from a
small town. You've got a. . . . " I trail off.

"A larger view of the world?" he finishes.

"Yeah. It's one of the best things about being a college professor,"
I say. "Watching that happen to kids, even when it takes *that* kind of
turn." I nod toward the angst-ridden boys and their superior female
companion. "Those dudes need to lighten up a bit."

We work off the breakfast by walking around Dinkytown, sticking
our noses into all of the shops—Varsity Bike Shop, Dinkytown News
and Campus Cards. Cheapo Discs is a warehouse-sized store with
two long walls featuring only local bands. Underneath a giant
blowup of the *Let It Be* cover (the Replacements' album, not the Beatles album), the store lovingly displays discs by Shaky Jake, the Sandwiches, the Roswell Incident, Spy Mob, Tulip Sweet & Her Trail of
Tears and scores of others. Never heard of any of these bands, but
think of all of the great artists who stomped these grounds: Bob,
Prince, the Replacements (you've got to love a group with a song
called "Gary's Got a Boner") and the Trashmen.

A cult surrounds the Trashmen, the celebrated Minnesota surf
band. In those pre-Beatle days, when the Beach Boys were cool and
not yet Republican, and even the rhythmically impaired could pinch
out the guitar line of "Wipe Out," the Trashmen hit the charts with
"Surfin' Bird." I was a kid living in south Florida, and I thought surf
music was the coolest thing in the world. The Beach Boys, Jan &
Dean and Dick Dale were at the top of the southern California pyramid, but from someplace much weirder came this howling jibber
called "Surfin' Bird." I didn't know until I was an adult—until I

started teaching rock 'n' roll history—that this surf music (*"A-well-a everybody's heard about the bird"*) came from Minnesota.

Greater dementia has never since been heard on the radio. The Trashmen were just a simple Minneapolis rock 'n' roll band, starting out as Jim Thaxter & the Travelers, but after a trip to southern California and surfing, they began playing surf music to a landlocked Minnesota audience. "Surfin' Bird" was the moment in the sun for the quartet. They recorded a lot of songs—imagine "Greensleeves" played surf-guitar style—enough to fill a four-CD box set retrospective, and disbanded in 1968 (the year Jimi Hendrix offered his famous benediction, "May you never hear surf music again.") They revived the act on a wave of perverse nostalgia in the 1980s and performed until drummer Steve Wahrer's death disbanded the group for good. He was the weird croaking voice on "Surfin' Bird." Whatever lives the survivors followed, they rest secure in the knowledge that they made two minutes and twenty seconds of insanity that will live forever in the annals of rock 'n' roll.

Graham and I go different directions in the store. He's over there in hip-hop, and I'm cruising through folk and blues, hoping to find some Bob rarity.

We're blissfully looking through discs, listening to tracks from the featured albums displayed on the wall, enjoying the parade of other shoppers. When we bump into each other in the pop-rock section— somewhere around the Allman Brothers—we're both nearly giddy.

"What a great store," Graham says. "I wish we had something like this back home. You have Hear Again, but this kicks Hear Again's ass."

"Most definitely," I say. As soon as Graham hits town on vacation, we're usually off to the massively disorganized used-CD store down by campus. "But you know what this does to me?"

"What?"

I indicate a nearby section labeled "weirdness." "I remember when you guys were little and you had such shitty taste," I say. "You liked 'The Simpsons Sing the Blues' and Sarah liked Ace of Base."

"Don't remind me."

"Anyway, I just saw 'The Beavis and Butt-head Experience' over there and got all oogly and nostalgic."

We don't buy anything. The store is overwhelming, like an over-stocked hardware store—so much stuff that you can't focus on anything.

The Purple Onion is nearly vacant and we need more coffee. One of Bob's first steady gigs in his college days was at the Purple Onion in St. Paul. That place is long gone, but the successor here in Dinky-town looks like a reasonable facsimile of an early 1960s coffee shop.

Graham gets a Roadrunner and I get a vanilla crème. Ghostly echoing surf guitar rattles around the high ceilings, bare walls, soft pastels and painted, exposed girders. The dominant artwork is a psy-chedelic drawing.

The surf guitar ends and it's Bob, singing "Moonshiner," one of his early recordings. The echo gives his voice a phantom quality. Maybe he never sang here, but I'd swear Young Bob haunts this place. Bob's ghost begins "Let Me Die in My Footsteps." It's him as a stern, resolute young man, defying the world to incinerate itself. The little man's voice sounds so brave.

"So, the creek—that's all you remember about Oklahoma?" I ask suddenly.

"I remember getting peed on," Graham says nonchalantly. "One of those boys down the street. I was the littlest one, so they used to pick on me."

"I never knew about this."

"I remember the time I stepped on that branch and it went up into my foot. That hurt like hell."

"You went to the emergency room. Remember the time I bor-rowed the 'Top Dog' costume and wore it to your birthday party?" Top Dog was the university's courtside mascot for basketball games, and the kid who wore it was one of my students. The costume was hot and I was nearly faint with sweat after the party. "One of those boys—Ira, I think—kept hitting me in the crotch and I was getting so pissed. But I didn't want to ruin Top Dog's image by smacking him."

Our laughter mixes with Bob's singing, and one of the bookish types by the window looks up with annoyance.

"I wish you could remember more about that time," I tell him. "I remember everything."

Outside, a homeless man accosts us for change. Luckily, we have a buck fifty left from the five we used on the coffee. He accepts it graciously, doffing his grease-stained porkpie hat. "No matter how bad it gets with the economy," he says, "there is always charity."

The Mall of America

Being a heterosexual father-and-son bowling team, we loathe shopping, but we're still curious about the Mall of America. As soon as we get out of the car, God's Holy Bladder bursts and we're drenched when we sprint into Sears.

"Good God," I say to Graham when we step into the huge multi-level mall. "What have we gotten ourselves into?"

The Mall of America is monstrous. As we get to center court, an amusement park called Camp Snoopy with roller coasters, log rides and carousels, I wish for a moment that it was four-year-old Graham with me. His friend's father designed Camp Snoopy, he says. He does mall designs, and the amusement park was his biggest project.

We work our way through the jostling masses of whiney kids and pushy parents and find the relative safety of one of the shopping promenades and work our way up. As much as I might want to disparage the whole thing, I can't help but be awed. Looking up, there's a huge canopy of skylights nurturing four hundred fully grown trees and thirty thousand live plants. They look a lot better than the stuff on my porch back in Gainesville, and these things are in a *mall*—in Minnesota for God's sake. How can I be bitter and snobbish about something based around Snoopy anyway? Charles Schulz, the "Peanuts" creator, was from the Twin Cities. What a nice thing for a hometown to do for a native son. Bob probably feels pretty good about a restaurant in his honor back in Hibbing, but if he'd see this place, he might want Hibbing to at least upgrade to a strip mall.

No doubt we should be shopping for Nicole and Savannah and Sarah and Mary Grace, but as we go through the endless stores—pausing to play in the Sharper Image and to leaf through CDs at Sam Goody (bland after the character of Cheapo Discs)—we can't find anything to buy.

"This is just too much," Graham says when we sit down for dinner in the Café Odyssey. "I mean, can you imagine Mammaw saying, 'I'm going to run to the mall for a minute,' and then coming to this place?"

He chose the Café Odyssey after looking over a brochure about the mall restaurants. You're supposed to have a choice of three environments for dining—Machu Picchu, the Serengeti Plain and Atlantis. We pick Atlantis because it's the only place impossible to go otherwise, but it turns out there's no seating left in the Lost Continent. As we squeak across the Spanish tile to our table—his sneakers still soggy from the parking-lot dash—we're shivering in the air-conditioned rain forest. I'm trying not to worry about money—hell, when's the next time I'll be dining with my son in Machu Picchu, and so I decide American Express will pay for this one. We go for Katmandu Chicken and the featured fajita of the day.

"Where to from here?" Graham asks.

"Somewhere south on 61."

"I think I've had quite enough of this place," he says, mouth full of fajita. "The mall, I mean, not this place. This place I like."

The Walls of Red Wing

The highway crosses the Mississippi and dives south, but soon joins the river north of Red Wing. This is another near-homecoming.

"Red Wing could have been your home," I say. "But I suppose if I'd grown up here, I probably would have never met your mother."

Graham, eyes on the road, seems intent on the drive and not reminiscence.

I was here before, in that earlier life. My mother and father brought me along to look at this town on the Mississippi River, to see if we might want to live there. My father liked Red Wing, its surprisingly up-to-date clinic, and a particular hundred-year-old house on a bluff over the river, with a grand, butternut staircase that rose imposingly from the foyer, like something out of *The Magnificent Ambersons*.

One of the Dakota tribes settled the area, and several of the chiefs were named Red Wing. A dyed swan's wing was the tribal symbol and was later adopted by the shoe manufacturer based in town. It became a heavily trafficked port—look at it as you cruise into town on 61 and you have to thank the gods of geography for blessing the little village—and was for a while the largest wheat market in the world.

I remember our day in Red Wing so clearly that I can't believe it was more than thirty years ago that we drove these streets. I didn't know Highway 61 from Route 66 back then, Bob Dylan was not vital to my existence (so I was unaware of his obscure song about a reform school here, "Walls of Red Wing"), and parenthood—the defining role of my life—was more than a decade away. I just remember how much my father loved the town. He drove to the top of the bluff, where the grandest houses in town looked down on the painted river, as happy as I'd ever seen him. Where he chose to live and open his practice was entirely his decision, my mother said, but her silence registered her opinion of Red Wing, Minnesota.

Graham loves it too. We drive down to the banks of the river, then take a cross street to the top of the hill, to those old houses my father coveted.

"I could see living here," he says, nodding. "Might be cold in winter, but I don't think it would kill you."

We're parked on the hill, enjoying the view. The sun is going down behind us, casting huge shadows the way of the river. I call home.

"Hey, Mom. I'm in Red Wing."

"Red Wing, Minnesota?"

"Yep. You know, it looks exactly the same as it did when we were here in 1968. Nothing has changed."

There's a long pause on her end. "Your father loved that place. I just think I would have been so bored there, but I think that's what he really wanted. . . ."

The whole idea had been *fond-memory*, but now it seems I've made her sad. "Mom, I think he was perfectly happy with the choice he made. You know he had a happy last few years in Indiana."

"I know," she says, "but every now and then, he'd talk about that house with the butternut woodwork, and I wondered if he did what he did to make me happy."

"Isn't that what you're supposed to do in a marriage?"

"I suppose so." How rotten it feels to bring your mother to near-tears. I brag about Graham being a great driver and traveling companion. As I say this, I look at him and he's proudly surveying the Mississippi River from the driver's seat, a true Road Warrior.

"I'd better go, Mom," I say, "I didn't mean to make you sad. It just felt strange being here in Red Wing. I've got so many memories of those trips when Dad was getting out of the service."

"Yes," she says, and pauses again. "I miss that guy."

I hang up. "Did Mammaw get all sad and shit?" Graham asks.

"Yeah. I feel like a creep now. You know," I tell Graham, "memory is a funny thing. You heard me—it was a long-damn time ago we were here. And I remember driving up this street that day. It was the old blue Cadillac convertible. Dad was driving, Mom was shotgun, I was in back. We were driving up this street and there were three boys playing football in the front yard of this house over here." I point to a brick house with white columns. "And so when we drive by, I give the boys a look, you know—scoping them out. These guys might be my buddies. And this one kid sees me and makes a face and puckers his lips like he's kissing me. And I thought, 'What an asshole.' " I focus on the image for a moment; it's one of those odd incidents that persist in my memory. "I bet that guy's still in this town somewhere. I'd like to hunt down that little fucker and kick his ass."

Graham laughs, starts the car and eases it down the steep hill to Highway 61.

Goodbye, Norma Jean

Ten miles south of Red Wing is Frontenac, a small community on a narrow strip of land that fingers itself into the Mississippi. Even moderate rainfall floods these homes, and the shin-high watermarks indicate it flooded recently. Still, people walk nonchalantly down the gravel road by the village and wave at us, the intruders in the *much-too-clean-to-be-from-around-here* Explorer. They are obviously at peace with their lot in life. It has its inconveniences, but they live in the teeth of the Mississippi River, and if the price you have to pay for this gift is annual flooding, then so be it.

The river is beautiful alongside the highway. A few towns dot the scenery, but it's primarily water, asphalt and trees through here. The sun drops behind the tree line to the west, and we sniff out the motels in each of these small towns; but when we think we're ready to stop, we decide to try for one stop more.

A name on the map catches our eye: *Rollingstone*.

"Bob would want us to stop there," Graham says.

"It's off the highway," I say. "Too bad. That would be kind of cool—'Rollingstone' on Highway 61."

It's dark by the time we make it to State Road 248 and turn the five miles to Rollingstone. There are two streets and we pick the one with the two-story building. Lights indicate a tavern, so maybe the upstairs has rooms. At the corner, we pull up next to a pickup truck just as a tall man in a baseball cap gets out. I ask, "Hey, is there a hotel here?" The patch over his pocket says, "Ed." Before he can answer, Ed's wife comes around the truck. "There's no hotel in Rolling-stone." Ed advises, "If you want a hotel, you've got to go to Winona." Ed's wife herds their teenage daughter toward the tavern.

Back toward 61 and Winona. Rollingstone is a minuscule town, well cared for and hidden, but nothing like what its name implies. The place is covered in moss.

Winona Ryder was born here as Winona Laura Horowitz in 1971, her parents taking the town's name for their daughter. We can't find any place with a room. Six motels, all full. The state high-school baseball tournament has drawn the visitors, so we decide we'll take *anything*, and that category covers the Sterling Motel. It's off one of the main streets, and its marquee is dark, discouraging people from stopping. "Yes, there is room," the weathered woman behind the desk says. "Can I show you one?" She opens the door to the room behind the maid's supply closet.

Her name is Marilyn. "If you need a bite to eat," she says, "you might try the Happy Chef next door. They don't give me nothing for sending people there, but they should, I send so many." She's mastered the art of talking while holding a cigarette in her lips. It flaps at me like the handle on a slot machine. "Open twenty-four hours. Truckers like it a lot, so it must be good."

The Happy Chef is empty except for a cook and a waitress, a young girl about Graham's age. She seems ready to flirt but probably wonders if that's a good idea with the older guy around. *Father and son? On a Friday night? What's up with this?* We must seem like an odd couple. When a tableful of college-age kids comes in—Winona State University, Home of the Warriors—Graham probably feels, for the second time that day, odd in the presence of his peers. Maybe he'd like to join that table—one of the kids is a girl, very cute, and the other three, somewhat dorky boys, are trying to see who can be the most irritating, in some misguided ritual to win her affection.

Graham orders a hamburger and when it comes he says, "We haven't had a bad meal on this trip—even here."

The college kids are getting louder and more annoying, so we leave quickly, pick up a quart of Miller Lite at a convenience store and go back to our room: two double beds, with worn comforters in paisley explosions of red and green, cigarette burns in the side of the bathtub, a dish with the congealing remains of an earlier guest's soap.

We drink beer from Styrofoam cups and channel surf. I linger over Larry King on CNN, a rebroadcast from earlier in the evening, drawn by the anger in the voices—one of those verbal free-for-alls you expect from a political show, but this isn't politics. There's a face familiar but at first unrecognizable. Then the superimposition pops on the bottom of the screen: "Tony Curtis." I'd thought the angry man with the bloated face was some sort of drag queen, and I guess I'm right, considering *Some Like It Hot.* Larry King is refereeing the fight between Curtis in Hollywood and a couple of experts *du jour*— no doubt college professors—on the East Coast. The experts are saying she was murdered because she fell into the Kennedy-Hollywood axis and Curtis is saying she was just a troubled nymphomaniac. Another expert, near tears, says for Curtis to speak so vividly of his sexual encounters with her is to trample on her memory.

And then Larry King comes on to take us to commercial break and remind us of the subject: Today would have been Marilyn Monroe's seventy-fifth birthday, and his guests tonight are here to pick through her remains.

"Wow, first James Dean seventy and now Marilyn seventy-five. It's making me feel very old."

"She was some kind of sex symbol for her time, wasn't she?"

"She sure was," I say. "She was *the* sex symbol."

That whole world seems distant. I remember when she walked the earth; I remember the day she died. Seems like you can't read anything about her anymore that doesn't speculate on her life with the Kennedys. I remember standing by the runway at Homestead Air Force Base, watching Air Force One arrive and seeing President Kennedy walk down the ramp from the plane. "Hello, Jackie!" everyone yelled when the limousine passed by. And now they are both gone, their son is gone, Marilyn is gone. I am gone too—at least, that little-boy version of me standing by the runway. So is that other little-boy version of me, who grew into this unshaven young man in the next bed. Marilyn Monroe at seventy-five . . . tasteless as it may sound, maybe she died when she should have died. She'll always be young.

I toss the remote control at him. "It's all yours," I say.

He doesn't hesitate to switch channels, uninterested in Marilyn Monroe.

Big River

Next morning, I pull on my jeans and my Sun Records T-shirt and bowling shoes and jog over to the Happy Chef. The waitress brings me a pot, a cup, a metal container of cream and a jar of real and fake sugar. She knows I'm here for the long haul.

A chubby man in a black-and-red ball cap ("Muczee's 11th Anniversary" with white lightning bolts decorating the brim) is spread out in a booth, romancing his coffee. When he says hello I see what the hat says. He smiles at the waitress, a grandmother type with tight gray curls, huge black horn-rims and oversized Reeboks. He's leisurely working his way through a stack of four pancakes.

A chill as the door opens and an older man in a two-tone blue windbreaker enters, his distinguished gray hair combed back. He has an imperious look, and I wonder if he's a chamber of commerce dignitary.

The young waitress ("Cathy" pinned on her bosom) greets him: "You want me or Elaine?"

"Lord, don't make me choose," he implores.

He gets Elaine, the fastest thing in Reeboks. "Good morning, Elaine," he booms and efficiently orders oatmeal and toast. When she leaves, the friendly fellow in the ball cap raises his coffee cup. "Chilly this morning," he says.

"Hard on the crops," gray hair says.

"This is September weather."

"I know—fall." Gray hair lights a cigarette and holds it arrogantly, between thumb and forefinger, like a concentration-camp commandant in a World War II movie.

"How you been doing with the Indians?" ball cap asks.

"They took me to the cleaners," the commandant says, shaking his head. Treasure Island Resort and Casino is down in Hastings.

Ball cap asks Elaine for three more pancakes, then tells the commandant that he's just back from a trip to Otsego ("not a bad run") and he's been on the road since three o'clock. That must be his truck outside with the "Wall-Eye Pirate" plate on the front. When Elaine comes back, he asks her, "Say, you know what's going on up to the middle school this morning? I saw four buses there when I went past."

The oatmeal and toast arrive, and the commandant sits at attention and eats efficient spoonfuls.

Back at the room, I pull on Graham's toe. "*Time tuh rawk 'n' rowl, Dude.* Hit the shower. I'm going to clean out the car."

We've put down the second row of seats, and the boxes, clothes, newspapers and food remains have created a disgusting mess. I open the back of the War Wagon and begin heaving things into the Sterling's dumpster. Marilyn wheels up the maid cart and takes a look.

"I thought you worked the front desk," I said.

"I'm the maid, the check-in girl . . ." She looks in the cooler. "What're you going to do with that?

Grapes, yogurt containers, carrot sticks all float like shipwreck victims in the remains of ice, my own little *Titanic* diorama. I was going to heave it all but hate to see things wasted. "You want it?" I ask.

"Sure," she says, gathering up the food. "I'll give some of this shit to the birds—if you'll pardon my language." Maybe, like Elvis, Marilyn Monroe faked her death and now she works as the maid and check-in girl at the Sterling Motel.

We leave Winona on the last stretch of Highway 61 in Minnesota, a few yards from the Mississippi River. "Like a Rolling Stone" is blasting.

"Wouldn't it be cool to live in that house?" I say, pointing up on the bluff. "Everyday, you look out your front door and see one of the greatest things about the country."

"I want to live on the water someday," Graham says.

"I want you to live in the Keys, so you'll let me come visit."

An oriole watches us from the top of a Highway 61 sign as we blast by at seventy miles per hour, our fastest speed on the trip. "Tombstone Blues" is crammed with images, and Bob is at his name-dropping best—Ma Rainey, Beethoven, Belle Starr, Jack the Ripper. . . . Graham tells me that in his African-American lit class they read a play about Ma Rainey by August Wilson. I'm ashamed to admit I don't know a lot about her.

"The best part of the class was when we divided into black and white and made up ethnic notions about each other," he says. "It was like that scene in *Do the Right Thing* when they have all the name calling. So the white guys talked about how the black guys smelled and the black guys talked about how the white guys smelled. It was the craziest class. After a couple of classes like that, you got to know each other pretty well."

"Did I ever tell you about when I taught in the jail?" He gives me a blank look. "Down in Florida—I know I've told you this." It was the semester after the kids moved away with their mother. I taught at the county jail one night a week to keep myself busy. "It was supposed to be a class on the mass media or some shit like that, but it turned out to be a class on race in America. My class was the only time during the week that male and female prisoners could be together, but they couldn't talk. The guards just led me into a room, brought in the prisoners and closed the door. The prisoners could probably give two shits for the mass media, but they wanted to see members of the opposite sex. Anyway, I told them the first night, 'I don't care what you did to get here.' I *didn't* want to know. But I *do* read the paper, and so I'd see when they went to trial. The little-old country girl named Tammy, it turns out, was in there for skinning a hitchhiker she picked up. And this nice old gentleman, Mr. McDaniel—since he was older, I always called him that, *Mr.* McDaniel—he was in for trying to cut off his wife's head. The last class period, we get going on why there are so many black people in jail, way out of proportion to the population. And this guy was jabbing me in the chest while he was making his points, and we were all screaming at each other. Best single class period I've ever had. When it was over, we all shook hands and hugged, it was so intense."

Bob starts singing "Highway 61 Revisited."

"When I was your age," I tell Graham, "I was *obsessed* with this album. This is the album you must memorize when you're nineteen or twenty. It spoke to me, at least." The police-siren sound effect whistles through the car and we turn up the volume. "Everything happens on Highway 61," I say, as the police siren fades.

We gas up at a Wisconsin Pump 'n' Munch after crossing the Mississippi. "I think I'm going to miss Minnesota," Graham says. "I like that place."

"Sometime we should come back," I say, "and just stay for a week. Maybe we can all go to Lake Bemidji some time."

Maybe when he's older, maybe even married with kids, we can all meet here.

Fans

Dave's Guitar Shop in La Crosse is the size of a basketball arena, and inside there's a museumlike hush, occasionally broken by a Steve Vai wannabe. Over a thousand lovingly displayed models line the walls. A dozen customers mill around, and Dave's employees wear black T-shirts. For twenty minutes, we saunter through the store. Graham takes a Les Paul guitar from the wall and plays a few chords.

"Cool," he says. "No one comes rushing over to give me shit. Usually at guitar stores they get all weirded out when you actually touch the guitars."

You can comb your hair in the metal front of the gleaming National guitars. Graham tries out an acoustic Rickenbacker. We see a rare Merle Travis electic sunburst for twenty-five thousand. There's a Gretch Eddie Cochran in pumpkin orange for two thousand. There's also a prebattered Stevie Ray Vaughan replica of "No. 1," his lucky guitar.

"Look at this Bo Diddley," Graham says, showing me a red rectangular guitar.

Suddenly, a hyperactive solo from across the shop, obviously a speed metal fan.

"That's a PRS," Graham says. "What a waste of a great guitar." Paul Reed Smith is the preferred guitar of Carlos Santana.

We move a little closer and see that the show-off is a bearish, long-gray-haired man with spectacles. "It has such a great sound," the show-off says. "It's such a rockin' machine . . . that's what I'm excited about."

"You can wail with that," his friend says.

"Let's do a 'guitar-and-go,' " Graham whispers. The tone here is reverential, so we lower our voices.

"What's that?"

"Like a 'gas-and-go.' " With my blank face I must look like a shovelhead. "You know, you pull up, get your gas and drive off without paying. I had friends who did gas-and-go's all the way to Florida last year."

"So which one would you risk your life and career for?"

"I'll grab that Les Paul," he says. "You get the PRS—save it from that dude."

There's a raffle to win a Les Paul guitar, and the price is a donation to the local food bank. I tell Graham to get the unopened case of Captain's Wafers out of the car.

I bought Graham his first guitar—an acoustic—for Christmas one year. It took him a couple of years to really take an interest in it and when he did, he learned quickly. He had a great young guitar teacher and he soon wanted an electric. So we got a cheap Yamaha at a pawn shop. Soon he needed a better acoustic, and we got him an Alvarez. The next spring break, when he visited me in Florida, we went to a guitar shop in Jacksonville Beach.

As he fingered a Danelectro, I said, "Let me get you this one."

"You're kidding."

"No, just pick out one of these Danelectros. I think we can manage it."

So the credit card went to work and Graham got a decent electric guitar. The following Christmas when I was visiting Indiana, I was with him in his bedroom at his mother's house and he put on a Led Zeppelin CD and plugged in his guitar. I went down the hall to the bathroom, and all of a sudden I heard only Jimmy Page's guitar track. I wondered how he could isolate the guitar since his stereo wasn't that sophisticated. I stuck my head in his room and he'd put on head-phones. I was hearing him, not Jimmy Page.

Sometimes I think I must be a disappointment to him. Although I love music, I'm not a musician. Although I love fishing with him, I'm not a fisherman. It seemed whatever he needed help with was some-thing I couldn't do.

We're talking about our trip with Laun Braithwhite, one of the salesmen. "I did that once," he says. "At least, the pilgrimage to Hib-bing part. It was me and my friend Vince, my buddy from high school. You know, you like to drive around in high school, so we decided to drive all the way up Highway 61. We loaded up our car with Dylan tapes and off we went."

He's mid-thirties now, with long brown hair and a friendly Mid-western twang. "Highway 61 led up to Duluth, and I believe we had to get on another road to get over to Hibbing. Saw the high school first—it was night—and we made it to where Dylan's house was. We asked some people on the street. Some of them acted like, 'Dylan? Who cares?' We stayed at an old motel, kind of a nasty place; the cur-tains looked like they hadn't been washed since 1960. The next morning, Vince, being an outgoing type, just goes up and knocks on a door and says, 'This where Dylan lived?' And they said, 'Oh, you mean Bobby Zimmerman? He lived across the street.' So we had our picture made out in front of it."

"Those were the coolest guitars," Graham says when we're back on the road. "The places where we stop turn out to be very serendipitous."

"I am so impressed that you said 'serendipitous.' I didn't even know that you knew it."

Outside La Crosse, the highway pitches and heaves with the rolling hills, and deer stroll across the road without fear. Fields are green and lush and the trees' new leaves make me wish we had a sharper change of season in Florida.

Beer-Can Philosopher

The Fjord Bar in Coon Valley is empty except for a white-haired man with a Friar Tuck fringe, sitting on the customer side of the mahogany bar and reading the *Eau Claire Leader-Telegram.*

"You open?" I ask.

"As much as I ever am."

It's a steel-clouded Saturday afternoon, and Coon Valley's populace is invisible. Graham and I settle down at the bar, but Friar Tuck seems in no hurry to get up from his sports page. Eventually, he lumbers behind the bar.

"What can I do you for?"

"What's on tap?"

"Nothing. We only have cans."

"Well, what do you have in cans?"

"Miller Lite." I wait for more, but that's it.

"I guess I'll have a Miller Lite then."

He's wearing an all-denim ensemble—dark jeans, light blue work shirt—and he smokes Vantage. Should there ever be demand for a look-alike Dennis Franz of *NYPD Blue*, he should apply.

"Interesting name," I start. "Is there a fjord around here?"

"This area was settled by immigrants from Norway because it reminded them of their homeland. Look at a map of Norway and you'll see that it's made up of a series of bays—those are fjords. The people who started this bar many, many years ago called it the Fjord."

He takes a long drag on his Vantage. "This building is ninety-seven years old, built by a doctor, and it was a drugstore. The doctor lived upstairs with his family, and this area back here was his examining room and this is where they had the drugstore, in this part here in the front."

It's a dark room with high ceilings, and the bar is elaborate by

Don Ketchum, owner of the Fjord Bar in Coon Valley, Wisconsin.

modern standards—dark mahogany, the sort of look the Bennigan's chain tries to copy.

"I came here fourteen years ago, expecting to be passing through," he says. "I'm still here."

His name is Don Ketchum, and he proudly offers his business card:

USED CARS—LAND — WHISKEY — MANURE — NAILS

FLY SWATTERS — RACING FORMS — BONGOS

DON *"Have Knowledge, Will Travel"* KETCHUM

MARRIED WOMEN COUNSELED	TIGERS TAMED
SINGLE WOMEN REVIEWED	BARS EMPTIED
FINANCIAL COUNSELING	VIRGINS CONVERTED
GOVERNMENTS RUN	MEXICAN GOLD
UPRISINGS QUELLED	ORGIES ORGANIZED

ALSO PREACH AND LEAD SINGING FOR REVIVAL MEETINGS

FJORD BAR — COON VALLEY, WI

"That covers it all," I say.

When he learns that Graham goes to Indiana University, the talk turns to basketball. "Bobby Knight's old stomping grounds," he says.

"Remember that riot they had on campus when they fired Knight?" I ask, patting Graham on the shoulder. "My boy was one of those guys out there trying to keep Knight."

"That was my first week in college," Graham says.

A large woman comes in and plops down on a barstool.

"Want a beer, Marge?" Don asks.

She sighs heavily. "I guess." *Jesus, Marge, we don't want to put you out or anything.*

He sets a Lite in front of her and she braces it between her fingertips before resolving to drink. Don continues on sports for twenty minutes, working through basketball, baseball (he played on the Wisconsin State Championship team in high school), football and even women's volleyball. His daughter is the assistant coach of the team at the University of Wisconsin at Milwaukee.

Milwaukee . . . don't get him started. "I've lived in big cities all my life, but now you couldn't drag me out of Coon Valley. This is the best place I've ever lived."

"I love where I live too," I say. "My backyard runs into a state park, so I've got lots of privacy. Of course, I'm selling that place . . . I'm getting married next month."

"I solved that problem," Don says. "I said I'd never get married again, right Marge?"

"I haven't got a clue," Marge cackles.

"I saw the ex-wife two weeks ago," Don says. "It convinced me I was right. I've gone to the short-term lease program. Sort of like a library. I borrow one for a couple weeks. . . ."

"I've been divorced a long time." I turn to Graham. "How long? Twelve years?"

Don addresses Graham. "Kids your age, if you have some friends and their parents are still together, then that's kind of strange."

A rural crossroads in southern Wisconsin.

"Definitely," Graham says. "The divorce rate is fifty percent."

I've never talked about this with Graham before. "You know, your mom was worried that when we got divorced, you guys would be outcasts or lepers at school."

"He's OK." Don looks at Graham. "Boys . . . *sons* . . . you can treat them equal. But daughters . . . they're always your little girls."

As we drive deep into Wisconsin, we're deep into rural Scandinavia. In Westby, the bowling alley is Nordic Lanes, the signs says VELKOM-MEN TIL WESTBY and HILSEN FRA WESTBY. The town dates from the early 1800s, when it was an Indian settlement, but the Black Hawk War cleaned out much of the Indian population in the 1830s, and the Norwegians began arriving by the boatload in the 1840s. Say it loud—they're Norwegian and they're proud.

The sign says "PIES 'R' US" at Borgen's Café and Bakery, and when we sit at the bar—no table seating available, probably a good sign—I see that the pie of the day is sour cream raisin pie. We are apparently invisible to employees, particularly the cute waitress who seems to be covering the dining room by herself. Finally, a large woman comes out of the back and gives us the *you-must-be-strangers* look and takes our order. She then instructs the young waitress—probably the rural Scandinavian equivalent of a punker—to serve it. When it comes, she slides it in front of us with surliness. Maybe she was tired of travelers confusing Norway and Sweden and therefore blaming her home country for ABBA.

We order what sounds most Norwegian—bratwurst with mashed potatoes and kraut, and it's amazing. It's as if that stuff I've been grilling for football games for two decades was made from leftover Keds. We chase lunch with that pie, nearly vertical with whipped cream rising from the plate like a shark fin. The corners of my jaw tingle with sweetness.

An old man named Al sits at a table near our end of the bar. He's in his nineties, with his sunken eyes and a bucket hat, working his way through a mound of mashed potatoes, taking an occasional hit from an oxygen tank on the seat next to him. When he's finished, the large waitress—the one who'd looked after us—asks, "Al, do you need some help to your car?" He grunts a response, and she helps him up and pulls his arm around her shoulder and limps with him out the back of the restaurant, to his faded green Aires-K.

"I'm oddly comforted knowing we will share the road with that driver," I tell Graham.

A few more Stepford-like communities and then we stop and poke around in Boscobel, another frighteningly neat little town.

"Hey," I tell Graham, looking at a historical marker on the main street. "This is where the Gideons started. You know, those Bibles we find in motel rooms? The ones that say 'Placed by the Gideons'? It says here that it was a chance meeting between two traveling sales-men named John H. Nicholson and Samuel E. Hill. They shared Room 19 at the local hotel, and the chance meeting was on May 1,

1899. They decided that all hotel rooms needed Bibles for travelers. Wow, we just missed the 102nd anniversary. That's kind of cool. Can you control your excitement?"

"I'm not sure I can control my bladder," he says.

"I'm serious, though. How many times have you seen those Bibles in hotels, and here's where it all started. It's serendipity, man—we find history wherever we go."

Golfers have replaced rollerbladers along the highway, as waves of green fairways border the road as we head toward Iowa.

Fennimore claims it is a cheese capital. We're past the sign before it has completely registered, but it's something like the CHEESE CAPITAL OF EXTREME SOUTHWEST WISCONSIN. So we stop at the Fennimore Cheese warehouse, which has a huge statue of a bug-eyed mouse munching on a chunk of Swiss the size of a La-Z-Boy. Inside, the cheese is like a drug, and we're suddenly strangely fatigued, then a little surprised at just how expensive cheese can be. The Snackmaster box, for example ("Our No. 1 seller!"), includes a ten-ounce link of summer sausage, surrounded by a delicious combination of four-ounce brick, three-ounce Swiss, four-ounce Edam, four-ounce cheddar and two containers of wine spread and cheddar spread. It's nearly thirty bucks.

If I had the money, the Snackmaster or the Merry-Go-Round (a 10-ounce, red-waxed cheddar cheese in the shape of Wisconsin, surrounded by a variety of four-ounce wedges, nineteen bucks) would be the perfect gift for the hearty Midwesterners in my family. There's also a variety of cheese-related headgear—the classic cheesehead worn by Green Bay Packer fans, cowboy hats, baseball hats—along with neckties, bow ties, earrings, beer cozies. But even the baseball cap is out of our range at twenty bucks. Plus, where we live we don't often have the need to wear dairy products.

We pick up a half pound of cheddar for two bucks.

"This may be too fresh," I tell Graham. "I love the taste of cheese when it's begun to sweat. It squeaks on my teeth. Want to just gnaw on it together?"

Outside Fennimore a billboard says, WE NEED TO TALK—GOD.

"*Wasssssuuuuuuuuuuuup*, God?" Graham asks.

I've never seen him so happy. He's scanning the radio, gleefully deriding pop music but slapping his thigh in time when John Bonham hits the opening drum riff on "Rock and Roll," which he recognizes on the first downbeat and turns up. After a couple of overcast days, we are blessed with glorious weather—probably the confluence of God-related things in this part of the state (including a hand-painted sign: CHRIST DIED FOR THE UNGODLY)—and Graham's happy not to be ushering at the movie theater, or cleaning up his room at his mother's insistence, or sitting through a summer-school algebra class. He's a free spirit.

The Grotto

Dickeyville calls itself the "heart of the heartland," and although it's a small town (one thousand and change), it has a significant tourist trade because of the Dickeyville Grotto. We're still cutting our speed when we see the Holy Ghost Catholic Church. A scarlet-robed priest leads his congregation inside, and I see from the sign that it's time for the Saturday-afternoon mass and suggest to Graham that we go. "Don't we have to make it to Iowa tonight?" he asks.

We park across the street from the grotto, nestled next to the church. Built over a decade by Mathius Wernerus, a German immigrant who was the Holy Ghost parish priest, 1920–1931, it's a small castle encrusted with tiles, jewels and other ornaments.

"Mom should see this," Graham says, pulling out his camera bag. But he has only black-and-white film, so he picks up a roll of color at Kieler's Grocery ("Photo Finishing—Cheese & Meats"). Father

Father Mathius Wernerus spent a decade building the Grotto in Dickeyville, Wisconsin, with help from parish children. He began with no firm concept of what he wanted to end up with. The main building is covered with stones smoothed by the nearby Mississippi River, glass from broken bottles, and costume jewelry discarded by parishioners.

Mathius began his work on the grotto by pouring concrete into slabs, or molding it around metal forms, to give the building its shape—something reminiscent of an adobe church in New Mexico. He began his decoration with small bits of limestone from quarries on the Mississippi River, three miles away. Parish schoolchildren helped find pretty bits of stone and glass and, working with the nuns living on site, even assisted in the decoration. Father Mathius had no blueprint and no real plan, other than building a tribute to what he called two great American ideals—love of God and love of country. It took him twelve years. He went spelunking the caves along the river to find stalactites. He covered the exterior walls with fossils, bits of antique pottery, costume jewelry, heirlooms from townspeople, crystals, colored glass and shells from his travels. Turquoise from the

Southwest forms emblems near the cross on top of the entrance, placed high enough to shape a memorable silhouette. The grotto is really a collection of shrines. The main shrine houses the grotto of the Blessed Virgin, but there is also a patriotic shrine, a sacramental shrine of the Holy Eucharist, the Sacred Heart Shrine, Christ the King Shrine, and the Stations of the Cross Shrine. An eagle monument tops the Patriotism Shrine, which features statues of Abraham Lincoln, Christopher Columbus and George Washington.

Father Mathius worried that the grotto would become a place "with ice-cream parlors and God knows what." Fortunately, the grotto is well cared for by the parish and its priest, Father Francis Steffan.

"Actually, they did sell ice cream for a while, I'm told," Father Steffan says. "But that was just something done after mass in the rectory basement. We really haven't had any trouble with people trying to commercialize it. They respect it." Alas, visitors to the grotto usually walk through it, admire the work and move on. "Very rarely do they stay for mass," Father Steffan says. He doesn't mean to, but he makes me feel guilty.

"Imagine the commitment this took," I say to Graham when he walks up after finishing a whole roll of film. I'm sitting on a bench in the flower garden. "I'm not sure I could do something like that. *Twelve years*—can you imagine?"

"It's beautiful and tacky at the same time," he says. "I prefer it to those shrines people put up in their yards."

"Like those reflecting balls?" He hates those shiny, colored balls on pedestals that people put in their gardens.

"Exactly. The government issues those to you as a sign that you are now officially old and have bad taste."

Only two seats left at the U-shaped bar of Pat & Mike Valentine's Bar and Restaurant in Dickeyville, and the TV is tuned to the MBNA Platinum 400. Mike Valentine's the tall guy behind the bar in the stained yellow Packers cap, preceded by a friendly middle-aged paunch.

"What can I get you fellas?" he asks.

"This one here looks good," I say, leaning forward to touch a canoe-shaped tap. I figure it's special, because all of the other beer taps are Packer helmets.

"Leinie's Original," he says, smiling as he fills a schooner. It's made by Leinenkugel's, a brewery in Chippewa Falls. Graham gets a root beer.

A couple in their late fifties with their adult daughter and son-in-law are telling stories on the old man and his horrendous snoring.

"Remember that time, Ma?" the daughter asks in a nasal whine. "I had friends over and Dad was a-snorin' so bad, we had to go outside to the porch and then to the street, and we could still hears him out there."

Dad tries to change the subject, "Mike, will you mind changin' the TV to something else? I think the Brewers are on." Dad is wearing a Number 3 hat, but maybe he's lost all interest in NASCAR since Dale Earnhardt's death. Mike obliges quickly with his Saran Wrap–covered remote control.

"I swear," the daughter continues, "there were times when I thought you were going to die, Dad. It rattled them walls."

Dad forges ahead. "How about the Packers this year, Mike?"

The daughter jumps in. "They'd better get their act together," she says. Dad's ruse works. The Packers are a reliable subject changer.

Mike is quiet and diplomatic. His wife, Pat, is the gregarious hostess. They've been in business sixteen years.

"You ever get any non-Packer fans in here?" I ask her.

"Oh, *suuure*," she says. "We get Bear fans, Viking fans, on occasion St. Louis fans."

"You ridicule them?"

She laughs. "Aw, nothing more than some good-natured jibbing."

The grotto brings in people from all over, Pat says, "more West Coast than East Coast. And there are people who come from France, Germany, Spain . . . just to see the grotto, like it's the main thing of their trip."

Back in the car, we're almost in Iowa.

"They went from snoring to the Packers in no time," Graham says when we're pulling out of town. "I wish I would have packed my stopwatch."

Dubuque Blues

Dubuque, Iowa, grips the river and screams *old*, the downtown unchanged in fifty years. I see nothing built in my lifetime. Bright blue gas tanks crawl over the downtown buildings like aliens. Dark green trees march up the hills behind the town. Highway 61 rolls over the city, almost imperially, and we look down into a Lionel-like replica of a 1950s American town.

"Let's exit," I tell him. "We ought to go down on that Main Street and see what it looks like."

"Do we have to?"

The city nestles between the river and the hills. There are, apparently, no human beings. Downtown has the usual businesses, a plaza with a gazebo in the middle, the Knights of Columbus, the Dubuque Museum of Art. Green, no people. Dubuque has it all, the billboards say. "The only thing missing is protoplasm," I tell Graham. "It's like driving through the final reel of *On the Beach*, that movie about nuclear war."

"Never saw it."

"It came out when I was a kid," I say. "Scared the hell out of me to think how the whole earth could be wiped out in nuclear war. Everyone's vaporized, except the Australians. The nuclear cloud drifts their

way, so they know they're going to die. They send this submarine off
to explore the West Coast of America, and they go through San
Francisco at the end and they're walking along and there's no one
there. Everyone's been vaporized."

A waterless fountain downtown and an abandoned baby seat by a
garbage can lead me to conclude that there was indeed nuclear war.
The town smells like lo mein. In the car, we're listening to *Prairie Home
Companion*, but the laughs at Garrison Keillor's jokes emphasize the
absence of humanity in this part of the Great American Midwest.

A neon sign outside Paul's Tavern advertises BIG-GAME TROPHIES.
Inside, we're assaulted by the mixed aromas of smoke and stale beer.
A half-dozen cigarette smokers at the long mahogany bar watch a
television whispering a Cubs game. A jukebox belches Loretta Lynn,
and severed animal heads preside.

Bartender Maria Roling is seven months pregnant, her navel form-
ing a crescent against her T-shirt. I ask her about Paul. Turns out he
no longer owns the tavern.

"How could he give up all of this?" I ask.

"He didn't give up the heads," she says, pointing at a startled
bighorn. "Those are still his."

"How does that work? Does he get visitation?"

"When Tom Koch bought this place, he had to cut a deal that the
trophies were still Paul's."

"Does he have self-esteem issues?" I ask. "Why didn't he change
the name to *Tom's* Tavern?"

She shrugs. "Paul's already had a following," she said.

"I should say so."

Busch Light, Bud Light and Old Style are on tap. I pick Old Style—
it's Iowa, after all. The beer is throat-numbingly cold. I drain it in two
gulps and ask for another. Maria puts down her Camel to work the
tap. I want to quote the surgeon general, but think better of it.

"Are the animal heads that big a draw?" I ask. "They brought us
in. The beer too, of course."

"I think it's one of our main attractions. Paul shot most of these, you know. Deer, elk and a weird rabbit."

A sign over the bar says, THEIR WILL BE A $10.00 CHARGE ON ALL RETURNED CHECKS.

I order a cheeseburger and chips for Graham. Maria takes the order back to the hissing kitchen pass-through window, and I prick up my ears to eavesdrop on her talking to the cook about a customer request: "Someone asked for a 'male Hershey's.' I said what's that. He said, one's got nuts, one don't." Maria laughs, dragging at her cigarette.

She walks back to us. "Where you guys from?"

"I live in Gainesville, Florida."

"Oh, that's close," she says, brightening. "I just moved back from Ocala." It's about a half-hour south.

"'Back'? You from here originally?" She nods. "What brought you back?" Florida is rampant with fault, but Ocala is beautiful north Florida horse country. I think you'd have to be a lunatic to prefer Dubuque to Ocala.

She shrugs. "Just from here," she says. "It's the town, the people." *Ah, the missing people . . . they must be nice.* "I like the people up here better."

I understand. Growing up rootless, moving every couple of years, I always wanted someplace outside the universe of change. But as I grew older, I realized change had become a comfort. Maybe I like Florida because it's a Velcro state—it attracts and keeps people from all over, but few actually think of it as home. Home is somewhere else, it's somewhere you go for the holidays. It's always been where I go to see my children.

Ray Stevens finishes up "Everything Is Beautiful" on the jukebox, and Conway Twitty growls, "Hello Darlin'."

The cheeseburger is served on a napkin and is splendid. Graham murmurs congratulations and Maria smiles.

While Graham and his taste buds commune, I inventory the tavern's walls: a white-tailed deer, shot in Wisconsin, 1960; stone sheep from British Columbia, 1964; bighorn sheep, Montana, 1959; Dall sheep, Alaska, 1962; white-tailed deer, Saskatchewan, 1961; pronghorn sheep, Montana, 1958; polar bear, Fort Hope, Alaska, 1966; and finally, a jackelope.

Walking back to the War Wagon we see a couple of life-forms—two kids about five or six pushing an infant in a stroller, followed by a twelve-year-old on a skateboard. No adults in sight. This can't be good.

The sky is still deeply overcast, clouds active, like boiling dishwater. We still have a long way to go.

The Bonus Room

The drive south from Dubuque takes us through rural, unremarkable country. It's not as pretty as Wisconsin, with few small towns and religious grottos to distract us.

It's a straight shot from Dubuque to Maquoketa, a slight bend between there and the Quad Cities. The beers work through my system and with no towns or gas stations, I ask Graham to pull over so I can pee by the side of the road, shielded from the occasional driver by the opened car door. My urination seems to last for weeks.

"You all right there, Bro?" he asks. "First time you've actually peed on Highway 61, isn't it? We ought to take note of this."

I look up from my stream. The overcast sky is threatening. "Look at that," I instruct Graham over my shoulder. "Look at those burbling clouds."

" 'Burbling'?"

"It's a Lewis Carroll word—it 'Came whiffling through the tulgey wood, / And burbled as it came!' I love those lines. So I say these clouds are burbling."

A semi–tractor trailer speeds by and acknowledges me with a blast of the horn. At first I think it says "Fore-Play Express" on the side, but it's "Four-Way Express."

Trucks. When Graham was little, he used to sit up front with me and pump his arm at truck drivers when we passed. When the drivers blasted their horns in response, Graham smiled up at them and waved so hard you'd think his hand would fall off. *It doesn't take much to amuse some people.* I said that to him because my father used to say that to me.

Back in the car, Garrison Keillor is reading off the names of obscure towns on the radio, and I suspect we're passing through them. We drive through Zwingle, Otter Creek, Maquoketa, Welton and Long Grove—bypassing Grand Mound—and when we get close to the Quad Cities, we start trying to reach our host for the night, Terry Quinn, on the cell phone. We try for over an hour but can't get through.

"We might move on to Plan B," I tell Graham. "We'll look up their address in the phone book when we hit town, and then we'll get a map and stalk them."

The Quad Cities are clustered in a bend on the Mississippi—Davenport and Bettendorf on the Iowa side, Rock Island and Moline in Illinois; total population 360,000, with four daily newspapers, four television stations and twenty-one radio stations.

We sit at a picnic table at a riverside park for a while, watching kids play on swings. I'm sure it strikes Graham as odd to stay with total strangers. I work with Terry's sister in Florida, and she made the arrangements for me. I've never talked to the guy.

Finally, we get through and learn that one of Terry's teenage daughters has been on the phone. Terry seems genuinely excited about our visit and gives us good directions.

Terry and Kim Quinn's house is so clean, I suspect they're about to sell it. Terry seems to grasp the awkwardness of the situation as much as I do. His wife, Kim, small and lovely, seems shy or preoccupied; I can't tell which. There seems to be some controversy about their daughter Emily's plan for the evening, and we have walked right in on it. Terry apologizes for being unable to get through on the phone and mutters something about "teenagers." Graham turns on the charm in this awkward situation. "They've got to do their pregame planning," he says. Terry smiles weakly. They have a younger daughter, Kristen, who is over at a friend's house. *You have a long road ahead, my friend,* I think.

American Express buys us all dinner at a Mexican restaurant, and after a couple of drinks we all relax. Graham, to his credit—and to my surprise—vividly tells about our adventure on the road, his life in college and his academic ambitions (something in environmental studies, he thinks).

At home, they set us up on the sleeper sofa in their "bonus room," and I pass out. Graham stays up surfing the Internet.

Terry and Kim see us off the next day, and I realize it's Sunday.

"You want to go to church?" I ask Graham. I'm driving, since he was up late on the Quinns' computer. The look on his face is my answer.

Down Other Roads

"Are you looking forward to Keokuk?"

"Keo*what*?"

"It's a town way down in the corner of the state, and we'll hit it in an hour or so," I say.

"Not soon enough."

"Funny, everyone who sees us—like Terry and Kim—they think we're exactly alike. I think what you got from me is your temper," I tell him. "It explodes, but when it's over with, it just goes away. I think I'm pretty easygoing, but then I reach a point and I go . . . " (shouting now) " . . . *fuck it.* I just let it all out in this tornado of blasphemy, and then it's gone."

"I think this year I held in a lot of stuff, which wasn't good," Graham says. "At school . . . at home." He stares at the road ahead. "It was a really weird year. I became friends with a guy who died shortly after I got to know him."

"Tell me about it."

"Ron died from hitting his head while he was drinking one night at a fraternity party. He didn't think much of it at the time, but he was bleeding internally and there was a blood clot in his brain. A few days later he went into a coma and died."

Those last few days, the kid was dying and he didn't know it.

"I had hung out with him just the night before that party and met him a few weekends before that through two of my friends. Ron was the nicest of those new people I met and was the only one who remembered my name the next weekend when we hung out."

"Did we get off the highway?" I don't mean to intrude on his sorrow, but it appears I made a wrong turn. After doubling back, we make it back on 61 south. We've gone around in circles. I think it's poorly marked roads; Graham thinks it's because I'm incapable of following directions.

We talk about other trips, and he wants to hear stories about my dad and trips with my family.

"I got a good deal, being the last kid at home," I tell him. "Dad wanted me to go with him and Mammaw for a trip out West. And we drove all the way out to Montana and Idaho. The Little Big Horn was one of the spookiest places I'd ever been. I think Charlie and Suzanne were a little jealous because when Dad got out of the service and they went off to college, he had more time to take trips and I was the kid who got to go along."

"You got to hang out with him more."

We stop in Muscatine for gas—at $1.68, cheapest on the trip so far—and Graham wants to switch and get behind the wheel. "It's funny," he says slyly. "I drive, we're fine. You drive, we get turned around and lose an hour."

Muscatine calls itself the "pearl of the Mississippi," and it's a pretty river town that lists "sunsets" among its attractions. The town has a river walk for nightly sunset viewing—not quite as large or as busy as Mallory Square in Key West, but the same idea. Mark Twain said, "I remember Muscatine . . . for its summer sunsets. I have never seen any, on either side of the ocean, that equaled them."

Another straight, flat patch from Muscatine down to Burlington, where the road jags westward, following the will of the river.

"I know we burned up the road between Indiana and Florida, but what other trips do you remember most?"

He remembers the time we were visiting a girlfriend's brother in West Virginia. He was a semirecluse and lived on top of a mountain. Another brother came to visit, and we stood in a mountain stream and fished. Graham, who was seven then, caught fourteen fish in twenty-nine minutes—probably his personal best.

"The trip when we went to Washington, that was good," he says. "I liked that drive. And that time we came back to Indiana through New Orleans and Memphis, that was the coolest. We met that mime that talked."

Graham's driving, so I have time to study the atlas and realize we've just passed a red-starred attraction—Riverside, Iowa, "the Future Birth-place of James T. Kirk." Apparently, the people in this town decided to cash in on a passing reference in a *Star Trek* script to where the captain of the starship *Enterprise* was born. The bundle of joy does not arrive until March 21, 2228, but the town already has an annual James T. Kirk Birthday Celebration and Trek Fest, a plaque to honor Kirk and a scale model of a spaceship that bears a remarkable resemblance to the USS *Enterprise*. The town fathers who thought up this idea balked at the forty-thousand dollar licensing fee Paramount Pictures wanted. Telling Graham about this, I note that thousands of *la-hoooo-sers* descend on the town to honor that overrated television program.

"Then let's not be among them," he says. He's eager to get out of Iowa.

Harold

The highway skirts Burlington, and Dillon's Real Pit Bar-B-Q whets my appetite for pork products, but I want to hold out to Keokuk. The road rides the top of the river bluffs again, giving us glimpses between the trees of the river below, before the road dives back down to the riverside at Fort Madison. This time, there's no bypass, and we get the grand tour of the little town and come across the Iowa State Penitentiary at a turn in the highway. Graham gets out of the car to take a picture, and a guard shoos him away. "It's an execution area," the guard says. "No pictures."

"What a pisser," I say. "Here's where some killin' is actually done along Highway *Sixty*-One . . . and they won't let us take any pictures."

Harold Pratt, volunteer on duty at the Fort Madison Visitor's Bureau, is in his late seventies, with slick silver hair combed forward to a point, thick black-framed glasses, a camel-hair sports coat and a cranberry-striped dress shirt. I love old men from the Midwest. After Thanksgiving dinner on the family farm, Uncle Russell, Uncle Red and Uncle Gene sat around talking politics and football. Harold's from their generation.

"We brag of twenty-three different factories in this area," he says. "Schaeffer Pen Company is right across the street. We're the home of Schaeffer Pen. They have factories *all over the world*. But you know Bic" (conspiratorially) "—that three-letter word—they bought them

Harold Pratt, volunteer at the visitor's center in Fort Madison, Iowa.

out, but they still go by the Schaeffer name. I have a pen or a pencil
of every model that they ever sold. Have you ever had a Schaeffer pen
with a white dot? That means it's a lifetime pen. No matter what you
do to it, it's good for life. You drop your pen, it gets run over and you
think, 'Goodness, there goes my Schaeffer pen. What do I do now?'
Fear not! Schaeffer Pen will replace that pen free of charge, because
it's supposed to last *you* a lifetime, not the lifetime of the pen.

"Now," he continues, and I sense a punchline coming. "Right behind us over here is the Iowa State Pen. Now, to my knowledge, you people are in the only city in the world that can brag of two life-long pens."

Harold seems lonely this afternoon, so we get more than just the usual Fort Madison jokes. As much as he loves telling stories about the town, his real love appears to be selling a cube of dirt from Nauvoo, Illinois, across the river. I don't mention my Highway 61 gravel concept, in case he has some sort of lock on this dirt-for-sale market. He's already registered the dirt cube with the U.S. Patent Office.

He works the combination on his battered briefcase and pops it open to show us his valuable dirt. There's an assortment of stuff inside the briefcase: a Ray Stevens videotape, a collection of early 1990s NBA trading cards, some Master Locks, a few Mothers Against Drunk Driving ribbons and some Q-Tips.

He tells us he has two brothers—Harry and Tom—and speculates on why his parents didn't name him Dick.

"Two brothers named Harry and Harold," I say. "Wasn't that a little confusing around the house?"

He looks at me like I'm a lunatic. "No. He was Harry and I was Harold. No confusion a'tall."

After loading us with brochures, he walks us to the car. "This is a great thing you're doing," he says. "A father and a son need to spend time together. *Beautiful, beautiful.* You might not have as much time as you think."

Town of Big Shoulders

The small finger of Iowa that intrudes into Missouri was prime hunting and fishing ground for the Sac and Fox Indians. The Des Moines River flows into the Mississippi at that point, and Chief

Keokuk's name was chosen by white settlers who built a town on that point.

Between November and March each year, Keokuk has the largest concentration of eagles in North America. They must like the view when they migrate from Canada, not to mention the hospitality: Keokuk hosts Eagle Appreciation Days. The town is also the north-ward satellite of Mark Twain territory. Since he worked there as a young newspaperman, the city mildly exploits his name, and Twain impersonators are so thick, you bump into them on the way into the men's room.

On those many family trips through Iowa, we stopped here to eat and to let Dad shop at the downtown bookstore. To a child, every-thing looks big, so when Graham and I arrive in Keokuk I'm shocked: It's Dubuque all over again, a dead city. It's disorienting to find that the world I remembered so clearly has changed so much. To a child Keokuk might as well have been Chicago: big shoulders on busy streets.

The moment I step into the Covered Wagon restaurant, it hits me—I was here before, and nothing has changed in forty years. There are bridles on the wall, a big mural of a Conestoga wagon, longhorns over the bar, and that woman behind the cash register . . . even *she* looks familiar.

I turn to Graham. "I was here before, with my dad . . . with every-body. We used to stop at this place."

It reminded me of the Keys. The summer before, Graham and I pulled off to the side of the road on Long Key and by accident found Dad's old fishing spot—just the highway's shoulder. My mother and father and I fished the Gulf, my brother fished across the road in the Atlantic and my sister reclined by the car and worked on her tan. I couldn't believe I'd found it.

We take a booth near the back. The walls are knotty pine with shellacked burlap wallpaper from waist up. Our table is worn smooth by generations of hands, maybe even mine.

"I knew when I saw the name on the sign. It triggered this memory," I say. "It's scary when you realize your memory goes back forty years. If you can remember 'Thriller' being on MTV all the time, that's when you were two. I can remember things back to that age."

"What's your first memory?" Graham asks after we order.

"Lying on the couch in the Quonset hut in England, where we used to live. Do you know what a Quonset hut is?" He nods. "I heard these kids outside singing, 'Nick nack paddy wack, give a dog a bone, this old man came rolling home.' I've never forgotten that moment. You know, Bob recorded that song. I used to sing it to you guys when you were little. Now I sing it to Savannah. Promise me you'll sing that song at my funeral?"

"I thought you wanted 'Ripple.' "

"You play that so well. Play this one too, since I'm your old man."

Graham gets a Chuck Wagon Steak Burger, mashed potatoes, baked beans and a dinner roll fluffy as a feather pillow. I have a huge omelet stuffed with peppers, mushrooms and three varieties of cheese.

Graham sips his coffee. "Looks like a nice piece of pie," he says, as he watches the woman behind the counter slice a pie into six pieces with one stroke of an appliance. I get a piece of strawberry, and Graham gets apple. They're both delicious.

Pie baker Helen Harvey comes in at five every morning to do her work, but owner Linda Houston makes the strawberry pie. I tell her about coming to the restaurant as a child; she nods politely. When we say good-bye, she says, "Thank you. Come again."

"I promise not to wait so long next time," I say.

We walk around downtown Keokuk for a while, but it's depressing: the backs of the Main Street buildings crumble into glass-strewn, overgrown lots. An appliance graveyard—TVs, stoves, refrigerators—is overgrown with weeds. Loading docks decay, and garbage is knee-high in one of the basement entrances. Two boys in vintage 1964 bikes with banana seats and spider handlebars ride up next to us in the alley. One of them looks our way and points to his buddy and shouts, "He's wearing a condom!" And indeed the other 10-year-old is—it's filled with water and tied around his neck.

Main Street of Keokuk is Business 61, so on our way back to the main highway, we pass the Keossissippi Mall, with Western Auto as one of its anchor stores. We have found the shopping center on the opposite end of the continuum from the Mall of America.

"This is Sunday, a day when we might be communing with God," I tell Graham. "Maybe you should thank God you don't live in Keokuk."

Odd how things can change so suddenly when you cross a state line, how man-made divisions still follow the general geographic character of a place. When we cross the Mississippi, we end up in beautiful, flat, intensely rural Missouri. The highway follows the river closely, and it's flowing especially fast here, much wider than when we crossed it up at Dubuque.

Walk along the river, sweet lullaby. . . .

It's that fluid, wonderful voice of Dickey Betts from the Allman Brothers Band. We're looking down on the river ("not a commonplace river," Mark Twain wrote), and the sun has broken through the dirty clouds just as we cross into Missouri. Mark Twain seems suddenly thick with us.

"What Mark Twain did you read in high school?" I ask.

"None," Graham says. "I read parts of *Huckleberry Finn*, that paperback we have at home."

"Jesus. I thought they'd at least have you read *Huck Finn* or *Tom Sawyer!* Do they consider them racist?"

He shrugs. "I saw the movie. *Slugbug!*" It's the first one in Missouri, a red one parked at a Phillips 66 station.

The Rolling Stones come on the radio with "Jumpin' Jack Flash." As required by law, we turn it up.

"I sure wish I could see them before they die."

"They're getting old," I say. "They had the Voodoo Lounge tour, the Bridges to Babylon tour, then the No Security tour . . . next time will probably be the Handicapped Parking tour."

"You've seen them twice?" he asks.

"Three times now. It's funny, I turned forty and I thought, 'Well, it's been a good life, but I wished I'd seen the Rolling Stones.' Then all of a sudden they're everywhere."

We stop at what looks like a homemade rest stop called Mound Roadside Park. As we get out of the car to stretch, a light rain falls, though to the west it's perfectly clear. But for the namesake mound, the landscape is flat and we don't see or hear other cars. It's beautiful here, but the ground is littered with a Hiland orange juice container, a Budweiser can and a spent box of Lusianne tea.

"When I used to make those long drives, like twenty-six hours straight, Florida–Oklahoma, I'd be driving on fumes—*mental* fumes, I'm talking, not gas. I would hit a wall of exhaustion around three in the morning, but I'd still have hours to go. That's when I'd put in a Mojo Nixon tape. It wasn't pretty, but it got the job done." I start singing:

I married a Bigfoot, I gave birth to my mother. . . .

"It's a song made up of entirely of Weekly World News headlines. That would always give me the push to make it home. If it weren't for Mojo Nixon, I might not be here today."

Until now, all of the Highway 61 signs have been on metal poles, but in Missouri they're on thick wooden rails. Graham's already plotting vandalism. "I'll get a saw and chop down one of these," he says.

Safe Water

Mark Twain, writing about home: "In the small town of Hannibal, Missouri, when I was a boy everybody was poor but didn't know it; and everybody was comfortable and did know it. . . . Everybody knew everybody and was affable to everybody and nobody put on any visible airs; yet the class lines were quite clearly drawn and the familiar social life of each class was restricted to that class. It was a little democracy which was full of liberty, equality and Fourth of July and sincerely so too; yet you perceived that the aristocratic taint was there."

The Huck Finn Motel signals arrival in Hannibal. The highway forms the western border for the older part of town, and we turn off on Harrison Hill Road to get down to the river. Everything is Mark, Tom or Huck related—at least on the outskirts of town. Hannibal High School is grand-looking, nearly in the league with Hibbing High. Above the Mark Twain Dinette is a huge rusted rotating mug of root beer. We park and walk around the historic district. The old town has been well preserved with an acceptable level of exploitation.

From the Mark Twain Boyhood Home, the bricked street slopes gently down to the river. Two children dressed up as Tom Sawyer and Becky Thatcher pose for tourists in front of the fence that young Sam Clemens whitewashed. A busload of sixty tourists from Chicago—half adults, half kids—has just arrived, and we hold back for a while to avoid the crowd. After letting that group amble through, Graham and I have the museum lobby all to ourselves, except for an elderly attendant and an early-thirties blonde woman with bowl-cut hair and an olive-drab jumper.

Laurie Britt is a local. She grew up in Hannibal, and she's just begun work in the museum as a host and guide. But the tours are self-guided, so a better job description is "question answerer." The main qualification for the job is liking Mark Twain.

"A lot of people think he was a happy man who wrote stories for children," she says. "But he was actually pretty dark. The death of his wife . . . losing so many children at an early age . . . all of that contributed to his outlook."

"I think it started with his sister Mary," I say. "As I recall, she was his hero when he was a very little boy. She came home from school one day, said she didn't feel well and lay down. She never got up again. I think that was when he was four."

Laurie says what surprises her is that foreign visitors—from the Netherlands, New Zealand, Slovenia (that's just today's guestbook)—are pretty well versed in Mark Twain, in some cases better than Americans.

I ask her: "Growing up here, now working here, did you ever get sick of Mark Twain?"

Quickly, without a whiff of public relations: "No, not at all. I enjoyed Mark Twain growing up; I really did."

The museum tour includes a short film, some exhibits and then a self-guided tour of the Clemens home. It's so well labeled and laid out that the tour is dummy-proof. Hallways are open, but rooms are enclosed in Plexiglas. A recorded voice—friendly, not mechanical—tells you about each room: "Mark Twain described this as Tom Sawyer's room. In the story, Huck Finn would catcall and meow outside, and Tom would sneak out of bed."

Across the street is another museum, the home of Laura Hawkins, Twain's model for Becky Thatcher in *Tom Sawyer*. Twain wrote about Tom's first sighting of Becky: "He saw a new girl in the garden—a lovely little blue-eyed creature with yellow hair plaited into two long-tails. . . . The fresh-crowned hero fell without firing a shot."

Wherever we go, we seem to be right behind that party-of-sixty from Chicago. We amble, so as not to intrude on the group and preserve a little peace and quiet. A young woman with two kids in tow comes jogging by in orthopedic sneakers, catching up with the group.

"We went back to the hotel for a potty break," she yells in explanation.

Good Christ, I think. *Do people have no shame?*

Down the street, The New Mark Twain Museum exhibits paintings by local artists and a replica of a riverboat pilot's perch. The annoying Chicago kids repeatedly pull on the riverboat whistle, and the parents are either oblivious to their children's horseplay or rude, knuckle-dragging morons themselves. One big kid, shorts nearly down to his ankles, with a chain looped so low it skirts his shoes, pushes the smaller kids out of the way to have his turn aggravating people. Several display cases show the breadth of Mark Twain in popular culture: Tom and Becky rag dolls, plates, comic books, and old Hal Holbrook LPs of his "Mark Twain Tonight!" one-man show. There's a small gallery of Norman Rockwell paintings—in the 1930s he illustrated valuable editions of *Tom Sawyer* and *Huckleberry Finn*— as well as a room full of Thomas Hart Benton sketches on loan, for his illustrated editions of *Tom*, *Huck* and *Life on the Mississippi*.

No shortage of Mark Twain pictures. Graham stands in front of a late-in-life picture of Twain in his white suit, eyes saddened by age, hair a model for Albert Einstein.

"Mark had a pretty good 'fro," he says. "For a white guy, I mean."

Not much open in Hannibal other than the Mark Twain Dinette, under the giant rotating root-beer mug. We score some Mark Twain fried chicken, which is like Kentucky Fried Chicken on steroids. We also have the best, frostiest root beer we've ever had.

At the next table a pear-shaped father with Coke-bottle glasses presides over his family's spaghetti-all-around order.

"Are they nuts?" Graham whispers to me, chicken crust on his chin. "You eat *chicken* here."

The paunchy man's trailer-ish wife and their children—two beautiful little girls clutching green cellophane bags of Mark Twain goodies—noisily slurp spaghetti.

"You think in a hundred years, people will be going to Hibbing to see Bob Dylan's boyhood home? They'll sit in the Bob Dylan Dinette, eating Bob Dylan fried chicken."

After the meal, we return to Twain's boyhood home. "So he was there," Graham says, pointing up at his bedroom window, "and his girlfriend was there," turning toward the Hawkins house, "and his other love was just two blocks away."

"He had another girlfriend?"

"The Mississippi," he says.

We walk down to the river, through the floodwall and onto the landing, bricks covered by a veneer of mud from recent flooding. We gingerly step out onto the landing, hoping not to slip and fracture a hip. My bowling shoes take on a layer of mud.

"Hey, look at this," Graham says, leaning over as we cross the railroad tracks. He holds up a spike. "Something from Mark Twain's hometown. This'll look cool on my desk."

A riverboat casino docked nearby is vacant, and the landing is strewn with trash, bottles and oxidized Natural Light beer cans. This is probably a party place for Hannibal teens, same as it was 150 years ago.

The Indians called it the Father of Waters, and Mark Twain called it the crookedest river in the world. Here is the Mississippi in all of its greatness. We'd been crossing and recrossing it ever since Minnesota, never failing to marvel at it; but here it was, a few feet away, a reminder of its power caked to the bottom of my bowling shoes.

No accident the river is bound with this highway we're traveling. Study the maps, and they're wrapped like shoelaces down through the middle of the country. The river, the road and the rail all tie together much of American culture.

Mark Twain stepped ashore here on his sentimental journey up the river he wrote about in *Life on the Mississippi*. When he disembarks in Hannibal on an early Sunday morning, he sees the city at it was at the moment and also sees it as it was twenty-nine years before, when he moved away. He has that strange experience of retracing his steps, which I'm feeling on this trip. "I passed through the vacant streets, still seeing the town as it was," he wrote, "and finally climbed Holliday's Hill to get a comprehensive view. The whole town lay spread out before me then, and I could mark and fix every locality, every detail. Naturally, I was a good deal moved." The trip home had made him feel like a boy again, he wrote. Life since leaving Hannibal had simply been "an unusually long dream."

When he lived in this town, he was Sam Clemens. His older brother, Orion, had led him into journalism, employing him at newspapers in Hannibal and Keokuk. Sam gave up journalism to work as a riverboat pilot for two years, until the war closed the river. After short service in the Civil War, Sam followed his brother out West, where he was territorial secretary of Nevada. That's when Sam started writing for the *Virginia City Territorial Enterprise.* So as not to embarrass his brother, he decided to use a pen name. "I want to sign my articles 'Mark Twain,' " he told his editor. "It is an old river term, a leadsman's call, signifying two fathoms—12 feet. It has a richness about it; it always was a pleasant sound for a pilot to hear on a dark night; it meant 'safe water.' "

There's a light rain when we leave Hannibal, and Highway 61 impersonates an interstate down to Wentzville—four lanes, heavy traffic. Along the way we're passed by a battered white pickup truck going well over eighty. A golden retriever chained in the back of the truck can't get purchase with his paws on the slick metal of the truck bed. One slip and he'd fall out of the back of the truck, hanging himself on the chain.

I point west. "That's where Mark Twain was born," I say, "over there in a little town called Florida. His daddy settled there thinking that some day the Salt River would be dredged and there would be a lot of river traffic. He would be one of the longest-lasting residents and so he'd have it made. Never happened, though. I get the impression Judge Clemens was a hard-luck guy."

I check the map and see that they dammed the Salt River and created Mark Twain Lake, with Florida still in existence on a peninsula. Poor Judge Clemens was 150 years too soon.

"It sucks, all the death Mark Twain suffered," Graham says. "His three daughters and his wife all died before he died. The little girl died."

"When he was four and his sister died, I think that broke his heart.

He had a tragic life. I think a lot of people just look at him as a 'spinner of heart-warming tales.' They might not think a lot of that stuff was sarcastic. He wrote this story called 'The Man That Corrupted Hadleyburg.' All these innocent people are turned greedy, victimized by an evil stranger who comes along. And there's this Bob Dylan song, 'Man in a Long Black Coat,' that seems connected to that story. I think Bob and Mark have a lot in common."

At Wentzville, we leave Highway 61, turn east on I-70 and head toward Indiana to spend a rest day. We skirt St. Louis and pick up a free-form community radio station playing great old rhythm and blues, and the music gets us thinking about the second half of the trip, when we'll dive down through Memphis, Mississippi and New Orleans.

There's no pleasure in this part of the drive; it's all business. We're racing across Illinois, and although we're well over the speed limit, the car is nearly blown off the road in the backwash from semis hurtling by. We listen to a great local show on a St. Louis station, KDHX, *Nothin' But the Blues*. The host has great taste in music. I'm hearing things I've never heard on the radio: Brownie McGhee, Pegleg Sam, Lonnie Johnson singing "Tomorrow Night."

"This is the first blues we've heard on the radio," I say.

"And it took us all the way to St. Louis," he says.

Right after crossing into Indiana, we get on a winding state highway that takes us to Bloomington. I go to Graham's mother's house first and spend some time with the girls. They want to hear all about the trip, but we're too tired to talk much.

Rock 'n' Roll Heaven

After a full day at home, we hit the road early the following morning for a quick interstate ride back to St. Louis to pick up Highway 61 again.

I used to pass through St. Louis all the time. When my father was stationed in Texas, we came through at least three or four times a year. Same thing when I taught at the University of Oklahoma. I'm used to seeing the Gateway Arch. For Graham, it's a thrill when it comes into view. It means he's no longer in Indiana. We go through town to where we left Highway 61.

Wentzville is an outer suburb, and we find a bottom-of-the-food-chain motel fronting Highway 61, with a little café across the road. It's dumpy and perfect.

"It's going to take us a day or two to get back into our road rhythm," I tell Graham, admiring our splendid view of the parking lot.

"Maybe we should hang out here for a while," he says. "I've always liked St. Louis."

I remembered another St. Louis trip, years before, to visit a college friend. He'd taken me to Blueberry Hill, a bar with the best jukebox I'd ever heard. I was underage, so just being in there was a thrill. Blueberry Hill isn't hard to find—it's on Delmar Boulevard in the University City Loop, a brief walk from Washington University.

"This is like Dinkytown, only upscale," Graham says.

The neighborhood's grown since I was here. Back then, Blueberry Hill was a bar with two side rooms, but as we walk up to it—stepping over stars patterned after the Hollywood Walk of Fame (Bob Costas . . . Scott Joplin . . . and, right in front, Chuck Berry)—we find that it consumes most of a city block.

"This place was here way back in the day?" Graham asks when we step inside.

"Yep, I was here in 1974."

"When did they start the Hard Rock Cafés? You think they ripped him off?"

You have to wonder. The walls are crammed with memorabilia, but it has a warm, homemade quality. It's mostly rock 'n' roll, but some display cases are devoted to Howdy Doody, the St. Louis Cardinals, old campaign buttons and The Simpsons. It's not clinical like

The arch in St. Louis, Missouri, honors the city's role as the "Gateway to the West." We discovered it was also the Gateway to the South.

the Hard Rocks, with gold-plated labels for donated stage costumes, platinum records and autographed photos. This place is run by Joe Edwards, and this is Joe's stuff. It's like sharing your family room with a bunch of strangers.

Blueberry Hill seems to please everybody and has a wildly mixed clientele—businessmen in suits, kids with purple spiked hair, a weekly lunch group of elderly women.

Joe asks us to sit with him in a booth by the bar (solid mahogany, 135 years old). He's in his fifties, with long brownish-gray hair pulled back into a ponytail. He looks like a customer, and he doesn't treat the waitress like an employee. You wouldn't think we were sitting across from a guy who almost single-handedly took a slum and turned it into a mini-boomtown. Joe's fingerprints are up and down the boulevard, lined with the stars he placed to honor some of the city's best-known citizens. Blueberry Hill has grown, adding two concert halls downstairs, but Joe also bought and refurbished an old theater down the street, the Pageant. This is why they call him the Mayor of Delmar.

"I was here . . . whew, almost thirty years ago," I tell him. "This place has grown."

He nods, modestly. "Little by little we expanded, took over some storefronts, and then we went down into the basement, and built the Elvis Room. And three and a half years ago, we built the Duck Room."

"You still have that great jukebox?"

"Better now," he says. "Two thousand songs."

Joe's modest. *Cashbox Magazine* named it the best jukebox in America. In one of its "American Culture" reports, the BBC went further, calling it the best jukebox in the world.

This is Chuck Berry territory, so I ask him if the Duck Room was named in honor of Berry's famous duck walk.

"We named it after the duck walk, and it also rhymes with a lot of words rock 'n' roll bands can remember. So there are two rooms for live music now."

Joe's father was a heart surgeon, and Joe seemed headed for a more traditional professional career, earning his degree in psychology from Duke in 1968. He kicked around and did a few things, but his heart belonged to rock 'n' roll—and to his wife, Linda. She'd earned her degree in architecture and together, in the early 1970s, they started looking at buildings in the decaying Delmar section of St. Louis. She encouraged him to start a place devoted to rock 'n' roll and all other things fun.

He'd been collecting all of his life. Rather than stick his collections in an attic, he built his dream restaurant around his stuff.

"They opened the first Hard Rock in London in 1971," Joe says, "around the time I was set to open here. I was delayed a year. At the beginning, Hard Rocks didn't have any rock 'n' roll memorabilia. I don't know if they ever scouted here or not. Who knows?"

Hard to believe this wonderful clubhouse kind of place in this idyllic neighborhood was run down when Joe opened Blueberry Hill, and it makes you appreciate what one guy—and a few friends and fellow businessmen—can do.

Joe gives us the tour. The Duck Room downstairs is where the big-draw acts play. Joe lowered the basement floor to give the room more head space, and he's built a nice concert hall. We've just missed Levon Helm and the Barnburners.

"How's he doing?" I ask.

"He still puts on a great show. His daughter Amy's in the band, and she's a hell of a singer."

Levon Helm came out of the Mississippi Delta back in the 1950s and joined up with Arkansas rockabilly star Ronnie Hawkins, following him to Canada. One by one, young Canadian musicians joined the band until Ronnie Hawkins and the Hawks became the best-known band in Canada. The band split from Hawkins and gigged up and down the East Coast bar scene as Levon and the Hawks. They were playing a bar in New Jersey when Bob Dylan found them and took them on the road for his raucous 1965–1966 world tour. Bob's fans couldn't deal with the fact that he was playing rock 'n' roll and booed the band at every show. Levon couldn't take the abuse and returned to Arkansas. After a motorcycle accident forced Bob off the

Joe Edwards, owner of Blueberry Hill, created the St. Louis Walk of Fame and led the restoration of the city's Delmar neighborhood.

road and back home to Woodstock, New York, Levon was summoned to rejoin the group, now known as The Band. They made several critically acclaimed albums and even accompanied Bob when he came out of seclusion in 1974 for his triumphant comeback tour— playing essentially the same set that had gotten them booed eight years before. But since the late 1970s, The Band has been split by bitterness—Helm and guitarist Robbie Robertson wouldn't even speak to each other—and marred by tragedy. Pianist Richard Manuel hanged himself after a show in Winter Park, Florida (Levon had to cut down his friend's body), and bassist Rick Danko died in his sleep at fifty-six. Now, Levon had throat cancer, silencing his splendid singing voice. He speaks only in whispers, Joe said.

There's a lot of Chuck Berry memorabilia on the walls—movie posters, album covers, pictures with fans. He lives about five minutes away, Joe says, and he plays the Duck Room once a month. His guitar from the 1950s (labeled "the guitar that shook the world") is displayed in a glass case by the front door.

"That's awesome," Graham says. "You can tell that's the guitar he used in his early years. Look at the pick guard." It's scratched from heavy use.

The Elvis Room, on the other side of the basement, is newer and since this is a Tuesday, it's set up for dart night. "We have the biggest dart tournament in North America," Joe says proudly.

Forty-five r.p.m.'s are glued to the walls, and there's even more Simpsons memorabilia here. "I just think there's something real positive about them," Joe says. He also collects old postcards, mostly with local angles—the 1904 World's Fair in St. Louis, historic local buildings, a whole series on the construction of the Gateway Arch. Joe has a collection of every single Top-10 rock 'n' roll recording, and his home stash includes thirty thousand recordings—albums, 45s, 78s, cylinders and compact discs.

Joe has to go upstairs to work but invites us to look around as much as we want and to promise to have dinner there.

For an hour, we explore the place, with its long hallways filled with smiling photos of Joe at Blueberry Hill with a staggering array of visitors—some musicians, some actors, some athletes and one chairman of the Federal Reserve: Ben E. King, Bob Costas, Jackie Joyner-Kersee, Sheryl Crow, Buffalo Bob Smith, Robert Plant, Natalie Merchant, Steve Tyler, Jimmy Page, Ike Turner, Ray Charles, Melissa Etheridge, Gene Chandler, Lou Brock, Joe Perry, Chrissie Hynde, Lisa Loeb, James Caan, Kate Pierson, Whoopi Goldberg, Bruce Springsteen, Kathleen Turner, Laurence Fishburne,

Don Rickles, George Clinton, Solomon Burke, Plácido Domingo, Alan Greenspan, Donald Sutherland, Morgan Freeman, Kurtis Blow, Little Richard, John Goodman, Mandy Moore, Jakob Dylan, Keith Richards, Dave Grohl, Yogi Berra and Jerry Lee Lewis.

One exception to the Smiling Joe rule is a photo of him standing menacingly in front of a vintage car. Next to it is a framed satirical essay by his daughter questioning why her father identifies with West Coast rap culture. First of all, she notes, he's a middle-aged white man from St. Louis. "I think anyone would agree this is not a natural progression," she writes. "Granted, he's been driving a '64 Chevy Impala since 1986 and even drove one when he was in college, 'way before the likes of Dr. Dre and Ice Cube popularized this car for a nation of gangstas. However, in this photo of him and his Impala, the pose is distinctly that of a West Coast rapper."

It's a beautiful afternoon, so we explore the whole neighborhood, looking at the stars on the sidewalk as we go. The earliest is dedicated to Pierre LaClède, who founded St. Louis in 1764, but many of the stars are for St. Louisians who made a mark in the twentieth century—lots of actors and musicians, but also *Wild Kingdom* host Marlin Perkins, poet Maya Angelou, Negro League star Cool Papa Bell, *Naked Lunch* author William S. Burroughs, poet T. S. Eliot, the author of "Wynken, Blynken, and Nod," Eugene Field, feminist author Kate Chopin and sex therapists William Masters and Virginia Johnson.

One of the stars triggers my memory: On childhood rainy-day Saturdays, I'd watch Dizzy Dean and another Hall of Famer, Pee Wee Reese, do play-by-play on major league baseball. It made me fall in love with the game. With Graham, it was Nintendo that got him hooked. Times change.

"Dizzy Dean," I say. "I can't tell you how cool this is. I remember listening to him when I was kid."

Graham knows his baseball history. "He and his brother won all four games for the Cardinals in the World Series once, right?"

"Yeah, probably 1934. By the time I was watching him on TV, he was old and sometimes he had trouble getting into the broadcast booth. Those guys used to drink beer and call the games. Of course, I didn't know that at the time. Man, I wish they'd rebroadcast those old games. I'd probably understand the jokes now."

"I don't like many announcers anymore," Graham says. "I miss Harry." As a Cubs fan, he was devoted to Harry Caray.

"Once, during a slow part of the game, the camera pans to a couple making out in the stands, really going at it, and Pee Wee says something like, 'Diz, how would you call that play?' and Dizzy doesn't miss a beat; he says, 'Well, ole buddy, I guess I'd say he kisses her on the strikes and she kisses him on the balls.' I guess Pee Wee spit his beer all over the booth after that one."

People bump into each other walking down Delmar, because they keep looking down to see whose star they're stepping over. Graham's wearing his Miles Davis T-shirt today, so he's especially impressed when he finds Davis on the walk of fame.

When we get back to Blueberry Hill, we order chicken wings and onion soup. Graham's eyes look like honeydews when the wings are laid before him. I get a burger with iceberg-sized chunks of bleu cheese.

"This is the most decadent meal I've ever had," I say. "I would be a lardass if I ate here more than once every twenty-five years."

"Best food of the trip so far," Graham says. "Hell, best meal ever."

The only blemish on the evening: Of the two thousand songs on the jukebox, some mental pygmy has chosen "Vehicle" by the Ides of March, truly a wretched piece of music from 1971.

Graham dabs at the corner of his mouth with a battered, wing-sauce-covered napkin. "I want to throw it up and re-create that meal."

Joe comes by and, fueled with a couple bottles of Blueberry Hill's Rock & Roll Beer, I'm effusive in my praise. He's drinking a vodka, so maybe I don't seem too gushy.

"Over the years," Joe says, "Chuck Berry has become a friend."

Berry is a sometimes ornery reclusive man, distrustful of people who've ripped him off. As one of the founding fathers of rock 'n' roll—a title he could share with Little Richard but few others—he's had a difficult career. As a handsome young black man admired by white teenage girls in the 1950s, he was a target for a lot of white anger. He was convicted in 1962 of violating the Mann Act for transporting a minor across state lines for "immoral purposes"—and his prison term stunted his career. He'd already secured his spot as a charter member of the Rock and Roll Hall of Fame in his first five years, as the singer-songwriter of "Johnny B. Goode," "Roll Over Beethoven," "Maybellene" and scores of others. Out of prison, he never really recovered professionally and was relegated to the oldies circuit. He got popped in 1979 for income-tax evasion but used the time in prison to write his autobiography, perhaps the best rock-star memoir yet written.

"He did that all himself," Joe says. "No ghost writer, no help, nothin'. Typed it all out himself. You can hear him talking when you read it."

When Berry first hit as a rock 'n' roll artist in 1955, he was nearly a decade older than Elvis and aware of what he wanted to accomplish. Elvis had instinct and pure, raw talent. Berry had more of a creative imagination. For commercial reasons—he wanted to make a buttload of money—but also for social reasons, he made his songs race-generic. He wrote "School Day" about things both black and white kids could understand: the frustration of waiting for the bell to ring, for school to be over and to hit the streets in a burst of freedom. He was consciously trying to erase barriers between black and white kids.

So when I think about that Mann Act case or the recent charges of hanky-panky at his nightclub, I don't really want to believe them. Someone once referred to head Beach Boy Brian Wilson, another flawed man, as "a genius musician but an amateur human being." For me, the same thing goes with Chuck Berry. His accomplishments outweigh all of that other stuff.

Joe honors the graffiti writers at Blueberry Hill by periodically reproducing the bathroom comments on T-shirts. One of my favorites from above my urinal: "Fuck this honky-ass West Country tourist blowhole. *Rock and roll?* I don't think so."

When it's time to leave, Joe comes by again with another vodka.

"61 is the real 'gut' highway," he says. "There are so many great people from St. Louis in music and literature and stuff. Not only is St. Louis the gateway to the west, the same thing was happening from south to north—both directions. All of the cultures collided here. And that's when you get creativity. Everyone's exposed to other cultures, other ethnic groups, other everything. St. Louis is where the arts exploded—Scott Joplin, Miles Davis, Chuck Berry, Tina Turner, Albert King. . . . I think it is a cultural collision. St. Louis is such an important part of the cultural history of the United States."

It sets me off to a short, slurred version of my radio-is-subversive lecture, which I'm not used to delivering after drinking a couple beers. Joe picks up on it right away. "WLAC!" he shouts. "Wolfman Jack—coming to you from Del Rio, Texas!" He leans back and howls like the Wolfman.

"Glad to see we're on the same wavelength," I say.

There's a place across Highway 61 from our motel called the Set 'Em Up Saloon. It's smoky and raucous.

I sit down at the bar and the woman behind the counter, dealing with stools full of drinkers, says, "I'll help you in a minute, Hon."

"Can I get a six pack to go?" I yell when she comes back.

"Oh Lordy," she says. "Our six packs are really expensive. Whyn't you try the Conoco station around the corner?"

I get us each an oil can of Foster's and we drift off in our room, still talking about our visit to rock 'n' roll heaven.

Solace

The next morning, I sleep in—8:30 is "sleeping in" for me—and I cross 61 for breakfast at Ryan's Grill. Graham was up late watching *SportsCenter* again, and I'm not sure I'll get him motor-vatin' for a while, but I need my coffee.

The waitress has tight brunette curls and is built like a boxer. I must look like hell, with my mushroom cloud of hair carrying the stale smell of cigarettes and beer from Blueberry Hill. I order coffee and wheat toast with raspberry jelly.

The waitress pads around refilling coffees, and I sit at the bar, listening to six women at the table closest to me, yapping. They vary from late middle age to elderly—there's a walker parked in the aisle. They have concluded that Suave is OK, but if you've got the extra fifty cents you ought to try that Pantene stuff. Another source of concern is how Crystal Gayle cuts her hair. I'm struggling to find something interesting in the *Wentzville Journal*. The café doesn't even have a *Post-Dispatch*.

I got to be a pretty good eavesdropper during my days as a reporter, but I struggle to hear the waitress when she lingers at one of the booths. It's frustrating for an audio voyeur when the hearing starts to go. She's talking to a sinewy blond man in a sleeveless faded blue T-shirt with glasses and Elvis-length sideburns.

I hear him say, "Aw, it's just the same old same old."

"Yeah, I know what you mean," the waitress says, and starts to walk away. Then she says, "We talking about the same thing?"

"I'm talking about eatin'," the man says.

"I'm talking about men," she says, winking.

I must be the only person in the place she doesn't address by first name, so finally she asks my story. I tell her about my sleeping son across the street. "I'll be mad if you don't bring him over here for breakfast," she says.

After I rouse him, we return and both order the Gonzo—four scrambled eggs, with onions, green peppers, chilis and cheese, side orders of bacon and American fries.

When the waitress sets the mound of food down before us, I ask: "How come it's called the 'Gonzo'? Just curious."

"I have no idea." She looks at me as if I just offered to spay her cat without anesthetic.

St. Louis used to frighten me when I was a kid. I remember staying a week at the Howard Johnson's on Lindbergh Avenue, out in the safe suburbs and watching *Psycho* on local television every night. Its network premiere had been canceled because CBS feared a negative reaction after the recent high-profile murder of Valerie Percy, daughter of Senator Charles Percy. But a St. Louis independent picked up the rights and ran the film every night at nine. I managed to avoid the horrible decaying image of Norman's mother every time.

Whenever we drove back into the city to where my sister Suzanne was attending the St. Luke's Hospital nursing program, the Howard Johnson coziness was lost. St. Louis was a war zone, with bombed-out buildings and survivors limping through rubble.

That was the ghost of St. Louis past. Every visit since, it seemed like a great American city with so much character, preserved by the well-intentioned historic societies, with grand Victorian mansions on Lafayette Square called the "painted ladies" and the splendor of the old, well-preserved public buildings, concert halls and schools.

But as Graham drives into the heart of the city on Delmar Boulevard, I'm reminded of that forbidding St. Louis when I was a child. That was the era of cities in flame—Detroit, Newark, Watts—and even though my view was from the safe back seat of my father's ice-blue Cadillac, I still carried that impression.

Scott Joplin's house is on Delmar, close to downtown, a beautiful two-story lovingly preserved state historic site.

Scott Joplin and my father. I never hear his music, even when it's played poorly ("It is never right to play ragtime fast," he said), without thinking of my father and mescaline.

My father was ordered to relax after his first heart attack, but he was incapable of napping, so my mother suggested he take music lessons. *Why don't you both take lessons,* she suggested one Sunday afternoon while helping me with my college-boy laundry.

And so we bought a keyboard and took lessons one after another every Tuesday afternoon. I struggled through the Irving Berlin songbook. My father picked it up easily and before long was playing some of his favorite standards: "September Song," "Stardust," "Georgia on my Mind" and a lot of Rodgers and Hammerstein. But Scott Joplin frustrated him. He bought recordings to help: *The Red Back Book* by the New England Conservatory Ragtime Ensemble and Joshua Rifkin's *Piano Rags by Scott Joplin.* Rifkin played Joplin slowly and mournfully.

I borrowed that record once and took it to the Maggot Kingdom, my last college home. One Sunday night, I returned from a day at home with my parents. Three of my roomate's friends were in the living room, everyone awaiting my arrival. "Want to take some dope?" my roommate Mike said. *Take?* "Smoke" I understood. "Take" was different.

It was mescaline, and the ensuing night—evening ran into the next morning—was one of the most wonderfully bizarre of my brief but active drug-taking career. The lingering image is of Wayne, Mike's friend, playing darts to *Piano Rags by Scott Joplin.* He'd step forward with a dart, measure the distance to the board with his eyes, step forward again, prepare to throw, then step back and measure the distance again, all to the lovely syncopated accompaniment of Scott Joplin. When he finally threw the dart, it took three minutes to cross the room.

My father died that year, and our music teacher played at the funeral. There were no hymns. She started with "September Song," then followed with "Stardust," which Hoagy Carmichael had written after a desultory brokenhearted walk through the campus a mile away. Then she played "Solace," my favorite Joplin composition. I heard a few murmurs from the rows behind the family. "Odd music for a funeral," one man whispered. I smiled. They didn't really know my father.

"This looks like the crappy part of town," Graham says, steering through a burned-out block of stores and a roofless church. Desolation interests him, and so he parks and takes a few pictures. These are the kinds of tragic urban images his mother likes. *The Destruction of Lower Manhattan* by photographer Danny Lyon used to sit on the coffee table when we were married.

Graham works fast with the camera, a little ill at ease in the rubble, afraid some crazed crackhead will make a grab for his mother's second-string camera.

It's a bit of oversell to call the brick two-story "Scott Joplin's Home" since Joplin and his wife, Belle, merely rented an apartment upstairs. There, by gaslight, Joplin wrote most of his famous rags.

Graham knows who Scott Joplin is. I have a portrait of him in my rock 'n' roll room at home, and he knows he's been dead a long time. I could tell him how much that grandfather he never knew liked this man's music, but I'm not sure he'd be much interested. He'd probably like the mescaline story more, but that wouldn't be a prudent-parent thing to do.

"Scott Joplin here, he might have been the first crossover artist," I tell Graham. "I doubt there were too many black musicians before him who got their music heard by white audiences. After him, jazz made the first real dent in white culture—Louis Armstrong, King Oliver. . . ."

Joplin was born near Linden, Texas, and raised in Texarkana and Sedalia, Missouri. His family was musical and his parents, though not rich, recognized their son's talents and bought him an upright piano. He followed the path for a lot of black pianists—certainly the New Orleans variety—by playing in whorehouses. While in Sedalia, he played at the Maple Leaf Club, creating his most famous melody, "Maple Leaf Rag," while there. He sold it to a white music publisher who appreciated Joplin's talents. He then went off to St. Louis, where Joplin turned out scores of pieces and reached musical adulthood with longer works such as "The Ragtime Dance" and "The Chrysanthemum." He put all of his energies into his opera, *Treemonisha*, considered a failure when produced in 1910. It received its world premiere at Morehouse College in Atlanta in 1972 and made it to Broadway in 1975 and was the reason that, five decades after his death, he was awarded a special Pulitzer Prize.

The house is immaculate, and the downstairs is used for exhibits telling the story of Scott Joplin's life. The upstairs apartment is re-created as it must have appeared in his time and there is, of course, the player piano in the music room. You can play rags that Joplin cut himself.

In his last years, Joplin was diagnosed with terminal syphilis, suffering dementia, paranoia and other symptoms. By then, he was living in New York, and he died there April 1, 1917. His death passed unnoticed. Ragtime was a forgotten form of music then, and his passing was overshadowed by America's entry into the First World War that day. "Maybe fifty years after I'm dead my music will be appreciated," he said a few years before he died.

The Shredder

Graham is more interested in living musicians. In this morning's *Post-Dispatch*, he discovers that Dick Dale is playing that night. The thought of sharing air space with Dick Dale gets him excited.

Dick Dale was and always will be the King of the Surf Guitar. Surf music was one of the most misunderstood subsets of rock 'n' roll. It predates the most well-known surf group, the Beach Boys, by several years. For all of their talent and charm (considerable) the Beach Boys weren't really part of the surf culture. The group's leader, musical savant Brian Wilson, was a great composer who needed subject matter. His brother Dennis, a genuine surfer, suggested he match surfing jargon to his music. He did, and the Beach Boys became a surf band by default. They certainly had the greatest success of any surf band, and it makes you wonder how innovators like Dick Dale felt about that.

Dick Dale is probably one of the reasons the electric guitar sounds the way it does. When he met guitar manufacturer Leo Fender in 1954, Fender handed Dale his new creation, the Stratocaster, and asked him to try it out. As was his custom, Dale turned the right-handed guitar upside down and played it left handed. Fender thought he was nuts. Dale didn't change the strings, so he had to transpose the music in his head in order to play the guitar his way. Fender asked Dale to try out his amplifiers too. His piercing guitar playing took on its characteristic sound when he suggested to Fender that they work the reverb option off a Hammond organ into their amplifiers. Dale's intention was to enhance his singing voice, which didn't have a natural vibrato. Fake vibrato would have done just as well; but when he heard what it did to his guitar sound, Dale stopped singing and played his guitar louder than anyone ever had before. "Dick, why do you have to play so loud?" Leo Fender asked him. Dale said he wanted people to hear the ocean's roar in his music. He played so loud he destroyed forty-nine of Fender's amplifiers—several burst into flames.

Graham knows this history. Since he first showed interest in guitars, I'd been getting him *Guitar World* subscriptions. He can recite a guitarist's equipment with the same deadly accuracy with which he once recited batting averages.

He also knows Dick Dale's story—that his real name was Richard Monsour, that he was of Middle Eastern descent and that he really surfed. He started playing his distinctive style of music, aimed at audiences of surfers, nearly a decade before the "surf music" boom and when the Beach Boys were still in elementary school.

The Broadway Oyster Bar is a hole in the wall with a narrow hallway leading to a small dining room in back. There's an enclosed patio nearly as large as the interior, walled by lattice. A small stage opens to a side street with a White Castle hamburger stand in the next lot.

We sit down in the dining room, the only customers. It's early afternoon and we plan to wait out Dick Dale.

"This is a nice place and all," I say. "Still, don't you think Dick deserves more—like an auditorium?"

The concept behind the place is New Orleans in St. Louis, so we order a quarter pound of alligator tail battered with buttermilk, covered with cornflakes and flash fried. I also order Voodoo Wings, rolled in hot sauce.

Erin Rawlings, our waitress, brings me a Schlafly Pale Ale, with a lemon sunk into its amber neck. It's from the St. Louis Brewery and its slogan wraps around the oval logo: "Beer the way it used to be."

"How is it?" Graham asks, eyeing the bottle.

"Great. I'm glad we're going to stay put for a while though. I get some heavy beer in my system, I won't want to go anywhere."

"Come on, Dad. Maybe we can stay in St. Louis for another night. Free spirits and all?"

On road trips growing up, my dad always thought the day was wasted unless you got in five hundred miles. "All right," I say. "We'll stay."

Since we're here for the duration, I order Graham a B.O.B. Burger with grinder sauce, three cheeses and spicy fries. I order a dozen oysters and another beer. We move outside to the patio, where Dick Dale will play. It's a beautiful day and there's a fully stocked outdoor bar.

The patio's stereo system plays a jazz version of "Ding-Dong! The Witch Is Dead." Behind the bar is a huge mosaic of what looks like a man and woman fornicating on the back of a ram.

John Johnson was a painting contractor who just liked the Broadway. When the owner mentioned casually that he wanted to sell, John saw it as a chance to keep his favorite bar open. "The funny thing is," he says, "I'm not really much of a bar person. I'd go out every now and then. But now look at me." He's a large balding man with a gray goatee who books blues bands. "It's so much more interesting than painting and contracting. And the painting business is much harder."

By dusk, the patio is filling, and Dick Dale's bus pulls up on the street separating the Broadway's patio from the White Castle. He stays on the bus until announced, and when he steps onto the sidewalk my son is there with his camera. Dale points at him and says, "I don't want to see that shit on eBay!"

In the early days, Dick Dale was movie-star handsome in that anonymous television actor sort of way, resembling Robert Horton, Ward Bond's hunky sidekick on *Wagon Train*. Now in his sixties, Dale is striking in a different way: a tall man, still with a sculpted face, but with a high forehead and gray hair in a ponytail to the middle of his back. He wears a headband in keeping with the "tribal" themes in his recent recordings, and he dresses entirely in black.

As soon as he hits the stage, he grabs his guitar and starts playing. The bottles of whiskey and vodka across the bar from me rattle with the thunder from his Showman amplifier. He has a drummer and a sleepy-eyed bass player as the perfunctory rhythm section, but the show is all his. In a career spent listening to rock 'n' roll music, I've never heard anything as loud as Dick Dale. Not only are the bottles rattling—my heart reverberates in my chest, and my testicles resound with each gut-wrenching low run he makes on the strings. It's as much a sonic assault as a concert.

I'm content where I've been for the last few hours, sitting at the corner of the outdoor bar. But Graham stalks Dick Dale with his camera, roaming the front of the stage and, for part of the show,

Dick Dale, the king of the surf guitar, in concert at the Broadway Oyster Bar in St. Louis. The only thing louder may have been the Big Bang.

standing onstage, trying to get a shot of Dale's mobile face as he plays. I remember when I took him to his first spring training game, how wide-eyed he was when he saw Orioles pitcher Rick Sutcliffe up close. Once, we literally ran into Bob Feller under the bleachers—

looking like any other retiree snowbird except for the baseball uniform. Back then, when Graham said "Thanks, Mr. Feller" after getting an autograph, he wore the same little-boy wide-eyed expression as the kid at the side of the stage. Occasionally, Dick Dale looks his way and smiles.

The patio is packed. I'm surprised people in the nearby apartments and upscale remodeled homes in the Soulard area haven't called the cops to complain about the nuclear war at the oyster bar.

Dick Dale doesn't mess around between songs. No long introductions, no background on his inspiration, no philosophical indoctrination.

"Hey you," he nods toward a girl about twelve yards back from the stage. "You come up front, will ya? I like to have the pretty girls up front when I play."

He's old enough to be her grandfather, even though he has a nine-year-old at home in California. He bows and she leans forward to run her fingers suggestively down the long neck of his Stratocaster.

"I'll stick around and sign autographs and talk after the show," he says into the microphone. "Anyone who wants their tits signed, line up over here at the side."

His signature tune, "Misirlou," is known to the youngest of the audience through its use in *Pulp Fiction* and in Domino's Pizza commercials. Dale doesn't play the standard version—he improvises, toying with the melody for twenty minutes. On one of his recent albums, he does the same thing with Duke Ellington.

The place is so crowded that it's hard to get a clear look at the stage, so for a while I close my eyes and listen. But I'd like to know how Graham's enjoying it, so I ask Erin to protect my barstool and I walk around to the backstage area to watch Dick Dale in profile. There's Graham, smoking a cigarette.

He can see the shock on my face. He leans over and talks directly into my ear, since Dick Dale is louder than the Big Bang right now. "I'm sorry, Dad."

He stuffs the cigarette down the longneck of a nearby Schlafly's. I suppose it was inevitable I'd see him smoke sometime, but I can't get over my surprise enough yet to offer up a lecture.

I mill around near the front of the stage and look at the fans. There are the well-groomed gray-haired blues enthusiasts in plutonium-white T-shirts, longnecks held at nipple level, doing the white-boy bob-and-weave in approximate time to the music. The night produces an astonishing array of beautiful single women—they've come in bouquets of twos and threes—but as an engaged man, I have little interest. Then there's a very odd slack-jawed middle-aged guy—I'd guess forty—wearing a corduroy sports jacket on what's turned into a humid night. His haircut is pure Ringo, circa *Rubber Soul*, a bowl with wings. He's also dancing, but not to music Dick Dale is playing. His fingers move as if he's contemplating air guitar, but then they take on a horizontal motion and now I think he's sorting socks. He insinuates himself nearly onto the stage, and while he does his odd sorting dance his hands are three inches from the bass player's fingers. I've never seen anyone be so nonchalant about being so strange. He's obviously in touch with his inner weirdo.

Dick Dale sits in on drums and grabs the sticks to play the bass, showing off for the crowd. I return to my barstool, order another drink and settle in for the rest of the show.

I still can't see him well over the crowd, but I notice a change in the texture of the sound—not Dick Dale's sound, which remains thunderous, but the sound of the audience. I strain to see, and when I step up on the leg of the bar stool I see Dale walk offstage, toward the street. He's got a wireless guitar. He still rumbles through his amplifier onstage, but he's on the prowl. Graham is right behind him as he crosses into the White Castle parking lot.

There's a car at the drive-through window and Dale lines up behind it, still playing frenetic ski-slope runs, eyes closed, leaning back in concentration. When the car in front gets its order and drives off, Dale walks up to the window. He doesn't say a word, but begins jamming his guitar neck at the bewildered minimum wager behind the cash register. She laughs nervously, and Dale strolls out in the middle of Broadway. It's not busy tonight, but he still has to dodge a few cars. You can imagine the drivers' fright when they see this tall guy dressed in black, with a headband and Rapunzel-like hair, walking down the centerline. He walks back through the front entrance of the Broadway, where all of the people who couldn't fit onto the patio are surprised that they finally get to see the guy. When he comes back out onto the patio—*he hasn't missed a note* the whole time during his stroll—he asks Erin to get him a beer. She grabs a bottle, opens it, then pours it down his throat. *Never misses a note.* Graham's behind him, eyes big as pie plates, like Dick Dale's the ponytailed Pied Piper.

True to his word, Dick Dale sticks around afterward. Graham tells him about the trip and the serendipity of finding Dick Dale in town.

"Oh man, that sounds so cool," he says. "I'd love to do something like that."

"My son's a guitarist," I tell him, putting my arm around Graham. "We're just lucky we were in St. Louis tonight to see this show."

"You tell your friends to come out and see Dick Dale sometime," he says.

"That was awesome," Graham says.

A blonde woman with mascara sweat-pasted to her cheeks pulls down her shirt and presents her breast.

"Oh, baby," Dale says. "You don't know what this means to me." He signs "All the best, Dick Dale" in Sharpie across her flesh.

Trail of Tears

We spend the night in the suburb of Arnold, a succession of Taco Bells, AutoZones and Amoco stations. They smother the highway, known in town as Jeffco Boulevard, but as soon as we leave the gravitational pull of St. Louis the next morning, Highway 61 emerges again into splendid, sun-drenched countryside, and we see the road's personality again in all of its two-lane blacktop glory. Wide fields of grain border the highway and we pick up speed, heading south, the Mississippi River just two miles to the east. It's nearly as beautiful as it was in Minnesota, but here there are more towns, more trailers, a few more eyesores. For forty miles, our highway plays tag with I-55, which also runs down to Memphis. They cross each other down toward the Missouri boot heel, the notch into the northeast corner of Arkansas.

Before the kids knew their letters well enough to read billboards, I kept them amused with auto-bingo games with pictures of houses, schools and railroad tracks. But Graham always wanted to win and would cover up things he'd seen before we'd started playing. "Remember that cow we saw yesterday?" he'd say. "I think I will count that." Then Sarah would slug him and tell him he was cheating and we had to put the game away.

We got into the travel habit of reading signs aloud—the weirder the better, of course. Here's a tavern advertising itself as a "Famous Bah." Here's a road called "Ernie and Rick Lane." A drive-in wants us to try its "Quad-zilla," a four-patty monster hamburger. A billboard advertises a truck competition: MUDSTOCK 2001—BRING YOUR RIG!

Thank God we're still picking up St. Louis radio. There's an exceptional oldies station playing Van Morrison's "Moondance," The Trashmen's "Surfin' Bird," The Cornelius Brothers' "Treat Her Like a Lady" and "My Boyfriend's Back" by the Angels. To my surprise, Graham knows all of the backing vocals, which he sings in a girlish register.

We're still groggy and I'm not sure where we are.

"I'm too tired to look for the map," I tell Graham. "I trust you're on top of things."

"We're somewhere in Missouri, Bro," he says. "Free spirits on the loose."

The houses settled sporadically along the highway have manicured yards patrolled by concrete deer sculptures and the bad-taste reflecting balls in the flower garden. Occasionally, we see a Virgin Mary presiding over the marigolds.

"I just checked the odometer," Graham says. "In one-half mile, we had three monuments to Mary, Mother of God."

Down the road is another set of twin cities, Festus and Crystal City. In the 1840s a geologist found silica near Plattin Creek and, since it was near the Mississippi and its shipping lanes, the American Plate Glass Company built a town and then a factory. The town of Crystal City came first, in order to attract the workers, and soon there was a satellite town on the outskirts, called Limitsville. Later in the 1880s, in need of its own identity, it became Tanglefoot. But after a few years the Tanglefootians wanted something more dignified. One of the Bible-toting women in town opened the good book one day and the first proper name she came upon—Acts 25:1—was "Festus." I'm disappointed. I thought it would be cool for a town to name itself after the sidekick on *Gunsmoke*.

Highway 61 keeps wrapping around I-55 and when we cross over, we look down on the trucks and the family minivans with some pity. They're not seeing what we're seeing, not learning what we're learning. Trees line our highway, then there's an expanse of farmland. Here's a house wrapped in toilet paper. They don't see things like this on that damn generic interstate.

At a roadside rest area—just a gravel pullout with an oil can for trash on hinges—I take a picture of Graham in his faded Led Zeppelin T-shirt, with a beautiful valley down below, zippered by I-55. The sign says we're 583 feet above sea level. As we peer down the cliff, we see rusted refrigerators and bags of rotting garbage chewed open by animals.

State boundaries do strange things through here. Illinois claims a good chunk of land on the Missouri side of the river but doesn't care enough to have more than one town—Kaskaskia—to mingle with the Show-Me villages.

The radio picks up the percussive opening of "Sympathy for the Devil," and Graham turns it up and manages not only to play lead guitar but also to expertly handle the backing vocals. We seem to have Highway 61 to ourselves today, ripping through hay fields, putting a golden fringe on a bright green grassland.

The towns are all different. Sainte Genevieve has the first brick building west of the Mississippi. It's the oldest settlement in the state, and the Inn St. Gemme Beauvais is the oldest bed-and-breakfast in Missouri. With a coat of white paint, the two-story six-columned mansion could be a dead ringer for Tara. This B&B and a few others around here have made the cable travel shows and the magazines.

After Perryville and Old Appleton, we take a turn at Fruitland to the Trail of Tears State Park. From high-school history class, Graham knows some of the outlines of the story—how gold was found near the north Georgia homeland of the Cherokees and how the tribe was "removed" to Oklahoma on a thousand-mile death march. Every Florida-to-Indiana run takes us by New Echota, Georgia, the Cherokee capital and home of the tribe's newspaper. They weren't nomads like other Native American tribes. They had their own language and alphabet, and many had a Western education.

In 1838, more than fifteen thousand Cherokees were marched across the country, in thirteen separate bands, to Indian Territory, now Oklahoma. Nine of the thirteen bands crossed the Mississippi here, and during the harsh winter of 1839 thousands died—many here, on the land we walk.

Now RVs and tent campers dot the site, and we poke through the exhibits in the ranger station before heading down to the river's edge. The river must have flooded recently, because the banks are scarred with debris. I'm hesitant for Graham to drive right onto the bank, but the War Wagon doesn't sink.

"Let's see if we can catch anything in this mighty river," Graham says, pulling out his fishing rod and tackle. He searches for a lure and we both know he's not likely to have much luck. He's always done better with worms in fresh water.

The wind is blowing and whole trees speed by in the current.

"Dang, the river's moving fast," he says. "I doubt I'll get anything."

"It's a wonder you like fishing so much," I tell him, "considering the first time."

I'd come up to visit at the end of the semester when Graham was five, and I'd brought him a Snoopy fishing rod. There's a huge lake south of Bloomington, so I rescued one of my father's rods from the basement, bought some worms at a bait store and took my son fishing for the first time. The fact that I was a lousy fisherman didn't faze me. This is the sort of thing fathers and sons do.

We'd set up on the muddy banks of the lake, much like this place here, and I baited his hook for him. He needed help casting, but after a while he had the hang of it and tried it himself. When my back was turned, he ended up hooking something—his forearm.

He never cried, even though he had a worm hooked into his arm. I ripped the worm in two while pulling it off, but the hook was so deeply imbedded I thought I might cause more pain if I tried to pull it out. Since I saw him only once a month, I didn't want him to associate me with agony.

I quickly packed the car and drove Graham into town. He held his left arm, hook jutting out, on his lap. "This really hurts," he said. "How soon until we'll be there?"

Convenient to have a brother as a doctor, but when we burst into his waiting room, the receptionist told us he was in surgery. I went to the next office over—a gynecologist—and though they didn't know me, the nurse was happy to help the little boy. She removed the hook, and Graham had a story of immense bravery to tell friends.

The hook incident didn't affect him. We went fishing every summer, and he fished two or three times a week during good weather at a pond near his mother's house. He thought it was funny that my dad used to take me fishing in the Florida Keys and I never caught a fish.

One summer when he was eight, we went to Cedar Key, a fishing village on the Gulf of Mexico. He and Sarah were fishing, and I was observing and drinking beer. Then Graham insisted that I fish, since he was having such luck. I'd just put the line in the water when I hooked a toadfish, one of the ugliest creatures on earth.

Graham insisted I hold it up and that Sarah videotape the fish before we threw it back in the water.

"Is this the greatest moment of your life, Dad?" he asked.

There'd been a lot of fishing since. When Graham was in high school, a friend took us out in the Gulf for an afternoon on his boat, and we caught more than forty fish apiece. Graham kept well-supplied tackle boxes in Indiana and Florida. When we talked on the phone in the fall, when the weather was good and the king mackerel still running, he'd ask me if I'd gone back out in the Gulf.

"No," I'd tell him. "You know I wouldn't go without you."

He seemed to think that the thing I liked about fishing was the fish.

Highway 61 hadn't brought us by many lakes, other than the huge Superior—and that didn't seem to have much in the way of a fishing pier. "I've never fished the Mississippi," Graham says, tying on a lure. "Don't think I'll get anything, but I want to say I tried."

He casts his line and it's immediately snagged in one of the tangles of branches rushing downriver. Graham fights for a while, not wanting to lose the lure, but finally cuts it loose.

"Oh well," he says, walking back to the car. "So much for the Mississippi."

As we head back to 61 on a gravel road, a spray of stones pelts the windshield. One of them ricochets off Graham's knuckle—he drives with his arm braced in the window—and strikes the glass, giving us a spider's web view of the world. We wash the windshield at every gas station, but it's still battered with insect remains. Now the glass is cracked, and to the casual observer the once-proud Explorer looks even more like a pummeled wreck. I prefer to think of the cracked glass as another scar in fine leather. If the War Wagon survives this trip, maybe we'll put it in a museum.

Throwed Rolls

We're on the gravel road for twenty minutes, trying to find our way back to 61. On the crest of a ridge, we stop at a little farmhouse shaded in the canopy of spreading oaks. There's a garage sale presided over by three kids, all under twelve, and no adults.

"This gun is *not* for sale," the boy says, snatching up a BB gun from the tree trunk. There's not much of anything for sale, and that which is we've outgrown—Beverly Cleary books, Leonardo DiCaprio posters, a broken gumball machine. There's a dollhouse Savannah might want in a couple of years. The kids can tell when something catches our attention, and they start talking it up. "Nothing wrong with the dollhouse," the littlest girl says. "I just don't need it anymore."

We don't really want anything other than to imagine what it's like to live in this farmhouse at the crest of this hill.

Wib's Drive-In ("Barbecue At Its Best") specializes in pork shoulder sandwiches on toast. It's an astonishingly quiet and clean little restaurant, which doesn't bode well for the food.

"When they spell it with *C-U-E*, it's not supposed to be as good as the Bar-B-Q," I tell Graham. "At least, that's what the barbecue snobs tell you."

Looks like this place used to be a Dairy Queen. Our waitress, a teenager named Lauren, gives us a few minutes with the photocopied menus. She's an Elisabeth Shue look-alike with a huge engagement ring.

We want the special, and Lauren drops our order off in the window to the kitchen. A gray-haired, somewhat prim woman picks up the order, frowns at it, then disappears from the window. In less than two minutes, Lauren brings us two barbecue sandwiches on toast, presented on butcher paper on a lunch tray. It's an anal-retentive barbecue sandwich; the meat lined up with the crust of the toast, no sauce or meat hanging off the edge.

"White people's barbecue," I whisper. "We can do better than this."

Cape Girardeau is ahead of Hibbing on the whole exploit-our-native-son thing. The town is poised to capitalize on its stature as the birthplace of Rush Limbaugh with a Rush Limbaugh Hometown Tour, which dispenses Rush facts ("Shined shoes at the College Barber Shop when he was 13" . . . "See where he cruised Broadway, traditional during Rush's high school days" . . . "first disk jockey job was under the name Rusty Sharpe" . . . "disliked school"). Hibbing could learn from this.

Rush no doubt approves of Cape Girardeau County Park, with its rolling expanse looking more like a golf course than a scrubby-grass playground. We'd need to bathe before we could take a walk there.

Ahead of us in traffic is a beige Ford Ranger with a tinted back-window with "Fear This" and Confederate flag stickers.

"I think we have just crossed over into the South," I tell Graham.

"I haven't seen any black people today," Graham says. "At least not since leaving St. Louis. It's kind of weird, don't you think?"

"I know. How weird to be in a barbecue place and it to be all white. It's like white gospel music—you've got to ask *why*."

We've been holding out for real food until we get to Sikeston, site of a regionally famous restaurant. It's a half mile off Highway 61, at the I-55 exit for Sikeston, with a sign even higher than the Cracker Barrel signs that drive zoning boards wild: "Lambert's Café, Home of the Throwed Rolls."

The décor also looks like the model for Cracker Barrel, walls festooned in license plates and other rusticana. The menu is ledger sized, with a note at the bottom: "Our pass-arounds today: hot rolls and sorghum, fried potatoes and onions, macaroni and tomatoes, black-eyed peas and okra."

The serving staff looks like they haven't made it through junior college yet, but they work like seasoned Disney World pros. This is an act, a country-hick routine put on for tourists.

A roll thrower comes around in the Lambert's uniform: Blue work shirt, red suspenders, red bow tie. He wheels a cart. "Hot roll!" he yells. Graham and I learn quickly from watching our fellow diners: Raise your hands and he'll toss you one. They're hot and glorious.

The roll throwers don't use their bare hands and instead rely on Reliance Powdered Vinyl Examination Gloves, product of Thailand.

"They've got this pretty well down," Graham says, nodding at his red-suspendered peers. "We've got the guys who order the food, then they have this babe who brings around the drinks, which are iced tea, iced tea and more iced tea. Then you have the okra guy, the sorghum guy . . . it's all pretty well organized."

"*Hot roll!*" All across the nonsmoking dining room, hands shoot up like we're robbery victims. A woman in an embroidered Snoopy shirt shakes her head *no* when the roll thrower gets insistent. I should tell her about the Reliance Powdered Vinyl Examination Gloves.

"It'd suck to be a paraplegic in this place," I tell Graham. "You'd starve to death. I wonder if proponents of the Americans with Disabilities Act know about Lambert's. Enough with ramps . . . we're going to require prosthetic devices to catch flying food."

You need fried chicken to properly judge a place like this. When it comes, the drumstick is the size of a cocker spaniel. The tunes are all old rock 'n' roll. Biting into a huge, crunchy chicken leg with Bruce

Channel warbling "Hey Baby" on the overhead (that's Delbert McClinton on mouth harp) is pretty damn cool.

A beautiful blonde girl with epidermal blue jeans comes around with a nearly empty bowl of potatoes. "'Taters?" she asks, but she can't fool me. She's never called these things 'taters' outside of this place. She's probably from southern California and just here to attend the CIA's top secret cheerleading camp outside town. I motion to Graham, thinking I'm doing the gallant thing. "I think he needs some," I say.

"I got the ass-end of the bowl," he complains after she leaves. When the blonde beauty returns with a hot, steaming mound of potatoes, she plops huge spoonfuls on my plate, and as soon as she leaves I transfer most of the pile to his plate.

"Happy now, you whiner?"

His fork stops its flashing movement long enough to give me a thumbs-up.

"I really have the feeling that we have crossed over into the South," I say.

"Me too," he mumbles through potatoes. "Ever since St. Louis, it's just been different."

"This could be in Georgia, for all we know. A bunch of kids hickin' it up for tourists. Would you do that? Would you dress like that?"

"I already dressed like a dumb ass in the movie theater. I had to wear a fuckin' beret. I hated it when my friends would come to the movies."

From the menu, we learn that Lambert's has hand washed, wrapped and baked over 68,000 potatoes along with 33 tons of French fries, and also used over 130,480 pounds of onions in "Old Norm's Fried Potatoes."

"Old Norm" was Norman Lambert, whose parents started the restaurant in 1941. Norman took it over when his father retired, and began the roll throwing when a customer got impatient waiting for Norman to pass a basket of them his way. "Just throw the damn thing," the customer said, and Norman obliged. Thus was roll throwing born. It got the restaurant—and Sikeston—in all of the major newspapers and tour books and on the nightly news programs. The place with the throwed rolls became a tourist attraction.

Twenty years later, Norman and his wife, Patty, spent an early-summer evening looking for deer on their property. When it grew too dark, they went back to the house, and a little before ten Patty went to the kitchen to make herself a snack. She asked Norman if he wanted something. No, he said, he just wanted to go for a walk.

A couple of minutes later, Patty heard what she thought were fireworks. When she yelled for Norman, he didn't answer. She went out to the driveway, where she found him sitting in his jeep, a pistol still in his hand.

When he died, all the businesses in Sikeston closed as his hearse passed on the town's main street. He was buried under a pear tree on his farm. No one has any idea why he killed himself.

Welcome to the South

New Madrid, at the edge of Missouri's boot heel, is a dirty little village deeply rooted in the South, with antebellum mansions and shacks within yards of each other. There's a plaid couch on the porch of one hut, with a woman in gray slacks lounging between the open springs, smoking a cigarette. Nearby there's the Hunter-Dawson house, an imposing two-story white home with fifteen rooms, a mixture of Georgian, Greek Revival and Italianate styles. The assortment of forms works, in part due to the spectacular setting near the Mississippi. Because it's at a 180-degree bend in the river—looking across at one of those weird geographical bubbles from Kentucky—the town was a river trading center dating back two centuries.

But we didn't stop to look at architecture. Two hundred years ago, there were three great earthquakes centered around the New Madrid Fault. We know now that they were all above eight on the Richter scale—which, of course, would not be invented for more than a century.

The great San Francisco earthquake of 1906 was 7.8, the most powerful California quake of modern times. The New Madrid quake was stronger, sending shock waves so powerful that church bells rang in Boston. The crew of the steamboat *New Orleans*, moored to an island in the middle of the Mississippi, awakened to find the island gone. The river itself reversed its course and ran backward. California quakes are brutal, but when geologists talk about the "big one," they say it will have this little town in Missouri at its center.

We stand on the street, near the riverbank, and I put my hand on Graham's shoulder: "In those dark days before cable brought HBO carnalities into our homes, son, we had things called TV antennas."

"I've heard of them."

"Well, my father—your grandfather—was a big football fan. And Bloomington had only one TV station, so if he wanted to watch the NFL, he knew he'd need a big antenna. You know us, we have to have the biggest everything. So he bought this huge TV tower like a radio station would have. He was at the hospital the day the guys were putting it up. So I'm sitting in the living room with Mammaw when the house starts shaking and I figure it's them, so I say, 'What in the hell is going on?', and I'm on my way out the door, like I was going to kick some ass—funny, considering I was thirteen or something. Anyway, the workers were gone, but there's all of this shaking. Then I learned later on the radio that there had been an earthquake centered here, and that's when I learned about the New Madrid Fault. There's still that big crack in the living-room window at Mammaw's house. That happened that day."

"Cool. Kind of wish I could see an earthquake."

"You have the weirdest ambitions. They say the next one that hits here will be deadly. Perhaps this is a good time to get back in the car."

First we decide to walk down to the river. A black family—mother, father, teenage son—fish off the platform over the river. We watch for a few minutes.

The son struggles with his line, and the father says, "What you hung up on?" There's so many branches flowing down the river, he figures it's caught. "Not letting you get away," the son says, and a few moments later pulls a ten-pound carp from the water. The fish flops on the shore and the son grabs him, runs a gaffe through him. He turns around to show it to us, and Graham waves.

"That's a cool fish," Graham says under his breath, "but I wouldn't eat anything out of that river. PCPs and all."

"Maybe that family has no choice." We get in the car and drive around a little more. "This is the most depressing place we've been so far," I tell him.

Grass grows down the centerline of Highway 61.

"All these interstates nearby," Graham says, "yet this road is still here. Since it's just two-lane it doesn't get paved much."

"People got too impatient for roads like this. On the interstate, it's like you're looking *at* a painting. Here, you're *in* the painting."

Lots of local color in this painting: the Te Roy Motel in Portageville, Chubby's BBQ (finally, spelled right) in Hayti, right next to R&P Package Liquors, with its cardboard front door.

First in New Madrid and now in Hayti, we see more black people—mostly kids—on the streets.

Club Zanza is a Quonset hut with a cardboard door. Graham had seen a rusted old-school Dr. Pepper sign on the way into town and was thirsty.

Inside, it's a stranger-in-a-strange-land scene. "Am I just paranoid," I ask Graham, "or does everyone know that we're from out of town?"

"Well, Dude, we have Florida plates on the car, and this town's so

A home by the side of Highway 61 in northern Arkansas, on the way down to Memphis, Tennessee.

small they know they don't *know* you." He sips luxuriantly from his Dr. Pepper. "Damn this is good."

Graham's Zeppelin T-shirt draws a few stares, and of course it makes me wonder. There's a Latin dude with a near-beehive pompadoured to his head and he's wearing an *Evil Dead* T-shirt. How come *he* isn't under the microscope?

Back on the road, Graham simultaneously drives and dances like the Ringo-haired dork in the front row of the Dick Dale show.

We slip out of Missouri through the boot heel, crossing into Arkansas just north of Blytheville, taking a turn like something out of the Indianapolis 500 and driving under a replica natural bridge. Irrigation tractors span the fields like huge mutant insects from an old science-fiction film. We're eager to get to Memphis, and this two-lane stretch is slowgoing. Over a ridge, we narrowly avoid hitting tractors using the highway while switching fields. One rusted John Deere has a Confederate-flag sticker on the wheel cover.

Everybody waves. Driving through the country south of Blytheville, we look out at the porches of the houses along the highway. An old couple salutes as we pass. A farmer nods as we pull around his tractor.

We've come from the part of the country where we could count black people on the fingers of the hand of an amputee to here, where we are the only white people we see. Osceola is a Oster blender of nice, well-maintained homes and rusted-out trailers. An anal-retentive resident apparently cuts his grass with manicure scissors to accentuate the difference between his yard and the overgrown weed patch next door. Petunias on the porch widen the gulf between the aesthetic haves and have-nots.

The sun sets over the open field to the west, and we speed through a collection of small, depressing Arkansas river towns. When we get to Frenchman's Bayou, I think we've driven into a Faulkner novel. Thousands of birds cover the branches of the trees along the highway. At this point, Highway 61 nearly joins the interstate—it's ten yards away—but we're in a different world. Poverty lines our road.

Graham's never seen *poor* quite like this. "You'd think Clinton could have helped his people more," Graham says. "Heck, he was president *eight years*."

Under Control

His full name is Charles Howard Blake Fontenay. With so many names, I figured his family was filthy rich. "Oh, hell no," Blake said. "My parents just couldn't decide on a name."

Blake didn't flinch when I'd called, asking if we could stay with him in Memphis. "Sure," he drawled. "I have a spare room, as long as you promise not to throw beer bottles against the wall."

He should talk. I'd met Blake when he came to college a dozen years before. I figured he was a Marine, with his buzz cut, reserved bearing and almost courtly manners. He always seemed older than the other students, so I thought maybe he'd done time at a military academy. He was bright, one of the better reporters in our program, an absolute straight arrow.

Then I got to know him better. In those prehomeowner days I threw huge parties in my rented puke-proof houses (linoleum floors) and invited all of my colleagues, friends from the local newspaper and three hundred students from my classes. I used to have a party every first weekend in February, to honor the Beatles' arrival in America. My last Beatles party was *too* wild. I had warring girlfriends, an out-of-control crowd and three visits from the cops. My neighbors wanted to kill me. Yet that party eventually landed me in *Playboy* as one of America's eight "most-fun profs."

Blake was at that party. While I was occupied with the girlfriends and keeping three hundred guests happy, Blake took a couple dozen eggs from my fridge, got my golf clubs from my shed and teed off in the front yard. Punctuated by sips of Jack Daniels, Blake sent yokey residue into my neighbors' yards.

Straight arrow in the classroom, a hard-drinking, sometimes confrontational guy when not at work—I knew he'd be a success in journalism. He got into the habit of calling me when he was drunk, usually around two in the morning. I got into the habit of turning off my phone.

But that was years ago. Blake had graduated, worked for newspapers in Jacksonville, Sacramento and now Memphis, where he'd covered city government for the *Commercial Appeal* for five years. I'd seen him on his rare visits to Gainesville for football games, so it wasn't too much of a stretch for me to call and ask him to put us up.

As 61 crosses the bridge from Arkansas to Tennessee, the Pyramid, all lights and glass, becomes visible.

"This is really where the Rock and Roll Hall of Fame ought to be," I tell Graham. "No accident the city built that thing after Cleveland got the Hall. Looks exactly like it."

Turns out Blake lives around the corner from the Pyramid, the big sports and rock-concert arena near Mud Island. The name "Mud Island" isn't attractive, and I seem to recall one of those nasty rock-festivals-gone-wrong there when I was in high school. But when we turn down the street, it's an upscale development. The houses, generally large and expensive looking, are right on top of each other. It takes about twenty minutes of driving down the storybook streets, but eventually we find Blake's house—a neat two-bedroom single-story home. I make introductions and, like everyone else, Blake marvels at the resemblance between Graham and me.

Blake's still in his necktie when we get there. He's been covering the move of Vancouver's NBA franchise, the Grizzlies, to Memphis. The Grizzlies want to hold up Memphis for a new arena and promises of financial windfalls. Blake's covering the business side of this sports story, and he's getting pretty disgusted with the team owners' demands.

"What's wrong with the Pyramid?" I ask.

"They haven't even played a game here," Blake says, "and already they think the place is too small."

"I just hope they change the team's name," I say. "What's grizzly about Memphis?"

"Probably more than you realize," he says.

"It's like when the New Orleans Jazz moved to Utah, though. The only thing they ever had in Utah that remotely resembled jazz is when a Donny Osmond tape got stuck in a cassette player."

To my horror, Blake suggests we hit Beale Street. This is what I was afraid of—a night of heavy drinking. I just want to sleep.

"Sounds great," I say, beaming.

We squeeze into Blake's Mustang convertible and within five minutes, we're at Silky O'Sullivan's on Beale Street.

———

Graham's been to Memphis before. A few years earlier I took the kids back to Indiana by way of New Orleans and Memphis. It was a thousand miles out of the way, but I wanted to show them more of the world than the usual I-75 scenery. I took them through Graceland and the Sun Studios, and then we came down to Beale Street. "What's going on, Dad?" Graham asked, looking over the huge crowd. "I think it's called Friday night," I said. Graham never forgot that as we walked by Beale Street Barbecue a man came out, wiping his hands on his apron. "Get your asses in here and eat some barbecue," he said.

Tonight Beale Street isn't quite as wild, but it's still the busiest place we've seen on the trip. Blake wants us to meet Silky, his Memphis mentor.

One of the exterior walls at Silky O'Sullivan's is held up by girders, and that part of the building has no roof. It's the oldest standing wall on the street and a forlorn link to the past. We find the owner on a stool at the end of the bar in the half of the building with a roof. He has the regal bearing of a hookah-smoking caterpillar.

Silky—a massive man in a black smock of a polo shirt with slicked-back gray hair and a droopy moustache—eyes us carefully while matching names with faces and, in my case, occupations. "This guy was actually my professor," Blake says.

"I know where you work," Silky says, pointing at my chest. "Right south of that football stadium there, Florida Field, there's a building—I think it's the engineering building—and you're up next to that, right? Second or third floor?"

"Second," I say. "Used to be third. How do you know that?"

"Silky knows everything," he drawls.

"That's pretty amazing, I mean for you to. . . ."

I might as well be talking to the lonely brick wall outside. Silky glazes over when something catches his eye behind me, and he follows it until it's next to me. *It*, of course, turns out to be two nubile college-age girls—both blonde, each with a pert bottom, one showing much cleavage, the other more modest. For Silky, the world stops as the girls pass me, making the turn toward the patio.

Silky reaches out and gently touches one on the arm. "Hello, Darlin,' " he says. "How are y'all this evening?"

"Fine," one of them giggles. They can see he's no threat. Blake, Graham and I gorge ourselves on the scene—hair-flipping from the girls, walrus tusk–sharpening from Silky.

"You gettin' everything you need here tonight?" he asks.

"We just got here," one of the girls says.

"Well, I'm Silky," he says. "This is my place. You need anything, you just come to me."

"We sure will." It comes out *we-ill*, and I glance at Graham: *our first Southern belle.*

"You have a good time here, will you? Check on my goats out there, let me know they're doing all right."

"We sure will."

They sashay to the patio, heads bent in conversation. Silky doesn't speak again until they are safely outside.

He turns to me, looking for a moment like he has no idea who I am, as if the encounter with the beautiful young girls has erased his memory. "Let's all go sit on the patio now, what do you say?"

He orders the bartender to bring us some drinks, and we get the first table outside the door so Silky can continue to monitor the comings and goings of his female patrons.

Specialty of the house is a drink called The Diver. For eighteen bucks, you get a gallon of "Southern Fun" served in a yellow bucket. This is Silky's secret blend of alcohol, "sure to make you go down." On the menu, drinkers are advised, "Keep the bucket—it may come in handy." Vomiting has never appealed to me, so I suggest we all get beer.

Silky sits before me, his shirt drooping off the side of the chair but his fingers knotted above his considerable belly line.

"Where you from, 'riginally?'"

"I grew up in the military," I say, "so I sort of grew up all over. Indiana, I guess."

"I.U." It comes out *Ahhh Ewe.*

"My alma mater," I nod. "That's where my son goes."

"Best student union in the world," he says. "It's like going to Camelot."

"You *do* know everything. Not many people know that."

"I got someone I want to put you on to." Silky makes a call, chats for a few moments, then hands the phone to me. "You'll love this guy."

"*Haaaah*," I hear a scratchy old black man's voice.

"Hi," I say. "Who's this?"

"Lil' Howlin' Wolf. Silky, my man Silky, he say you want to talk to me."

Dumbfounded, I say, "Sure, I'd love to."

"I can't come down there tonight. I'd love to, but I can't come down there tonight. My wife, she not feelin' too good and she'd—*heh heh*—she'd get after me if I leave her home late at night like this." It's half spoken, half growled.

"That's fine," I say. "To be honest, I'm dead tired. We've been driving all day. Maybe we can hook up with you tomorrow."

"Tomorrah'd be good, yeah, sho' you right." We set a time for the next afternoon—at Silky's, of course.

"Lil' Howlin' coming down?" Silky asks when I hang up.

"I'm going to meet him here tomorrow," I say.

Silky leans forward. "Silky'll set you up. If you're only in town a couple days, I'll try and make sure ya'll have a good time."

Silky's been a Memphis nightlife figure for thirty years, opening the original Silky Sullivan's in Overton Square in the early 1970s. When he opened the Beale Street place twenty years later, he added the *O*, meaning "son of."

———————

There's more to him than running a bar, I was to learn. He'd attended the Sorbonne and Harvard. He'd gone to LSU too, but then no one is perfect.

I tell Silky I'm just here for a brief visit, but he regales me with all the singers he wants me to hear and people I have to meet. I mention the *free spirit* thing and how Graham and I are interested in serendipity, not in getting into forced situations. But he is having too much fun reeling off great things about Memphis.

"You don't have to tell me," I say. "I love Memphis. I wish I lived here."

"Don't worry, Son," he says. "Silky'll set you up."

A woman who works for one of the local television stations comes in and Silky introduces me, fawning all over me as his new friend, the professor from Florida.

"They jus' been up your neck of the woods," he says, "Minnysota."

"Really?" she says. "I'm from Hibbing."

"Serendipity!" Graham shouts. "We were just there."

A duo plays white-boy blues on the patio and the crowd grows. Silky stops one of his waiters, gets an order book and starts writing names of places to see in Mississippi on the back side of the order form.

"I got a place down in the French Quawta," he says. "I want you to promise me you'll go there too. Silky'll set you *up* in Louisiana." He reaches into his back pocket and pulls out a bulky wallet, flipping it open to a badge from the Louisiana State Police. I start reading the card, but Silky doesn't want me distracted by his Christian name. "Just look at that number on that badge."

"My God," I say. "It's number one. You are what they call the Shit."

"I got it *under control,*" he says, stuffing away the massive pocketbook.

It's late and the kitchen is closed, so we head down Beale to find the burger Graham is craving. Silky starts to get up to walk us to the door, but then some lovely college girls walk by and they require his attention. "Hey girls," he calls, waving them over. "I'm Silky, where *ya'll* from?" He puts his arm around both of them— he's big and they're small—and points at Graham. "See this fellow here? He's a football player at the University of Florida. In fact, this boy's the *quarterback* for the Gators. Now what do you think about that? And tomorrow's his birthday. Come on girls, give him a *huuug*."

Every half block of Beale we hear new music. It's what I remember most about that earlier visit with the kids: music everywhere. This must be how Sam Phillips felt. He was a country kid from Florence, Alabama, at the end of the 1930s when he and some of his friends took a joyride over to Memphis. When he heard that beautiful noise on Beale Street, he was hooked. He moved to Memphis, got into radio and eventually opened the Memphis Recording Service. He made the first recordings of Howlin' Wolf, Rufus Thomas, Elvis Presley, Johnny Cash, Jerry Lee Lewis, Carl Perkins, Charlie Rich and Roy Orbison—not a bad achievement for a lifetime.

Silky insists Blake take us a few blocks down to Dyer's Burgers. ("Founded by Elmer 'Doc' Dyer in 1912 whose famous grease, strained daily, has produced the juiciest burgers for almost a century.") We're at Dyer's Burgers, drinking more beer and gorging on hubcap-sized hamburgers.

"It must be great to live here," Graham tells Blake. "I mean, all of the music . . . you must be out every weekend."

"Actually, I just work and drink," Blake says. "Going out to hear live music isn't a big deal with. . . ."

Blake suddenly stops talking, and I look up from my onion rings and see stone horror on his face. My back is to the door and he and Graham are across from me. Graham, too, seems suddenly trans-

fixed, pausing midbite, as if watching the head-spinning scene from
The Exorcist.

"You that fella from Florida?"

I see the hands first. The painted fingernails are nearly an inch
long, like slivered almonds. I follow the nails up through the hands
and arms to the body of a woman of considerable girth. Her breasts
are the size of fifth graders. If her huge head is the sun, her dark
brown mane is its solar system.

"Yeah, uh. . . ." But she can't mean *me.*

"Silky sent me. I wanted to invite you to see me tomorrow. My
act—Miz Zeno and the White Guy. It'll be over there at King's
Palace, out on the patio, 'round four. He told me he wanted you to
hear some good music while you're here . . . and I'm *good.*"

Blake and Graham haven't resumed chewing. They're still looking
up at her, in a mixture of fear and awe. Ms. Zeno is *imposing.*

"Will you be there?"

"Yes, ma'am," I say. "We'll build our day around it."

"Good. You won't be sorry." She bows slightly, turns and walks
out.

"Did you see those fingernails?" Graham asks. "They would have
made good lures."

"See what happens when I leave the safety of my house?" Blake
says. "This is why I go straight home after work."

Blake's home is a classic guy apartment, with a folding card table in
the dining room and a refrigerator stocked only with old pizza, beer
and orange juice. But it's clean and it's free, all that we require. Blake's
off work tomorrow—comp time for covering the NBA story nonstop
for weeks—and so he's in no hurry to go to sleep. He and Graham
stay up to watch a late baseball game from the West Coast. I excuse
myself to the spare bedroom, where I roll my dirty clothes up into a
pillow and fall asleep on the hard floor. When Graham steps over me
on his way to bed a couple hours later, I don't even stir.

The Thought Heard 'Round the World

*G*raham was a thousand miles away, so I stood in line for him.
I wake up thinking about the day he turned ten. The calendar never allowed me to be with him on his birthday those first few years after the divorce. I'd go up to Indiana for a week when the semester ended in May, and we would celebrate Graham's birthday then, in a flurry of autographed baseball cards, replica Negro League hats and video games. Dinner at Chi-Chi's, where they put a huge sombrero on his head and sang him "Happy Birthday." We just pretended May 8 was June 8.

When I talked to him on his real birthday, though, I always felt that it was never enough. No matter how much time I spent with the kids, it always hurt to miss a birthday or a school play or a triumph on the baseball field.

The day he turned ten, I was in St. Petersburg, working on the sports copydesk of the *Times*. I'd seen an ad for a baseball-card show in the paper the night before, and so I got up early and went to Clearwater Mall to meet Bobby Thomson.

Thomson's the man who hit *the* home run, the "shot heard 'round the world," the swing of the bat that changed baseball history, snatching the pennant from the Brooklyn Dodgers.

That was in 1951, three years before I was born, thirty-one years before Graham was born. Still, I know Graham will be thrilled to have Bobby Thomson's autograph. Baseball players don't live forever, but their acts do.

The line to see him is a quarter mile long, stretching by Thom McAn, Cinnabon, and Electronics Boutique. Set up in front of Burdines, the line so long it threatens to block the Saturday-afternoon department-store crowd.

Standing in line are kids with their fathers and grandfathers, some of them with replica 1953 Topps cards. Some are wily adolescents

with the sought-after originals. Others carry baseballs and bats for
him to sign. This is nearly a decade ago, a cutthroat time for baseball
collectibles. A lot of little kids read price guides like bookies, trying
to score with the most valuable autographs. But Graham is only
interested in cards of players he admires.

The guy in front of me works in a body shop, and the guy
behind me is a businessman, looking a little out of place on a Saturday morning with his tie and suspenders. I tell them both I'm a
rookie at this and wonder if Thomson might personalize the autograph. Body Shop says you never can tell. Suspenders is also
uncertain but told me of the nice guys he's met—Al Kaline of the
Detroit Tigers, my boyhood hero, was "a real gentleman." Ralph
Houk was talkative and friendly. Mickey Mantle was businesslike
and desultory. Joe DiMaggio was "just about the rudest man I've
ever met."

Mantle charged fifteen bucks per autograph, my new friend says.
We decide that was pretty reasonable, considering the bitterness the
guy had to have about modern players' salaries. He was one of the
greatest players in the game's history, yet made in one year what
today's players make in a week.

Older players like Bobby Thomson were really shortchanged.
He's only charging three dollars a signature, a small price to pay for
gratitude.

When Graham was a toddler and showed signs of being a lefty, I
told his mother he might be Major League material. I gave him a
plastic ball and bat and he took some promising cuts. By the time he
was six or seven, he was hooked. Soon I was as hooked as he was. I
began following the Cubs because Graham followed the Cubs. The
best we could do during my Indiana visits was to see the minor league
team in Indianapolis, but when he started coming to Florida for
spring training, we spent most of the days at the ball park. Sarah was
understanding—she could care less about baseball—but after months
of winter in Indiana, she loved to spend an afternoon in the sun.

Sometimes Graham and I would see two games a day. When he actually got to meet the ballplayers, he began to think of Florida as some place like heaven.

I've bought a picture for Thomson to autograph. I laugh because he looks like Al Bundy of *Married with Children*, decked out in a New York Giants uniform, getting ready to toss the ball, obviously posed.

I finally reach the head of the line and see that Thomson looks the same as he did in the picture—just grayer and bespectacled, Al Bundy in retirement. His eyes are kind.

"Hi," I say, intimidated by talking to a Major League ballplayer. I hand him the picture. "This is for my son. It's a birthday present."

Thomson looks at the picture, marveling at the young man he had been. He picks up his pen. "What's his name?"

"Graham," I say. "Like the cracker."

"How old is he going to be?"

"Ten. Today." I feel a need to explain his absence. "He's not with me," I say, but don't finish. In a way, Graham and his sisters are always with me.

"Ten," Thomson says, shaking his head. "Imagine being ten." He looks up and smiles, then writes, lingering over his work, wanting to phrase it just right. Then he hands me the picture. "Make sure you tell him Bobby Thomson wished him a happy birthday."

I shake his hand, then step back and grin at my autographed picture: "To Graham . . . Happy 10th birthday and good luck for many more. Sincerely, Bobby Thomson."

The picture still hangs on the wall over Graham's bed.

Show You Right

A car door slams outside, startling me. I look up from my pile of blankets and dirty clothes on the floor. The sun rudely blinds me, and when I'm able to focus I look over at Graham on the bed. He stirs, opening his eyes for a moment.

"Happy Birthday, Boy," I say.

"Thank you," he says, turning over. "I'm going back to sleep."

"You do that," I tell him. "I'm going to scrounge up some coffee."

Blake doesn't drink coffee, so I drive through the maze of his Mud Island neighborhood and find a bookstore that sells designer coffee.

Back at Blake's, the boys are coming to life. I give Graham a cup of coffee and a DVD of *Crouching Tiger, Hidden Dragon*, a frustrating gift since Blake doesn't have a DVD player. Still, Graham seems happy.

"I'd offer to take you to breakfast," Blake says, "but I figure if we wait any longer, it'll be lunch anyway." Sometimes with his laid-back voice, he sounds like Eeyore. "So I know where we should go."

To get to the Charlie Vergos' Rendezvous, you go down General Washburn Escape Alley. The strange name comes from a Civil War incident. While fleeing the city, Union General Washburn lost his pants, and they came into the possession of Confederate General Nathan Bedford Forrest, who gallantly shipped the pants to his adversary. Washburn recovered from the humiliation, going on to serve in the U.S. Congress, be governor of Wisconsin and to start the company that became General Mills. Forrest, on the other hand, is best known for founding the Ku Klux Klan.

The Rendezvous' ribs are different, and you can order them from anywhere in the states (1-888-HOGSFLY). If the place has a certain arrogance, that can be understood. If you don't eat here, someone else will, so get out of the way.

As they say around the Rendezvous, *Don't be wanting salad or dessert or be asking for espresso. We'll be bringing you what you need and a load of napkins.*

We're led to one of the back rooms and we place our order for dry ribs. The ribs are charcoal broiled, then rubbed down with the house mixture of spices, then served with a side of the homemade barbecue sauce. They call this place the "palace of pork." I'm sucking down my first beer—a Bud, nothing extravagant—when I notice that the watercolor on the wall is of a hog being slaughtered. "That's an unusual piece of art," I say to Graham. "This might be a good place to bring the kids when they ask, 'Daddy, what's a carnivore?'"

The waiters are celebrities, all showmen in one way or another, dressed in blizzard-white shirts and black neckties. As our waiter leaves the table after checking on our beer supply, he sings, "*My baaaaaaaaby*" in a cool falsetto. The song had obviously been playing in his head when he was talking to us; he just picked it up midchorus when he walked back to the kitchen.

The ribs are unique—dry, deliciously salty, even better when doused in the sauce. The meal is sloppy, and it must be horrifying for bystanders to watch the three of us eat, our chins dripping in reddish-brown sauce. To the kid at the next table we look like movie vampires. The waiter brings us enough napkins to reprint the World Book Encyclopedia, and soon they are coiled, bloody wads in the center of the table.

It's a Memphis cliché: The Mississippi Delta starts in the lobby of the Peabody Hotel. It's a massive hotel, reeking of style, grace and Southern culture.

"This is where Dylan stays when he comes to Memphis," I tell Graham.

"You've got to see the ducks," Blake says, apparently thinking we're the standard brand of geek tourists. "Every fucking visitor I've had always wants me to show them the damn ducks."

Every day since 1940, a parade of ducks marches from their rooftop quarters into an elevator and down into the lobby, where they frolic in a fountain. People line up to watch their red-carpet entrance before noon, and their exit when the working day is through at 5 P.M.

"The funny thing is," Blake says, "they serve duck at one of these fancy restaurants."

The ducks live on the roof, and we go visit their quarters and look around the city for a while. The streets are sweltering, but up on the roof there's a breeze carrying the smell of the river to us.

A friend wanted me to say hello to Judy Peiser at something called the Center for Southern Folklore. This is supposed to be my vacation from academe, and I figure it will be one of those places that takes something fun and shakes everything good out of it. But when we get there it's like a Disney exhibit inside—subdued lighting, raucous blues playing in the background, displays of books and CDs. The walls are lemon and the carpet an explosion of swirls of orange and tubercular blue, like a fun house.

"I know," Judy says. "*The name*. It's the most academic sounding name. Sounds like it should be stodgy, but it's the furthest thing from it. People come in expecting culture under glass, which is sort of the opposite of what I want to do."

She began as a filmmaker in the late 1960s and that led to the center, which she's been running since 1972. It's moved all over Memphis ("Every time the rent was due") and now it's across the street from the Peabody.

Her mission is to make the culture of the region meaningful to the next generation. "I'm trying to connect yesterday with tomorrow." This means putting on concerts, reaching out through the public libraries, taking the show on the road. "When people come to the center, I want them to think they're in a different world. Either you get it or you don't."

Back at Silky's, the proprietor has yet to show. We're the only early-afternoon customers, so we chat with the bartender and order a couple more beers. The wall with the supports outside is the only remnant of the Gallina Building, over one hundred years old and more historic than any other building on Beale. Once a saloon that employed fourteen bartenders, the building also contained hotel rooms favored by the theatrical figures who visited Memphis. Enrico Caruso slept upstairs. Bob Hope visited and so did Ella Fitzgerald, Tony Bennett, Tom Jones, Danny Thomas. . . . The bartender says Silky can reel off all the names and odd historical facts.

"Hey, while we're waiting on Silky," Blake says, "I'll show you the goats." He takes us to the goat pen, to feed Budweiser to Killian and Daisy. The goats lunge at the fence, sloppily sucking at Blake's plastic cup.

"Silky wanted to hire me as 'Goat Boy,'" Blake says. "I'd have to wear a cape and a mask and climb up that tower there and get the crowd riled up on Friday and Saturday nights. But the problem is with that mask on, you have no peripheral vision. I figured I'd fall and gore myself on a goat horn."

Graham takes a turn feeding the goats, and while we're at it, Silky comes up behind us in another tentlike shirt.

"You boys having a good time? You need you another beer?"

"Just about. Well, let's see . . . we celebrated Graham's birthday with some ribs."

Silky looks horrified. "Ribs? Where'd you get 'em?"

We're walking back inside. "The Rendezvous."

"Shit." Southern cliché or not, he pronounces it "*Sheeee-it.*" He barks at his bartender. "Get these boys some ribs and get me another pitcher right away here."

He sits us down. "I got some ribs that'll take the Rendezvous *out*," he says. "You'll think you ate some fuckin' Spam. Their ribs taste like sawdust."

Halfway through Silky's ribs—and they are more to my taste than the dry ribs at the Rendezvous (Silky calls them "good flippin', dippin' lip-smackin' ribs")—Lil' Howlin' Wolf arrives.

He's wearing brown nappy-on-the-thigh polyester pants, a faded yellow poly short-sleeve shirt with a hole in the armpit, and a white

Our Memphis host, Blake Fontenay, feeds Budweiser to Killian, one of the beer-drinking goats at Silky O'Sullivan's on Beale Street. He treated us with similar hospitality.

tank top underneath. A cream-colored riding cap tops his ensemble. He's carrying a briefcase, as I suppose all good bluesmen should.

Introductions all around. "Would you like some of these ribs?" I ask when he sits down.

"I can't hassle with them *riiibs*," he says. "And if I eat chicken, I got to take all the skin off. Now, I got something for you." He puts the briefcase on the table, sliding it through a small pool of barbecue sauce. It has a Masons' emblem on the outside.

"You a Mason?" I ask.

"Thirty-second grade," he says. "I got one more grade to go and I can't go no higher."

"He is probably the last living dusty blues singer," Silky says, "right out of the Delta."

Of course, I think, *a briefcase-toting member of the Masons* and *a blues singer.*

"I'm on the worldwide Internet. I been on the stage fitty-four years."

He's seventy but looks maybe late forties. His real name is Jesse Sanders and he was born in Florence, Mississippi, and spent most of his performing life in Chicago. He worked for the police department for forty-seven years, moonlighting in blues clubs on weekends. He met Howlin' Wolf—the stage name of Chester Arthur Burnett—fifty years ago and performed alongside him as Lil' Howlin' Wolf. When Howlin' Wolf died in the mid-1970s, Lil' Wolf met Howlin' Wolf's niece at the funeral and they married. When he retired from the police force, he came back to Memphis.

He's pulled pictures and press clippings from his briefcase. "I'm known all over, I don't care where yuh go. I met Mr. B. B. King in 1948. . . . *Show you right!* That was fifty-three years ago."

I order him a 7-Up ("Only thing I drink other than water"), and he pulls out another clipping. "I done shows for three presidents of the United States. I did a show for Jimmy Carter, I did a show for the vice-president, *Mondaaale,* I did a show for President Reagan. I've got the contracts." He pulls yellowed paper from his briefcase, marked with faded signatures. "I been booked in the *White* House. I used to live next door to the White House, I was living in the Capi-tol *Ho*-tel, that was the name of it, on Pennsylvania Avenue, I was liv-ing there."

He pulls out several copies of a blown-up clipping from an unnamed newspaper. The print quality diminished several genera-tions back in photocopying.

"That was thirty years ago," he says, looking at a picture of his younger self with B. B. King. "You can read this h'yere. That's me and my old man, B. B. King, Bobby "Blue" Bland, Koko Taylor . . . and anything you want to know, you can read it."

He's hoping that Blake can get a story about him into the *Commercial Appeal* but doesn't seem to understand Blake covers city government, not entertainment. "I'm in all the newspapers—the *Commercial Appeal*, the *Rolling Stone* magazine, the *Living Blues* magazine . . . I'm in all of them. When people read up *on* yuh, they know you're *real*. Talk is cheap, but I got it in black and white and people can read for themselves. *Show you right!*"

I sense that "show you right" is supposed to be his distinctive catchphrase, but I'm not sure it makes any sense. Still, it's great to hear him growl it—he smiles and his eyes gleam lecherously.

"They went crazy for him over in Europe," Silky says. "They tore the house down."

"They didn't want me to *leeave*," Lil' Wolf says.

He reminisces about Chicago, reeling off names of artists he's performed with: "Cab Calloway, Louis Armstrong, Dean Martin, Frank Sinatra, Sammy Davis Jr., Redd Foxx, Duke Ellington, Nat King Cole . . . I knew all them guys, when I was in Chicago. Tommy Dorsey, remember Tommy Dorsey? With his band out of New York City?"

"Wow," Graham says, "You've had a great life."

"All right, yes I have."

Back out on the patio, Lil' Wolf, Blake and Graham serve more beer to the goats. Graham pours Bud down Killian's throat.

A girl approaches, asks for Lil' Wolf's autograph and he beams. I survey the patio, beginning to fill with the Friday-afternoon beer-pitcher crowd, and watch through the lonely wall the goings on out on Beale Street.

"This property must've been outrageously expensive," I say. "Silky must be a millionaire."

"I thought you already know that," Lil' Wolf says. "I just did four

shows in the Bahamas last week. I just got back. He went with me. . . .
I had five millionaires with me."

The goats are known for their flatulence, but it doesn't bother Lil'
Wolf, who started life on a farm south of Jackson. "Mule farts made
a man out of me." He thrusts a forearm my way and asks me to feel
it. I touch something like a Sequoia.

"Holy shit," I say. "You don't feel human."

Lil' Wolf grins. *Seventy*, he reminds me. "I have never had a can of
beer *in my lif*e. I have never smoked a cigarette *in my life*." He was
Golden Glove champion in Milwaukee and for a time had the same
trainer as Joe Louis. He's always been strong. When he was a kid, he
was hired to work on a farm for fifty cents a day, and "I inhaled mule
farts all day." Never fazed him, he said. "I came up the hard way.
Twelve-hour day, five dollas a week. Kids today won't do that, it'd *kill*
them. I come such a long way and I want to tell the world God been
soo good to me. I just want to *thank* Him. I just want to *thank Him*.
God been so good to me. Like I said, my man, I been a lot of places
overseas. I thought I would never see the United States no more. I
been in some hellfire places on them damn airplanes. Always been
happy to get home here."

Graham asks to feel his arm again and Lil' Wolf gives him a killer
grip. Then he gives me the other hand. "How's my left arm feel?" he
grins.

I'm pretty sure he could dismember me without kitchen implements.
"Good Lord, that's a hell of a grip. How did you survive masturbation?"

He releases me. "I don't hurt nobody. You come to me wrong,
though, you gonna eat some *lunch*."

"I swear I would never come to you wrong."

Silky's back on his perch, looking through the *Commercial Appeal*,
watching customers come through the bar on the way to the patio.

"He's got a great job," I say to Lil' Wolf. "Have you ever noticed,
he just sits there and looks at women all night?"

Lil' Wolf hugs Silky. "See why I want to get with him?"

A couple of girls walk by and Silky takes one by the forearm. "Hey, Darlin', I want you to meet the greatest blues singer in the world . . . Lil' Howlin' Wolf." One of the girls, an already-drunk brunette, hugs the Wolf.

"Girls, you watch this," Silky says. "This man is seventy-two years old and now you watch this."

Wolf steps back, grins like a mischievous little boy and begins slowly moving his hips. From his thighs up to his chest his body ripples in a pantomime of slow-groove fucking. He winks at the girls while he undulates. A chunky blonde shrieks and covers her mouth, the brunette just giggles and takes another drink of beer.

"Seventy-two years old!" Silky could have been a carnival barker. "He just like a tick!"

When he stops, Lil' Wolf tells the girls, "I don't mean no harm now. I'm just like a tick. You know how a tick get on a milk cow? I'm the same way. I get on there and I jus' stick."

"This is the greatest blues singer alive, right here," Silky says.

"Show you right," Lil' Wolf says, winking at the girls.

Mojo Queen

Ms. Zeno's show has already started, so we ask Lil' Wolf to join us. He packs his briefcase and we head across the street to the King's Palace Café, following her voice to a garden concert area.

Ms. Zeno is *mmmmmmmmmm*ing her way through Robert Johnson's "Come On in My Kitchen," wearing a hot lime-green dress and a stalactite bra that could easily serve as a self-defense weapon. Her guitar player—Hawaiian shirt, Panama hat, wire-rimmed glasses and pointy white beard—picks out the tune with a delicate ferocity. Sympathy calluses form on my fingers.

Her voice is as imposing as her body. She stretches out the song,

Ms. Zeno and the White Guy (Guy Venable), onstage on the patio at King's Palace Café. Her full name is Verlinda Kertria Zeno, and she grew up in Louisiana, third child of eight. Guy owns a shoe-repair shop and moonlights as a musician.

does a few variations, and the guitar player—billed as "the White Guy," his real name is Guy Venable—improvises behind her.

She winks when she sees us and directs us to a seat at a table at the side of the raised platform. Lil' Wolf doesn't take his eyes off her, and she's ripping her way through the song, performing more for him, I think, than the rest of the audience.

When she finishes, she introduces him to the crowd, and he stands and steps up on stage. "We've played together before," she tells the crowd. "And we had them rock 'n' rolling, didn't we, Wolf?"

"Show you right!" he says, cackling.

"The secretary of state of Louisiana gave me a call this morning," she confides to the crowd.

"He called me too," Lil' Wolf says. "I'm booked down there on the nineteenth of this month. I'm in Baton Rouge, Louisiana, on the twentieth."

"Well, I leave for Italy June the twentieth," she says, "and I'll be gone for six whole weeks." She spread out *I-tah-lee*, savoring the word.

"Lord have mercy!" Lil' Wolf says, rolling his eyes for the crowd. He sits back down next to Graham.

Ms. Zeno turns to the crowd. "So ya'll should appreciate this while you got it, 'cause you sure ain't paying for it. They sure gonna pay for it there."

"There'll be a food surplus when she's gone," says the White Guy, drawing a modest laugh.

Lil' Wolf acts like it's the funniest thing he ever heard.

She writhes through a slow blues, punctuated by stinging Robert Johnson–worthy guitar. "Give it up for the White Guy," she says when he hits his solo. "Come on in and sit down," she waves to Beale Street pedestrians who pause at the garden entrance. "We got room."

Her full name is Verlinda Kertria Zeno, and she grew up in Louisiana, third child of eight. Everyone in the family played music—mostly gospel—but she found a home in the blues. Although she's almost forty, she looks late twenties at most.

She starts another slow blues, and Lil' Wolf shouts up at the stage: "Play some of that Jimmy Reed stuff."

"I'll get to you, honey," she says, then closes her eyes and sings so hard, I think there's going to be a protoplasm explosion. Maybe we ought to move out of the way. "Rock me," she pleads, "*Rrrrrrrock* me all night long."

"All right," she says to the crowd during the White Guy's instrumental break. "Let's see if we can get Lil' Howlin' Wolf up here."

I doubt it will be much of a challenge. I sense performer's competitive tension.

"Come show what I'm talking about," she says to Lil' Wolf. He stands next to her, turns to the crowd with the little-imp grin and begins the body wave—starts at the knees, works his way up through the belly and into his ribs. "I just want you to show me, Honey." Ms. Zeno steps back and lets the waves work their way through Lil' Wolf's ripped seventy-year-old body. She moves closer and begins singing again:

Roll me like you roll some flour dough

"Show you right," Lil' Wolf says. "Show you right, Baby. Don't stop once you get started."

Ms. Zeno is high maintenance: *"Rock me! Roll me! Kiss me! Love me! Lick me!"*

Lil' Wolf rolls his eyes, hitting a high note: *"Ooooooooooooooooo!"*

The song ends and Lil' Wolf has the microphone now. "How ya'll feelin' this evenin'? I tell all the ladies and men, have no fear 'cause the Wolf is here. The Wolf is here."

Whether Ms. Zeno wants him to or not, Lil' Wolf takes over the show. The White Guy hits the distinctive opening chords of the Jimmy Reed tune and Lil' Wolf starts grunting his way through "Bright Lights, Big City."

Ms. Zeno stands at the side of the stage, tapping her foot, showing a little impatience at the takeover. For the second chorus, Lil' Wolf looks her way and coaxes her to sing counterpoint.

"If a fight breaks out," I tell Graham, "my money's on Ms. Zeno."

"She'd crack his head like a walnut," he says.

She bills herself as the "Louisiana Mojo Queen," and she seems to be working her mojo on Lil' Wolf as they begin to mime more slow sex.

Either they need to get a room or we've got to douse them with our Miller Lite pitcher. The White Guy has a sixth sense though and he cuts into the chunky rhythm of "Shame, Shame, Shame," and the up-tempo stomp brings Lil' Wolf and Ms. Zeno back from the brink

When Ms. Zeno invited him onstage at the King's Palace, Lil' Howlin' Wolf was happy to oblige with "Bright Lights, Big City."

of penetration. It also gives her a chance to take back the show. After two choruses, she raises her hand and moves back to her spot due south of the microphone. "Lil' Howlin' Wolf, ladies and gentlemen . . . put your hands together!" He takes his cue and bows his way off stage, sliding back next to me on the bench.

Ms. Zeno takes back the show with a slow, moving version of Otis Redding's "Dreams to Remember," a song he recorded about ten blocks south of here.

I look over at Graham, over on the other side of Lil' Wolf. He turns and smiles, and I raise my glass. He recognizes the song and knows how much I love Otis Redding. Ms. Zeno may not approach the song with Otis's subtlety, but she rips the hell out of the lyric.

As the song ends: "Keep in mind we have a tip bucket, I'll be coming around with my tip bucket and if you don't have my CDs, we have those too. I am the Mojo Queen of Beale Street, and this is the White Guy."

While Ms. Zeno walks through the crowd cadging tips, the White Guy barks his way through the Sonny Boy Williamson tune "One Way Out."

After the show, Ms. Zeno talks with her fans and I have a beer with the White Guy, who owns a shoe-repair store—and who plays bass in a popular Memphis band called the Skyboys.

"Ms. Zeno and I, we were in a band about eight years ago and this"—he nods back to the stage—"grew out of that. I'm a bass player."

We can hear a trumpet player in another outdoor venue down the street. *What a great town,* I think. *There's music everywhere.*

Beale Street Can Talk

New Orleans can overwhelm. Memphis is cozier. The city has a long but historically accurate motto: "Home of the Blues, Birthplace of Rock 'n' Roll." Modern Beale Street is a tourist attraction, but a generation ago it was a crime-infested, charred remnant of what it had been in 1909 when W. C. Handy came to town and wrote the first blues song.

In the middle of the 1800s, Beale was a Memphis suburb—assuming they used words like *suburb* then—but it was a suburb with whorehouses and theaters. When the city fell to the Union troops during the Civil War, freed slaves settled along Beale. The Irish also moved in and when an Irish boy was killed the death was blamed on the blacks, and race riots erupted. The Irish went berserk, burning, looting and murdering.

Epidemics cleared out a lot of the city in the late 1800s, but the black residents seemed to withstand the diseases, moving back to Beale Street and making it nearly all black. Businesses prospered. The first black millionaire in the South lived on Beale Street.

George Lee, one of the first blacks commissioned as a U.S. Army officer in the First World War, wrote this in his 1934 book, *Beale Street, Home of the Blues:*

> Rising out of the Mississippi River, it runs for one mile straight through the busy heart of Memphis and loses itself in the muddy bottoms of East Street. The echoes of its fantastic music have been heard around the globe, for this colorful little thoroughfare is known the world over; its fame has penetrated into every nook and cranny where sound carries the echoes of the English voice. It has been talked about, written about, sung about so much that sightseers from every quarter are lured there in search of adventure or to gaze upon the scenes and surroundings that represent its vanished glory.

Until the years just after the Second World War, Beale was the center of commerce and art in Memphis. Other great blues artists followed Handy's path. At the west end of the street, B. B. King's nightclub is testament to the enduring popularity of its namesake, Riley B. King (a contraction of his original stage name, Beale Street Blues Boy). But the honor roll of blues artists here is long: Howlin' Wolf (the big one), Muddy Waters, Bobby "Blue" Bland, Furry Lewis. . . . How the list does go on.

But a slide into poverty, crime and drugs got Beale erased from tour guides. Like other cities, Memphis burned during the civil rights battles of the 1960s—but it may have been worse here, since Martin Luther King was murdered at the Lorraine Motel, south of Beale. There was talk of bulldozing the whole Beale Street area, tearing down what had come to resemble a war zone.

The comeback started when Beale Street was placed on the

National Register of Historic Places. In the 1970s and 1980s, businessmen like Silky Sullivan began to bring it back, investing in places that offered beer, barbecue and bands. New club owners traded off the street's past, both wicked and glorious. Now it's a safe haven for tourists, several blocks of music, booze and food. Imagine the folks at Disney World creating a theme park around prostitution and alcohol (let's call it *Skanky Ho World*) and you get the idea. Beale Street is safe. It's even safe enough for the gray-haired ponytailed attorneys in torn jeans who make six figures advising corporations about their taxes but who secretly wish they were blind black blues singers.

An Artist's Conception of Hell

B lake wants us to meet one of his friends for dinner. Mark Corley is starting a nonprofit corporation called A Friend in Need, to help children who have lost a parent. We meet him farther down on Beale, at Alfred's. It's not far from Silky's, and we sit on the balcony overlooking a busy corner. The music of the street mixes in the air, and we can pick out at least three tunes wrapping around each other.

Alfred's advertises that it serves "the hottest wings and gumbo this side of the bayou," and that it has killer ribs.

"What do you think?" I ask. Graham is having the same thought.

"Let's do it," he says. "How many times are we going to have a chance like this?"

So in addition to wings, we order ribs again.

We watch the crowd down below, and I tell Blake and Mark how much I like Memphis. "But I don't live here," I say. "What's it like as a place to live?"

"Memphis is a good city," Mark says, "but everything turns into a race thing. People bring the race card in and I just get tired of that."

"That happens a lot of places," I say.

"I think Memphis is worse because Dr. King got assassinated here and all that. A lot of the black people feel that the white people owe them because of that. And I'll just say, 'I don't owe you anything.' I don't owe anybody anything, except my parents and God."

I'm not sure that where I live is really the South—sometimes, Florida seems like a New Jersey suburb, judging from the accents in my classes—but I understand what Mark is talking about. Thirty-five years after King's assassination, and I'm not sure race relations are better. Every year on his birthday, newspapers crank out the *Dr.-King's-dream-yet-to-be-realized* clichés. Do we accomplish the goal by assimilating African-American culture into the mainstream? Or do we reach that goal by keeping that culture separate? If we want to truly see people judged by "the content of their character and not the color of their skin," why do we use every opportunity to call attention to the differences?

The waitress brings vast platters of food—chicken wings, ribs, fries and beer, all of the basic food groups. I'm hoping this is a good birthday meal.

The ribs are good, but Silky is still Memphis champion. The hot sauce on the wings swells my lips to the size of two frankfurters.

"My God," I tell Blake. "I look like Angelina Jolie."

After dinner, we take a ramble up Beale Street. There's a frenetic harp worthy of Little Walter blaring from the Rum Boogie Café, everything a homogenized middle-aged white guy might want in a juke joint. When my Florida friends visit Memphis every other year for a football game, this is where they come. Plus, it has the original Stax marquee over the stage. The music is good, driving and danceable, like Little Walter reincarnated. "Maybe he's an animatronic," Graham says. But we can't get past the doorway because, despite his height and stubble, Graham is clearly underage.

Blake and Mark want to take us in the other direction, to Neil's, a joint on Madison, in Midtown. It's ten minutes from Sun Studios,

One side of the sign from Stax Studios was brought to the Rum Boogie Café on Beale Street after the studios were demolished. The other side is in the Smithsonian's Rock 'n' Soul Museum in Memphis.

where Elvis Presley and Sam Phillips made those historic recordings the summer I was born.

Neil's is a sprawling place that mixes urban characters and country folk. We head to the patio, where Blake and Mark introduce us to more of their friends. There's a guy playing guitar and singing the Eagles catalog. Inside, a heavy metal band gets the tattooed crowd dancing. The disparate clientele mixes in the bathroom. Above the urinal are the usual hand-scrawled Confederate flags and "Forget hell" messages, but my favorite is "Your mom is a man."

Blake and his friends grab a central table on the patio, but Graham and I are restless, so we roam. We take a few bites out of the head-banging crowd—certainly, inside has drawn the greater number of females—but the music is so aggressively bad (the band plays covers of hair bands like Scorpions, Whitesnake and Great White) that after a couple games of a variation on air hockey— played with salt—we're driven outside to Mr. Peaceful Easy Feeling.

I resign myself to Holiday-Inn-Lounge mellow, but Graham remains twitchy, going back and forth between the Eagles and the head bangers. At least there are televisions inside, but the NBA play-offs can't be heard over the shrieking horror onstage. I follow Graham wherever he goes, determined to make sure the kid has a good time. But his restlessness makes me nervous. Standing outside on Madison after five minutes with the band, we agree we'd prefer to be back on Mud Island with beer and Marv Albert.

"How much do you think a cab would cost?" he asks.

The patio guitarist with nipple-length hair has moved on to the Steve Miller songbook. A beery middle-aged couple at the next table gets up and stumbles through the Caucasian two-step. Another man, a Hank Hill look-alike, pats his substantial belly in time, straining his "It's a Hog Thing" T-shirt, whooping whenever the guitarist fumbles through a solo.

Get us out of here, God, we beseech thee. It's like we're in an artist's conception of hell. Without the trusty War Wagon we're trapped. Of the two musical evils, the patio guitarist interests Graham more, but he closes up his guitar case early and rides away on a motorcycle with a peroxide blonde in genuine imitation leather. We're left with the sounds of traffic, endless conversations about people we don't know and the tattooed head-banging Mongol horde inside.

Anything, Anywhere, Anytime

Graham's up in time to go to the coffee shop with me the next morning. He finds a nice used copy of *Slaughterhouse-Five* in the small book section, and I buy it for him.

Back at the house, I suggest to Blake that we go to 706 Union Avenue.

Blake's face clouds. "What's there?"

"That's the delivery room of rock 'n' roll, Dumb Ass. *Sun Studios*."

"How could you not *know that?*" Graham asks.

"Oh," he says thoughtfully. "I've been wanting to see that sometime."

"That's kind of like living in New York and saying, 'Central Park? Yeah, I've heard of that.'"

"Some of us have real jobs," Blake says. "We don't get to drive around the country all summer, sponging off of our friends."

It's a gorgeous summer morning and at Graham's request, I'm driving. We've cleaned out the Explorer enough to put up one of the back seats, and Graham volunteers to sit there, giving our Memphis host the coveted shotgun seat. Waiting at a light, I turn to look at Graham. He's looking out the window, cradling a cup of coffee, perfectly content.

We were here before, with the girls, when we took that long way back from Florida a few summers before. Sun Studios a little hole-in-the-wall place—squeezed onto the corner of Union and Marshall, close to downtown. It's a wedge of brick in the middle of generic city streets. Seeing it is like rounding a hillside and seeing Mount Rushmore. That's how I first saw *that*, on a trip with my father and mother thirty-five years ago.

After sixteen-year-old Sam Phillips and his friends drove to Memphis in 1939 and heard the mixture of music on Beale Street, he was hooked. Out of high school, poverty forced him to give up his ambition of becoming a doctor. So he got his start in radio—working first in Alabama, then Nashville, and finally Memphis. He worked as an announcer at WREC, mostly doing remote broadcasts from the Peabody Hotel. He was also "Pardner," host of a country-and-western program. From the sound of it, he did just about anything at the station.

But it wasn't enough. He wanted something to do with music but wasn't a musician. He figured out another way to create music.

He started the Memphis Recording Service in 1950 with the motto, "We Record Anything—Anywhere—Anytime." That could mean weddings, funerals, barber-shop quartets . . . *anything*. These gigs paid the bills, but what he wanted to record was music. He did early recordings of B. B. King and Howlin' Wolf, but his real breakthrough came in 1951.

Ike Turner and his band, the Kings of Rhythm, were based in Clarksdale, Mississippi, and drove up to Memphis when they heard about Phillips's willingness to take a chance on new music. On the ride, the band's car hit a bump, and guitarist Willie Kizart's amplifier fell off the roof, hitting Highway 61 and cracking the speaker cone. Turner and his band went ahead to the studio, mostly to apologize to Phillips and to see if they could reschedule the session.

Why don't we hear what it sounds like?

"If Sam Phillips hadn't said that," I tell my rock 'n' roll history class, "we might be studying physics right now, because rock 'n' roll might not have existed."

The broken cone gave the guitar a rough, distorted sound like an engine, and Phillips amplified it on the finished recording. He sent the master tape off to Chess Records in Chicago, one of his regular outlets. Many critics consider "Rocket 88," credited to Jackie Brenston & His Delta Cats (Brenston was Turner's sax player and singer), the first rock 'n' roll record.

A few years later, Phillips had his own record company. When Elvis Presley came into the studio to make a recording for his mother, Phillips didn't send the tapes anywhere. For a year, he kept Elvis to himself, making the best music of Presley's career and the recordings that would launch rock 'n' roll.

Sun Studios is small and the tour doesn't last long, but it's augmented by a lot of the music recorded here—Howlin' Wolf, Rufus Thomas, Harmonica Frank Floyd, the very first Elvis recording

("My Happiness," an acetate cut for his mother), and sound bites from the Dewey Phillips radio show that introduced Elvis to the world. The tour also features a few Sun recordings from the 1980s— U2's duet with B. B. King, "When Love Comes to Town," and the Jerry Lee Lewis, Johnny Cash, Carl Perkins and Roy Orbison reunion for "Big Train from Memphis."

The girl behind the counter in the reception-area café is reading *Hellfire*, an excellent Jerry Lee Lewis biography by Nick Tosches.

"Great book," I say.

"I read it before," she says. When she talks, I can see the glint of a tongue stud. "You can't get everything in just one reading. People are always asking questions about Jerry Lee, so I've got to stay up on my Jerry Lee history."

She doesn't have any customers, so I ask: "Is it too much to hope that Sam Phillips is going to drop in this morning? Does he ever drop in for a cup of coffee?" My little joke; he's something of a recluse.

She doesn't dismiss the possibility. "He comes by for special events. Every once in a while we get to see him. If there's a meeting, he'll come for that. Sometimes people ask him to come by so they can take his picture."

Sam Phillips takes *eccentric* and squeezes it until it screams for mercy. He has also made a pact with the devil—or perhaps just the Grecian. Although nearly eighty, he has a full head of auburn hair, too messy, I figure, to be a wig.

The girl behind the counter is Cathy Gaffney. Karen Foster, who runs the gift shop, walks up and pitches in.

"He was just here for the fiftieth anniversary," Karen says. "We had a bunch of people come in—Rosco Gordon, Johnny Bragg, Scotty Moore . . . actually most of the guys who are still alive were here. And they all went in and just jammed. I guess they're going to release it some time."

There are only a few other customers, so we're not disrupting the tourist business. A somber couple takes the stairs up to the record store and souvenir shop. "Anything weird ever happen during one of these studio tours?" I ask. "People ever try to take one of the acoustic tiles off the wall?"

"About two years ago," Karen says, "we had a lady come in, a foreign lady, didn't speak any English . . . I think she was German. She goes in and Michael, this guy that used to work here, he was giving the tour and he looks up and she's trying to yank a tile off the wall."

"Those European fans are pretty obsessive," I say.

"We have Elvis impersonators coming in now and then," Cathy says, "and whenever we start playing an Elvis record, they start singing along. We say, 'People didn't come here to hear *you*.'"

"People will steal anything," Karen says. "They'll take ash trays off the table—Pizza Hut ashtrays we got down the street probably two weeks ago."

"They think, 'Elvis might have smoked here.'"

Graham checks out the Elvis books in the gift shop. "Learn anything interesting?" I ask.

"Yes. Elvis once ate meatloaf at every dinner for six straight months," Graham says.

"I was always impressed with the shower heads," Blake says. "Priscilla had all of these extra shower heads installed in the master bedroom at Graceland because she wanted the King to have a clean ass at all times."

"There must be a storehouse of Elvis folklore in this town," I say.

"It's not folklore," Blake says. "These are facts—true facts, as we say in the South."

We've been to Graceland before, and it's an otherworldly place. When Graham and I came with the girls, we'd taken the self-guided tour, filing through the museum annex silently, headphones spewing Elvis facts into our skulls. The house itself was a monument to bad decorating, tacky on a monumental scale.

This time, Graham, Blake and I content ourselves with the wall outside the king of rock 'n' roll's estate. Cops must look the other way when graffiti artists show up with their spray paint. New messages appear daily, exhortations for Elvis to return, regrets offered that he is gone, testaments of eternal love.

Tourists

Driving around Memphis, we breathe in the city's history. For the first time on the trip, I'm frustrated by not having a week to spend in one place. So there's a desperation today. I'm so frantic to show Graham as much as I can that we're using the interstate to get around town. I'm driving, since he's a little daunted by the laid-back approach to traffic laws on I-240.

We're just tourists, looking around at all the sights. We go back to Beale, to check out the Gibson guitar factory, a modern new building a block behind the historic debauchery on Beale. The twenty-five-minute tour is led by musicians, people who know the subtleties of making these instruments: shaping the wood, placing the frets, strapping on the pick guards. The factory makes replicas of B. B. King's Lucille, a bass that looks like a spaceship from a 1950s science-fiction film, even a Flying-V worthy of Bo Diddley. Graham is a man of simple taste—he covets a Les Paul Classic, the guitar of champions. In the small Gibson store, he fingers guitars (nobody stops him from strumming) and admires the peripherals—embroidered shirts, shot glasses, guitar straps.

"*This* is the place for a guitar-and-go," Graham says.

He stands in front of a wall of gleaming sunburst guitars, as if admiring great works of art in the Louvre.

The Gibson building also houses the Memphis Rock and Soul Museum, actually part of the Smithsonian. There's so much local music history that the museum clusters exhibits around different musicians and record labels. I spend most of the time looking over the memorabilia from Stax Records with the huge photographs of Rufus Thomas (in full flight, doing the Funky Chicken), Booker T. and the MG's and Otis Redding. Press a button and Isaac Hayes talks about writing and producing for Sam & Dave. Blake seems bored by this and Graham only moderately interested, but after Bob, Stax is my favorite music.

"This is all cool," I tell Graham. "In fact, it's very cool. But when you look at the Stax people, it touches only on the famous ones. I want to know about some of the others, like Wendy Rene. She's the one that sings that song about barbecue: 'I smell somethin' in the air . . . *Mmmmmmmmmmmm*, smells like barbecue.' " She sang it "*bobby Q.*" It was one of the most wonderful records Stax ever put out. "They don't write lyrics that incisive anymore."

"This place is for the casual fan," Graham says. "Not everyone is as into this as you are."

"That's their misfortune."

In blinding sunlight we take another stroll up Beale, looking at the names on the Walk of Fame. Hollywood puts its celebrity names in stars; in Memphis, the names are in brass musical notes. I lie down on the sidewalk so Graham can take my picture with Rufus Thomas's marker.

The department store A. Schwab has been on Beale since 1876. It's like a Dollar General Store on steroids, with horrifying bright neckties in ugly geometric shapes that might have my students running for cover. The motto is "If you can't find it at Schwab's, you're better off without it." We check out several other places—Elvis Presley's Memphis, W. C. Handy Park and B. B. King's Blues Club.

We end up at the Blues City Café, waiting for cheeseburgers. Graham goes to the bathroom, and Blake and I hatch a plan for the afternoon. I suggest a day trip to Mississippi.

"If it's all right, why don't you come along?" I ask. "We just want to bum around in Mississippi."

"I don't mind if I do," he says.

Soulsville, U.S.A.

There's a couple more stops before crossing into Mississippi. Blake gets a little antsy when I suggest we head down to East McLemore Avenue. It's not the safest part of town, he says.

But it's the neighborhood known as "Soulsville, U.S.A.," where Stax Records used to be. I'm obsessed with that record label and its artists. The house musicians, Booker T. and the MG's, may be the best studio band ever assembled. The first day of my rock 'n' roll history class, I ask students to tell me their theme songs, the tune always playing in their head. I tell them mine is "Time Is Tight" by Booker T.

I'd read a lot about Stax, absorbed as much as I could about the music, indoctrinated my children in the classics, such as "B-A-B-Y" by Carla Thomas, "I Thank You" by Sam & Dave, "These Arms of Mine" by Otis Redding. They'd all picked up on it, and when Sarah moved to Florida she had a black roommate who listened to Celine Dion, sort of the anti-Christ of today's popular music. Sarah, on the other hand, boomed Missy 'Misdemeanor' Elliot and was known on her floor as "the black girl." Moments like these make her dad proud.

George Orwell warned that politicians would use—or rather abuse—the English language in order to desensitize us. When you hear about people living in a *slum*, you are worried and you want change. But when you hear that those people live in a *depressed socio-economic area*, well . . . that doesn't sound quite as bad.

East McLemore Avenue, where some of the greatest records in the history of American popular music were made, has had a long history as a slum. We're a little uneasy driving the streets, but not from any real danger. It's just the shock of seeing the poverty you usually miss from the interstate.

All of this is about to change. This empty lot used to be the home of Stax Records. It was once an old movie house called the Capitol Theater, but by the late 1950s it was used for country-and-western shows and then, for a brief time, it was a church. When brother and sister Jim Stewart and Estelle Axton started Satellite Records in 1960, they needed a home, and this is the place they found. Eventually they changed the record company name, taking *ST* from Stewart and *AX* from Axton.

Blake doesn't understand why I'm so fascinated by a vacant lot. There's a few mounds of dirt, and I want to linger here while he wants to leave.

Graham understands. He might not share my devotion to soul music, but he knows guitar. Steve "the Colonel" Cropper is one of the all-time greats.

When they started this little record label at the dawn of the 1960s, everybody already had a day job, so there was a lot of weekend work, taking out the movie seats, hanging the sound-cushion curtains (Mrs. Axton stitched them herself), building the sound booth on the theater's stage. The sloped floor was never leveled, which gave Stax its unique studio sound—no wall was directly opposite another wall, so the notes of the music weren't trapped. Here, with that great house band, the staff songwriters (most of the production credits just read "Stax Staff") and a roster of unbelieveable homegrown talent, great soul music was made.

The *Capitol* lights were removed and replaced by *Stax*, and the theater's marquee was changed to read S O U L S V I L L E U. S. A. It became one of the icons of 1960s music. The theater wasn't air conditioned, so during the hottest part of the day the musicians would head down the street to the Lorraine Motel, where they'd have drinks and sandwiches and write classic songs such as "In the Midnight Hour," "Knock on Wood," "Soul Man" and scores of others.

Mrs. Axton turned the concession stand into the Satellite Record Shop. Steve Cropper started his Stax career behind the counter, before becoming the principal guitarist, songwriter and producer in the Stax house. A sixteen-year-old music prodigy named Booker T. Jones hung around the record shop until he was asked to sit in on keyboards. Deanie Parker also worked behind the counter. She says she used to walk to work and see Otis Redding and Steve Cropper standing on the street corner outside the studio.

The music came from a neighborhood with a strong personality. "Soulsville U.S.A." wasn't just a slogan or a record company. Al Green made all of his soul masterpieces a few blocks away, at Willie Mitchell's Hi Records Studios. Aretha Franklin grew up around here, and even Elvis Presley attended church in Soulsville.

Deanie Parker wrote songs and became publicity director for the company, and today, she's resurrecting it.

A month before we came to East McLemore Avenue, they had a groundbreaking ("ground shaking," she corrects me) for the Stax Museum of American Soul Music on the site of the old theater. It was torn down in 1979.

I ask if she had watched the destruction of the original studio. "I did not watch," she says, "I *could not* watch."

She grew up here, worked her way through college at the record company, put her heart into Stax, only to see it unappreciated in Memphis. "I always had a love-hate relationship with Memphis," she says. "Memphis was not mature in terms of its appreciation for cultural diversity, racial diversity, all kinds of diversity. All Memphis wanted to do was *not* change."

Stax had the golden touch for many years, but financial problems brought it down by the end of the 1970s. Like many Stax people, Deanie Parker moved away.

But then she came back. "I always felt very deeply that there needed to be some way to help Memphis to realize what a jewel it had—some way to express and demonstrate to the world at large how proud we are of our Memphis music heritage . . . and some way to help those who will come along afterward."

The Stax Museum is being built as a replica of the old theater-studio. Former artists and producers sorted through carpet samples to find the original pattern. A seamstress has re-created Mrs. Axton's curtains. "Steve Cropper has been a key person," Ms. Parker says, since Cropper practically lived in the studio. He's bringing Stax back to life.

But it's not just something of the past. Ms. Parker says the Stax Music Academy will help lead more generations of Memphis children into music. For a Stax junkie like me, I can't wait for the Wendy Rene exhibit.

It's two and a half miles between Stax Studios and the Lorraine Motel, another place with a second career as a museum. It was a supplemental office for Stax, but more famous as the place where Martin Luther King Jr. was assassinated in 1968. Today it's the National Civil Rights Museum.

"It was our home away from home," Deanie Parker says. "There were not nice places in the city of Memphis where black people and white people could congregate. There was a swimming pool at the Lorraine. Food could be catered in." It gave black and white musicians a chance to eat together, something many restaurants didn't allow.

When Atlantic Records sent temperamental singer Wilson Pickett to Stax to record, skinny white-boy guitar player Steve Cropper picked him up at the airport and took him to the Lorraine. The three of them—Pickett, Cropper and Jack Daniel's—wrote "In the Midnight Hour" there, the first in a series of great collaborations.

The National Civil Right Museum kept the look of the Lorraine Motel, but most of the museum is in a newer building attached to the motel: exhibits of abolition leaders, court decisions and rebellious slaves. The Montgomery Bus Boycott is portrayed by a real city bus, with a sculpture of resolute Rosa Parks sitting near the front. When you sit down on the bus, a recording of a driver orders you to move to the back. Sculptures also portray the abuse student dissidents felt at lunch-counter sit-ins.

Room 306, where King stayed, is preserved the way it was that afternoon in 1968.

Deanie Parker remembers that day. "I was driving from East Memphis, on my way back to the studio," she says. "Dark clouds were rolling over . . . the most turbulent wind that I could remember."

When the news spread about King's murder, rioters turned their anger on white-owned businesses in the Soulsville neighborhood. Despite the fact that Jim Stewart and Estelle Axton were white, Stax did not burn.

Lots of Stax artists and employees were affected by the murder at the Lorraine Motel. It was the assassination of a charismatic leader, but it was also a death in the family.

Isaac Hayes, Stax staff writer and producer, was deeply affected. "I went blank," he has said. "I couldn't write for about a year—I was filled with so much bitterness and anguish, till I couldn't deal with it." Immediately after hearing of the shooting, he and his writing partner, David Porter (together, they wrote "Soul Man," "Hold On, I'm Comin'" and other hits) drove to the Lorraine but couldn't get anywhere near the place.

William Bell, the label's great soul balladeer, was recording when he heard the news. Worried about the white musicians, he and other black musicians shielded Steve Cropper and Duck Dunn with their bodies until they were safely in their cars.

"That was the turning point," Booker T. Jones has said. "The turning point for race relations in America. And it happened in Memphis."

Outside the National Civil Rights Museum, I ask Graham how he feels.

"It's eerie," he says. "Those cars . . . it all seems unchanged." The parking lot has vintage 1968 cars, looking as they might have that afternoon.

Nearby, a woman named Jacqueline Smith sits on a folding chair, noisily protesting. She's black and thinks the museum symbolizes the entombment of the Civil Rights Movement. She calls "boycott the museum" toward tourist groups every couple of minutes.

Smith was the Lorraine Motel's last tenant and has been out front, protesting, since 1987. She says the museum has turned the Civil Rights Movement into "a Disney-style tourist attraction," with the re-creations of the Klan demonstrations and lunch-counter sit-ins. "Do we really have so little imagination that we need to spend thousands of taxpayers' dollars re-creating a fake Birmingham jail?"

I know what she's talking about. In the popular mind, King *was* the Civil Rights Movement. Tie it to him and when he dies, it's over. Bigots take pleasure in this, as closure. Activists wait for another King, but maybe the idea is to *be* another King.

T-Bone, Blind Blake and Sonny Boy

Just over the state line we stop for gas, and while I study the Mississippi road map Blake and Graham go into the convenience store to get some drinks, returning shortly.

Blake climbs into the shotgun seat with a forty-ounce bottle of Schlitz Malt Liquor in a brown paper bag. "You really missed it."

"The best-looking girl I've ever seen," Graham says, gazing back at the convenience store.

"She'll be out in a second, I bet," Blake says. "Don't pull away yet."

She is a parody of a wet dream—extravagant blonde hair, Ray-Bans, symmetrically perfect breasts in a lime-green top, and khaki pants barely restraining a glorious butt. She gets into a black Mercedes and takes 61 south. We follow.

"All right," Blake says. "Never let her out of your sight."

This is a first for me: I've never ogled a woman with my son before, even when I took him to Hooters for his birthday last year. Graham's never confided a sexual thought in me, and I'm kind of happy about that.

As we follow the girl down 61, the highway is littered with huge billboards for Harrah's Casino, the Hollywood Casino, the Grand Casino—all in Tunica, "the South's Casino Capital."

"All those people you thought were gone forever make comebacks in Tunica," Blake says. The towering billboards offer an appalling list of entertainers: Juice Newton, Billy Joe Royal, Paul Anka, Sinbad, Jethro Tull, Rick Springfield. . . .

This is all fairly new. As we drive through the sparse farmland south of Memphis, the casinos rise to the west like gaudy and bloated castles. The Hollywood Casino devotes fifty-four thousand square feet to gambling—fifteen hundred slot machines, fifty gaming tables. The hotel has 560 suites and there's room for 123 recreational vehicles. There's also a collection of movie memorabilia, including the biplane that tried to kill Cary Grant in that Indiana cornfield in *North by Northwest*, Arnold Schwarzenegger's jet from *True Lies*, and a motorcycle ridden by Harrison Ford in *Indiana Jones and the Last Crusade*. The centerpiece of the collection is a six-thousand-pound scale model of the *Titanic*.

"This all seems kind of weird," I say to Blake. "Look at the farmland and the houses, and it looks pretty darn impoverished around here. So they come along, build these big-ass casinos. . . . It just seems to exacerbate the poverty, doesn't it?"

"I think the consensus is that the casinos have been good for the area. Tunica County apparently had nothing before the casinos came along. Of course, what the hell do I know?" He takes a long drink from his bottle.

The highway is four-lane here, busy with gamblers. The wet-dream girl in her black Mercedes is long gone. The chugging old Explorer can't keep up with her.

Graham leans forward from the back seat. "Over here somewhere," he says, pointing west, "that's where Alan Lomax first recorded Son House."

Blake turns around to face him. "What are you, some kind of blues scholar or something?"

"He did a lot of research on the Internet," I say.

"I don't know who either of those guys are."

So I turn professor and tell him about John Lomax and his son Alan and how the two of them traveled the country, preserving and recording the music of obscure cowboy and country blues singers. "And Son House goes back so far, Robert Johnson learned from *him*."

Blake doesn't seem to know even the most well known of blues legends, the story of Robert Johnson.

"How could you live around here and not know that?" Graham asks.

Blake shrugs, taking another drink.

"Did you ever see that movie *Crossroads*? Unfortunately it starred Ralph Macchio. He plays this guy looking for a lost Robert Johnson song. Cheesy movie, but it might be a good place for you to start."

Blake looks blankly at me. I might as well be talking about the chair-selection processes of American air traffic controllers.

It's a recurring image in rural black culture: evil lurking at the crossroads. A black man on foot in hostile territory was an easy target. The crossroads legend had been attached to others before Johnson, but with him it stuck.

"I think history relies probably too much on the 'great man' theory, and so we've all seized on Robert Johnson as the 'great man,' meaning the key figure who pointed the way toward rock 'n' roll.

Face it, it was going to be some blues man . . . might as well have been him."

"How about Charley Patton?" Graham asks.

I turn around. "I'm *so* impressed you know about Charley Patton. Did I tell you that?"

"Yes, you did. The Internet is an amazing thing," he says. "And so is Morpheus. I downloaded some Charley Patton."

"So now are you going to tell me all about Charley Patton?" Blake drinks from the paper bag, pretending to be grumpy.

"Watch out!" Graham yells from the back seat. A car suddenly stops on the highway before turning off to the casinos, and I nearly rear-end him.

"You stupid fuck," I yell. "*You'll* meet the devil at the crossroads."

South of Tunica, away from the canopy of trees, cotton fields stretch in all directions.

"So . . . Charley Patton. He may be the man who started it all—rock 'n' roll, I mean. He worked on a plantation downstate but recorded some songs in the 1920s and 1930s that are still pretty unforgettable, haunting pieces of music. Maybe that kind of music existed long ago, out in the fields. But someone had the good sense to record Charley Patton. You ever think of giving up the world of journalism and becoming a sharecropper?"

"Every day," Blake says, nodding solemnly. "Every day I have to deal with editors on NBA shit. It's one day closer to pushing me into a life of rural agrarianism."

It's a straight shot through cotton fields and by small towns (Clayton, Dubbs, Rich and Birdie) down into Clarksdale. We're feeling suddenly, profoundly white.

"Listen to our names," I tell them. "*Blake. William. Graham.* You don't get more Caucasian than that."

"Maybe we should adopt assumed identities," Graham says.

"Perhaps we can blend in with the populace." I glance over at

Blake. "You're wearing sunglasses and there was a blues singer named Blind Blake. I dub thee Blind Blake. I'll be T-Bone. Graham, who do you want to be?"

"Sonny Boy."

"Graham is a pretty interesting name," Blake says, turning around. "Were you named after anybody?"

"I wasn't around for that part," he says, "you'll have to ask him."

"It was self-defense," I say. "His mother wanted to name him *Zed* or *Simon*. You lucked out, dude. If mom would have gotten her way and named you Simon, you would have had to kick much ass in your lifetime."

"So who was Graham, the namesake?" Blake asks.

"I was reading a lot of Graham Greene then," I said. "That was probably it. It sounded like a name no one would shorten into cutesy nicknames. His mother was convinced he'd be called 'Graham Cracker' all of his life and what's it been, Boy? One person called you that?"

"I had a teacher my junior year who called me 'Cracker Man.'"

"Of course, we called him 'Grambo' when he was little. He used to love wearing camouflage, when he was about three or four. Camo shirts, camo pants, hat . . . he even had camouflage socks. I thought he was going to grow up to be a psycho killer." I turn around to look at him. "Instead of the fine citizen he's turned out to be."

"There's still time," he says.

Standing at the Crossroads

Clarksdale, seventy miles south of Memphis, is the seat of Coahoma County and the largest city in the northern Mississippi Delta. Locals call it the capital of the Cotton Kingdom, and snowlike fields radiate from the city limits. The town draws people from throughout the Delta; eventually, everybody comes to Clarksdale. When we get to where 61 crosses Highway 49—*the* crossroads, the place where Robert Johnson gave over his soul for all eternity— we find a barbecue joint, a busy intersection by small-town standards. "Kind of bizarre," I say. "You think with all of this traffic around here someone would have noticed the Prince of Darkness hanging out at the corner—and I'm talking Satan, not Neil Diamond."

"I'm sure it was different back then," Graham says.

If you want to believe a legend, Robert Johnson went to this crossroads and sold his soul to the devil. That was the only explanation other musicians could give for his talent.

He was born, illegitimate, to a woman named Julia Majors Spencer. Already married to a man named Charles Spencer, Julia raised her son in Hazelhurst, in southern Mississippi, and the boy grew up believing Spencer was his father and going by his surname. Charles Spencer had a falling out with some prominent local landowners and left Hazelhurst just ahead of a lynch mob. He escaped to Memphis, where he began using the name Charles Dodds. Eventually, he sent for his wife and children—despite the fact that he was living with another woman, with whom he had more children. Robert then became known as Robert Dodds. It wasn't until he was a teenager that he learned that his true father was a drifter named Noah Johnson.

So he began calling himself Robert Johnson. As the family drifted back into Mississippi to labor on plantations, he had no attraction to farm work. Music interested him, and he strung wires on the side of a barn and thus taught himself the guitar. But he wasn't good enough to impress musicians who played juke joints and house parties. Son House and Willie Brown used to mock him. Then Johnson went away for a year. When he returned, he asked to play with House and Brown. After listening to him, Son House said, "He must have sold his soul to the devil to play like that."

Today we'd call it hype. What Robert Johnson did to solidify his image and give himself some glamour was to identify with the devil. He watered and manured the story with songs such as "Me and the Devil," "Hell Hound on My Trail" and "Cross Road Blues."

That crossroads image recurs in black culture. An earlier—and unrelated—singer named Tommy Johnson outlined the procedure: "You go to where . . . a crossroads is. . . . big black man will walk up there and take your guitar and tune it." When Satan gave you back the guitar, you could play better than anyone else—and he had possession of your soul.

In his western film *The Man Who Shot Liberty Valance*, director John Ford tells a long story in flashback in which the most esteemed figure in a frontier state admits, near the end of his life, that his whole career was based on a lie. He was not the man who shot the feared outlaw Liberty Valance; the town drunk did the killing. Finally, to cleanse his soul, this man—now a U.S. senator—reveals the lie to a journalist. At the end of the story the reporter tears up his notes and says, "When the legend becomes fact, print the legend."

Johnson never directly mentioned the pact-with-the-devil stuff, but it's a good story and it grew in the years after his death. Perhaps because so little was known about Johnson's life something needed to be invented. What is known is that he was poisoned to death in 1938 by a jealous husband.

Somehow, through myth or hype or chamber-of-commerce boosterism, the intersection of 61 and 49 has become *the* crossroads.

At the crossroads there's a signpost towering over the business neon—a pair of crossed blue guitars with replica road signs for 49 and 61.

"I was hoping for something bleak and rural," I say. "It reminds me of when I went to Nantucket, all psyched for the beauty and serenity of Cape Cod, and there was the Moby Dick Motel."

We look around at the businesses and read the signs.

Local attorney Bill Luckett saw that this sign was erected at the intersection of Highway 61 and Highway 49 in Clarksdale, Mississippi.

"Abe's Bar-B-Q says it's been here since 1924," I say, "so if this is indeed *the* crossroads, Robert and the devil could have at least sealed their pact with a two-piece and a biscuit."

Graham's being literal. "It's probably not the exact crossroads. They've probably moved the highway a little bit."

Other businesses at the intersection: Crossroads Laundry and

Cleaners, the Delta Donut Shop, Church's Chicken and Fuel Mart.

We drive through Clarksdale—stores closing on a late Saturday afternoon, vacant lots sprouting rusted soda cans, and car washes.

Oddly on display, three gawking white boys in an SUV drawing bored stares from the kids playing ball in the street.

We turn down another street and it's as if we've crossed over into the Twilight Zone—huge, columned houses with lawns that reach out to us in curtains of green.

"Methinks this is a honky street," Blake says.

"This seems wrong, though," I say. "Let's get back to that other 'hood. I felt we were bonding. I feel so much better about myself that I am no longer Bill. It's great to be T-Bone. If only I had musical ability." I pull out the harmonica and demonstrate my single blues riff.

I glance in the rearview mirror when we get closer to downtown.

"Dude, there's a Mercedes behind us," I tell Blake. "You think those are fellow blues *enthuse-e-asts*?"

"I'm hoping it's that woman from the gas station," Blake says.

"Alas, it's a blue Mercedes, not a black Mercedes." I start singing a song I know from John Lee Hooker, who was born on a farm outside Clarksdale: "One Bourbon, One Scotch, One Beer."

World Gone Black and White

Blake's malt liquor is drained, so we stop in at Toney's Package Store on Martin Luther King Boulevard. It's a narrow building, and the female clerk is behind bulletproof glass, all of the bottles displayed behind her.

"You mean you don't get to taste it first?" I whisper to Blake.

There's a narrow waiting room, where customers can examine the rows of booze under glass. The only actual customer has a ball cap, gray stubble and eyes clouded with drink but which instantly recognize the musician pictured on Graham's T-shirt. He stops making time with the woman behind the glass and turns to us.

"Man, that's some history right there," he says, pointing at the Miles Davis T-shirt. "That there's the genius man! I'm square with you."

"He's one of the greatest," Graham says.

"From St. Louis," the man says. "*I'm* from St. Louis."

"We were just there," Graham says. "Saw his spot on the Walk of Fame."

"Greatest trumpet player that ever lived. You ever hear of . . . 'Bitches Brew'?"

Graham nods, a little nervous when the man draws closer, breathing noxious fumes.

"Ain't that bad?" the man cackles.

"Yes, definitely," Graham says.

Blake is negotiating with the clerk-under-glass while the Miles Davis fan creates a trumpet mouthpiece out of his thumb and forefinger and begins playing a Miles-worthy solo.

"That's a nice trumpet you've got there," Graham says.

"Aw, no, man . . . I'm just a one-note blow call."

Blake walks away from the bulletproof clerk empty-handed and motions to the parking lot. "They don't sell malt liquor," he says. "They don't even sell beer." Every state's got a weird set of liquor laws. As we leave, I see a plaster statue of what's supposed to be Jack Daniel himself, and I try to talk the clerk out of it. "Graham, this would be perfect for your apartment." The woman behind the glass smiles but says it's not for sale.

Outside, we pile into the War Wagon and contemplate the oddity of the clerk-under-glass.

"Hang on," Blake says, and I look up to see the amateur trumpet player crossing the lot, coming toward us. He bends down to look in my car window, blowing bourbon into my face.

"There's a service station right there, on that corner." He points it out for us. "The Double Quick? You can get all the beer you want."

"You don't know how much beer we want," I say.

"Aw . . . hey, you can buy the whole damn store if you want," he says. "They got it by the cases." He leans down on the window. We couldn't back out now if we wanted to. "Hey, would you lend me a dollar?" He corrects himself. "*Give* me a dollar? I'll probably never see you again."

"Yeah, you probably won't."

"I always feel like being honest with a person."

I pull a couple of crumpled bills from my jeans. "There you go."

"Thanks," he says, doffing the crusty ball cap.

"Hey, mind if we take your picture?"

I can't tell if he's flattered or offended. "Look, we're on vacation, we're having a good time. We enjoyed meeting you and we just wanted to have your picture. I'll give you another dollar."

He poses, and when I get back in the car I ask for his address. "I'll send you a copy of the picture."

"You may have my picture," he says, "but no man may have my habitat."

"What's your name?" I ask.

"Uh, David Smooley Bill Bird the First."

"Wow. That's quite a name. What was it again?"

He repeats it, slowly. "The first born of my clan. *David?*"

"David."

"*Smooley?*"

"Smooley."

"*Bill?*"

"Bill."

"*Bird?*"

"Bird."

He punctuates it with the subtle toot from his invisible trumpet—*unh hah!*

As we pull out of the lot, Blake says, "Show you right!" I don my asshole-academic voice and say, "'That's what I should have said to establish my credentials as a 'brother.' "

"A black man wanted to talk to us," Blake says, in mock marvel. "He has accepted us as one of his own."

We pick up a forty-ounce of malt liquor at the Double Quick.

We're trying to find a few key sites in Clarksdale: the vacant lot where W. C. Handy's home once stood; the Delta Blues Museum (closed) and the Riverside Hotel, where Bessie Smith died in 1937 when it was a segregated hospital.

There's a disturbing slope to the roof of the Riverside. As a hotel, this place has housed a Who's Who of blues aristocracy. Right now, the only sign of life there is a maggoty looking guy on the porch. He could be a mean redneck . . . or perhaps a European tourist.

"What do you think?" I ask Graham. "Think that skinny dude is a Norwegian blues *enthuse-e-ast?*"

"Ya, you betcha," he says.

"Did you know 'Norway' is pronounced 'Norgay' in Norwegian?" Blake asks.

"I did not know that. As in, 'I'm neither straight nor gay'?"

I have the strangest feeling we're driving in circles. "We've been by here before," I say.

"We're been by everything before," Blake says. "It's a small town . . . what do you expect? Let's get out of Clarksdale. You guys're coming back tomorrow."

There's such a variance. A few blocks from leaning shacks are sprawling mansions.

"Now we're going to the wrong side of the tracks," Blake says. "These are the good neighborhoods."

We can't find too many things open. We cruise the street lucklessly looking for a bar, but they're all closed. JJ's Bar-B-Q advertises the best in town ("Quite a claim, I figure," Blake says) but is also shut.

"What do you suppose they do for a good time on a Saturday night in Clarksdale?" I ask Blake.

"Probably drink 40s and shoot guns," he says.

We can't seem to find any juke joints open—not that they'd let Graham in anyway. It seems that all the fun people must hang out at Toney's Package Store or the Double Quick.

We're heading out of town on Mississippi 1, toward Friar's Point. It's one of those names familiar from Robert Johnson songs: *"Just come on back to Friar's Point, mama, and barrelhouse all night long."* Graham says we need to find a certain drugstore here, something he read about in his research.

Originally Farrar's Point, Friar's Point was incorporated in 1852 and was a docking point for nineteenth-century riverboats. The post office contains the North Delta Museum—closed, since it's now Saturday evening. We see the police chief of Friar's Point and we wave to him. We can tell he's the chief because his black T-shirt has POLICE CHIEF printed on the back in big white letters.

The streets are crowded, and we are the only white people around. We slowly negotiate through the milling crowd, which doesn't seem to have any reason other than Saturday evening for gathering. There are no signs of street parties or dances or any sound of music other than thumping bass from a parked car.

At the edge of town, the levee rises and there's a dirt road angling to the top, but we can't get up there because of a gate with a large NO TRESPASSING sign.

Graham says, "I read where the Mississippi River levee is longer and taller than the Great Wall of China."

There are a few nice big homes with generous porches, but then we turn down Sycamore Street, which should more accurately be called Holocaust Street. It looks like a tornado ripped through.

We see a mutt in the middle of the street, gnawing on something. "That dog's chewing on a rib," Blake says.

"Think it's human?" I ask.

Two circuits through town, still looking for the drugstore. For the second time, we pass an elderly black couple reclining on their porch.

"Think they wonder what we're doing?"

"I'm sure they know," Graham says. "I bet they deal with this all day long."

He's probably right. Friar's Point is one of the stops on the American Dream Safari tours, operated out of Memphis. A guy named Tad Pierson leads tours through Memphis in vintage cars and has special package rates that take tourists—because of his background teaching English in Asia, he likes to draw on foreign blues fans—through the small Delta towns that loom large in blues lore, such as Friar's Point. No chain hotels for these tourists, either. He books his guests into hotels in keeping with the tour's theme. There's a place outside of Clarksdale called the Shack-Up Inn. The deluxe tour package is nearly a thousand bucks, but that starts in Chicago. Most of the multiday tours out of Memphis are in the two-hundred-dollar range.

But the tourists in the vintage cars probably don't look as out of place as the War Wagon, with its University of Florida plates, Bob Marley stickers and the father-and-son bowling team.

It was Graham who insisted we come to Friar's Point. He'd read that the only time Muddy Waters ever set eyes on Robert Johnson, it was here. Johnson was playing on the sidewalk in front of Hirsberg's Drug Store. Waters saw Johnson but was too intimidated by his ability and did not speak to him. The owner of the drugstore didn't appreciate Johnson's sidewalk concert blocking his front door. A pink brick building with no fanfare or historical marker turns out to be the site of this musically momentous near-meeting.

"If grinding poverty is a necessary ingredient for the blues," Blake says, "Friar's Point would seem to have plenty of it."

"Still, aren't you glad you came?" I ask. "It's like the only place where Robert Johnson and Muddy Waters shared air space. For a few minutes at least, they were breathing the same molecules."

We head south, toward Stovall. It's darker; the world's gone black and white. Even the Explorer is now shades of gray. The thick clouds don't allow any light except that along the horizon to our right.

"Malt liquor gets on top of your bladder and kicks its ass," Blake says suddenly. "We need to stop someplace . . . someplace soon."

We find the Stovall Store at the rural crossroads intersection of Stovall Road and Mississippi 1.

"I think I'll just stay out here," I say, getting out of the car. I see a show I want to watch.

"Can you bump me some money?" Graham asks. "I'd like to get a drink."

While Blake and Graham go in, I stand in the gravel of the lot. Across the highway, the sun is dying a magnificent death behind an imposing, spreading oak, cutting shadows through the rows in a bean field. The store is curious. The ancient, rusted sign advertises sandwiches, cold beer and fishing supplies. Afforded such a view across the fields and the perfect vantage for a nightly sunset, the store owner has chosen to brick up the two windows at the front of the store and five along the side. My feet on the crushed stone magnify the sound of my steps. I look down—tops of milk bottles, oxidizing Coors Light cans, cigarette butts. I feel that I'm back four decades.

Graham comes out of the store with his drink and we stand there, watching the sun.

"If there ever truly was a crossroads," I say, "I think it must have been like this."

He nods. "There's something about this place."

"It's so beautiful," I say. "I guess I never expected such beauty, at least not here."

His name was McKinley Morganfield, and he was born downstate, in Rolling Fork, but his mother died when he was three and he was sent up to his grandmother's home at Stovall's Plantation. He played so much in nearby Deer Creek that she named him Muddy. He started playing harmonica and singing at parties and fish fries while still a boy and he added Waters to his nickname. He saved his money from sharecropping and bought himself a guitar when he was a teenager. He bought seventy-eight rpm's of all the major blues artists of that time and place, including Robert Johnson, Charley Patton, Son House, Tampa Red and others. When he was eighteen, he opened up a juke joint and stocked the jukebox with his personal collection. When he was twenty-six, folklorist Alan Lomax visited him, bringing along his three-hundred-pound supposedly portable tape-recording machine, and made some recordings at the juke joint. Waters showed up barefoot, so Lomax took off his shoes as well. In between songs, Lomax asked Waters about Robert Johnson and Son House. Which one was better. "They about even," Waters said.

Soon, on the strength of the plantation recordings, Muddy Waters was off to Chicago. He recorded for Chess Records, became a recording star and one of the most celebrated and world-renowned ambassadors of the blues. Returns to Mississippi were rare. He felt he hadn't been appreciated here. When he died in 1983, he was buried in Chicago.

Driving down Stovall Road, we blast Muddy Waters singing "Sad Letter." The sun still hasn't given up and wrestles with darkness on the horizon.

Graham looks for the stand of trees where Muddy Waters's cabin stood. The problem is, the cabin's gone. It was removed several years ago and went on tour with the House of Blues to raise money for the Delta Blues Museum.

Graham's printed out a photograph of the site, and we make two turns up and down Stovall Road until we find what he's sure is the place. There are houses up ahead, but it's just us, alone on the road, with a sun raging against the dying of the light. We get out of the car for a moment and walk around by the side of the road.

"If I were the state of Mississippi," I say, "I think I would put up signs: 'Muddy Waters's cabin was here.' Like a Mississippi Blues Trail or something."

Sunset at Stovall's Plantation, at the site of Muddy Waters's cabin.

Graham disagrees. "Yeah, but then you'd miss the satisfaction of finding it for yourself."

We're back on 61, the old highway. No cars in either direction. For a moment, I think about the three civil rights workers killed across state. And Viola Liuzzo, another civil rights martyr, killed on a similar country road in Alabama, and Emmett Till, not far away in Money. Crossroads. *"Take a black cat bone and a guitar and go to a lonely fork in the roads at midnight."*

Graham has found the road sign he wants to steal. It's a green horizontal sign, not the classic black-and-white badge sign.

"Damn," I tell him. "I think I left my acetylene torch in my other pants."

"You just twist it the right way and those bolts will pop out," Blake says.

"Spoken like a true criminal. Don't be a bad influence on my son."

It's the intersection of Highway 61 and Dog Bog Road. I watch as Graham pushes on the road sign until it comes out of the ground.

Blake supervises, punctuating comments with sips from his brown bag. A few pulls and the sign comes loose in Graham's hand. He shoves the post back into the ground and we steal away. Graham proudly holds the green sign on his lap in the back seat.

We cheat on the way back to Memphis, taking US 278 over to Batesville, where we pick up I-55. It's a dull but quick drive up to Memphis. We stop at Batesville for more gas and malt liquor. We run through a swarm of bugs, turning our windshield into a gooey entomological exhibit. Sunflowers the size of power forwards line the road, silhouetted in the moonlight. It's an unfamiliar, wild world. We stop north of Crowder for more refreshments and to try to clear a line of vision through the insect remains. A woman in Tweety Bird house shoes is the only other customer at the convenience store. She's carrying one child on her hip, and another trails behind her to a pickup truck.

We see a couple of small, desolately brilliant concrete-block clubs along the road with a few cars clustered around, as if feeding on mother's milk. We slow down but can't go in, not with an underage passenger.

"So here I am, speeding through the Mississippi night with a vandal and a drunk," I say, sipping Dr. Pepper. We turn up Jimi Hendrix playing "Freedom," and our headlights cut our way through the darkness toward Memphis.

Billy Pilgrim

Blake can't get out of bed the next morning to wish us a proper good-bye, so we leave him a note on the kitchen counter and make as little noise as possible.

We plan to spend the day messing around in Mississippi, performing variations on a Highway 61 theme. We need to be back in Clarksdale the next day so we can go to the Delta Blues Museum. That's the only item on our agenda. We cross into Mississippi on I-55 and stop at the welcome center, which looks like a plantation house, for a detailed road map.

"You think they'd take some of that money they spend on places like this," he says, "and put it somewhere that needs it, like Friar's Point."

The first side trip is to Oxford. I'm driving and Graham's reading *Slaughterhouse-Five*—appropriate because I feel like Billy Pilgrim in that book, "unstuck in time." Billy finds himself waking up as a young man in the Second World War, but then having breakfast as a middle-aged father two decades later. Then he's old, living on another planet, then young and back to the war again. That's what happens to me when I drive. I travel miles, but I travel through time too, through my memory.

As I drive southeast, toward Oxford, Graham's intently reading, and I remember a trip with Sarah and Graham nearly ten years ago. It was the first time I was able to wrest them away from their mother for a quick spring-break trip. As soon as they got out of school that Friday, we started driving south because a big snowstorm was coming. Just north of Nashville, we stopped at a Days Inn. The storm hit in the night and snow was ankle-deep when we went out to the car the next morning, creeping onto I-65 and heading south. "Maybe in an hour, kids, we'll be out from under this," I told them.

But we weren't. After six hours, we were still inching along in northern Alabama, stuck on a frozen interstate in the middle of rolling, white hills. Bumper to bumper, all college kids heading to Florida for spring break. We saw back-window decals from Indiana, Purdue, Michigan, Michigan State, Wisconsin. . . . It was like a Big Ten convention.

I thought there was a chance we could freeze in that car—a little Mazda Protegé—and it seemed so fragile against the cruel weather. We moved at most a mile an hour, and so north of Birmingham I exited, but the car grounded in a heavy snowbank off the exit ramp. I was trying to dig it out when a pair of guys too ugly to have made the cast of *Deliverance* showed up and took a great interest in us and particularly in my blonde, cheerleader daughter. Sarah was thirteen but looked older. I told them I thought we'd be able to handle things ourselves. They hung around, watching me belly-crawl, trying to free the undercarriage of the car from the oppressive snow, not offering to help but feigning interest in our plight. Inside the car, the kids were terrified. Eventually, a guy in a Mitsubishi Montero pulled us from the snowbank and we inched our way into Birmingham on a state highway. We were nearly frozen again on a ramp trying to get out of town (I thought the road looked clearer and figured the gravel crews had gotten to the highway), and ended up abandoning the car. None of the hotels had rooms, but one of them had a large conference center. The kids and I were invited to bunk on the floor there. The front-desk clerk dug up two pillows and a few flimsy blankets.

We stayed three days, eventually moving to a room. The employees were trapped in the hotel too, and so they were punchy with fatigue and sleeping on the floor in the lobby. *This is Birmingham*, I thought. *This is the town that turned attack dogs on little kids.* But of course the *town* didn't do it; the old police commissioner, Bull Conner, did. That was spring 1963. Thirty years later, the people in Birmingham were good to us. They thought the goofy father and two kids were kind of fun to have around.

We eventually made it to Florida, and Sarah got her time on the beach in a bikini, and Graham got to meet some ballplayers at rainy spring-training games.

They both say that was one of their favorite vacations, but the thing they remember most is how scared they were and how I saved them. *I was their hero.*

We take the interstate down to Highway 6, a well-maintained road a few notches above 61 on the pavement food chain. It links the University of Mississippi in Oxford to Memphis and the rest of the outside world. We're relying on the radio this morning and picking up some good Holy Ghost preaching. The sermons must be carried on no-watt stations, because we lose them every ten miles. We catch a bit of one as the preacher screams about the Fox—Satan, of course—and how he robs the henhouse. I'd gone to an all-black funeral the year before when my secretary's sister died, and I wasn't prepared for the assault by tag-team preachers. When we got to the point in the funeral where us ritualistic Catholics would have a nice cut-and-dried sermon, the trio went off for an hour. There was call-and-response between the three preachers, one of whom was there primarily to growl. It was a deeply felt symphony of agony. I'd never felt anything so powerful in a church before.

South on the interstate, we find a dark blue Chevy Suburban, middle-aged white guy at the wheel with a Mississippi "Xroads" vanity plate.

"I bet those are highly sought after," I say to Graham pointing out the car to him.

"Yeah, and it's a white guy," he says, going back to his book.

I've never been to Oxford before. It was the home of William Faulkner. It's where James Meredith knocked down the color barrier in Southern higher education. It's the home of John Grisham, Inc. It's a little out of the way, but we don't mind; we're free spirits.

"How do you like that book?" I ask Graham. "Pretty cool, isn't it?"

"I haven't really gotten very far in it," he says. "I like how he shifts between all of these various moments of his life, though."

"I think it's a perfect book, like a soufflé. I'd put it up there with *The Great Gatsby* and *Fear and Loathing in Las Vegas*, one of those books where you can't find a single word you'd change. Every time I pick up *Slaughterhouse-Five*, it's like I'm gone for forty pages before I know it."

"And he knew Aunt Inez?"

My Aunt Inez and Uncle Cecil—my great-aunt and -uncle—had known Kurt Vonnegut as a boy in Indianapolis. My uncle was a builder and so knew Vonnegut's father, an architect and builder. "I doubt they were close pals or anything. But she gave me one of his books one time and inscribed it, 'We knew this young man when he was just a little boy.' I love that inscription."

Graham knows who William Faulkner is but has never read any of his books. I've read only a few—*Light in August* is my favorite—but I'm most fond of his short stories. I used to work at the *Saturday Evening Post*. While compiling an anthology, I looked through back issues and found Faulkner stories while turning pages. I'd turn to the cover, where he wasn't even mentioned.

Just as he was taken for granted by the magazine, he seemed taken for granted by his hometown during his lifetime. I try to interest Graham by making a Bob Dylan parallel. Now, forty years after his death, Faulkner is appreciated, even revered, by his hometown. The university keeps his house open for the curious.

We've lost preacher radio, so after stopping for sodas and switching places, Graham puts away his book and plugs in Radiohead—a sound that could be no more alien from the preachers unless it came from Jupiter. As we begin slowing for our descent into town, the singer whines, "Catch the mouse and squeeze its head." *The stuff kids listen to these days.*

Oxford Town

Oxford is a beautiful town, movie-set pretty, and the campus is quiet as a casket on this June Sunday. The campus mixes hideous 1960s academic buildings with classic university architecture, heavy on bricks and white columns. The Lyceum is where students gathered before the 1962 riot. A retired army general incited his student "troops" at a pep rally, urging them to protest James Meredith's enrollment. Two people were killed in the skirmish that followed.

James Meredith was thirty. I was a kid, watching President Kennedy address the black-and-white nation. When I think back on those grainy televised memories of childhood, they're always of doom-and-gloom things—the Cuban Missile Crisis (nearly in our backyard when we were stationed in South Florida), the integration of Ole Miss and the Kennedy assassination. Graham's childhood TV memories are legion: He-Man and Skeletor, Michael Jackson's "Thriller" and the Transformers.

So here I am, trying to be that dad/professor hybrid, telling him the James Meredith story, and I might as well be talking about something that happened on Mars. He can't believe that such a world existed. I plug in *The Freewheelin' Bob Dylan* so we can hear his song about Meredith, "Oxford Town." It's based on an old banjo melody, so the tune is upbeat, but the words are dark. "Lots of Bob's greatest songs in that era were based on real events," I tell him. "I make my class listen to 'The Lonesome Death of Hattie Carroll' every year. That's the most heartbreaking song ever."

Ole Miss was a battleground then, but today it's well groomed and innocuous. We might as well be on a tour of American universities. What is Ole Miss to my students back at Florida except a team in our conference we pound whenever scheduling permits.

"People were killed over this," I say. "I just had to see it. I've seen it in black and white, on TV and in books. I just wanted to see it in color."

"The Lyceum's kind of cool," he says. Three hundred federal marshals faced down the mob of two thousand white civilians in front of this building, I tell him. Just as we turn on to Fraternity Row our father-son spelunk into history is interrupted by a shot on my arm. "Slugbug," Graham says, pointing to a lime-green VW parked in front of Alpha Tau Omega.

A statue of a Confederate soldier still stands watch over the courthouse on the town square. We gorge ourselves on Uncle Buck's Records, which features framed autographed photos from any artist who comes within five hundred miles—and lavishly stocked Square Books, which outdoes many big-city bookstores.

The weather is the hottest of our trip so far, and so our around-the-courthouse promenade works up a sweat. The square's so pretty I feel obliged to stoop and pick up litter. It's a corsage, probably a remnant of a sorority formal.

Faulkner's home, Rowan Oak, is south of campus. We miss the small sign off of Lamar Street the first time, and Graham makes a three-point turn and runs up over a curb. "My bad," he says.

A dirt lane leads to a small parking area where a young man is unloading a carload of three elderly women. We wait until they have dislodged and then mount the steps to Faulkner's house, a grand home at the end of twin columns of oaks.

He bought this house in April 1930, on the first anniversary of his marriage. The house was well over eighty years old then and decrepit. The William Faulkner who bought it was a failed postmaster (he played cards more than sorted mail), failed Scoutmaster (he drank too much for the Boy Scouts' parents) and a failed writer (in terms of sales, of course, not talent). He turned Rowan Oak into a fine home and lived here, with time off for travels, academic appointments and Hollywood screenwriting, until his death in 1962.

Rowan Oak is open to the public, but it's not a stuffy museum. You might expect Faulkner to come down the stairway in his bathrobe and Pooh slippers, sleepily stumbling to the kitchen and brewing a pot of Folgers.

Curator William Griffith says they just got a half-million dollars to install a climate-control system to keep Mr. Faulkner's belongings fresh. There's no central air conditioning and they haven't so much as painted a doorjamb since Bill Faulkner himself was in charge of home repairs. Rowan Oak gets about twenty thousand visitors a year, and with all of that traffic you'd think they'd need to call Stanley Steemer every now and then. But it's a clean, well-lived-in house.

Griffith's a young man in a blue-striped Oxford (of course) cloth shirt, with precisely combed hair. He asks about us, and when we tell him about the trip, he perks up.

"Highway 61," he says wistfully. "So you're going all the way to New Orleans?"

"Yep. We started up in Canada . . . actually, I guess *I* started in Key West, and we drove up into Canada, around Lake Superior. Highway 61 actually starts in Thunder Bay, Ontario."

"That's a long trip," he says, shaking his head. "It's almost over though."

"I'm not sure I *remember* life before this trip. I know I had one, but I just don't remember it."

"Down in New Orleans, you should go to the bookstore in Pirate's Alley where he wrote his book 'Mosquitoes.' "

"A book I have but have never read."

"It's not one of his best." I nod, happy to have that on authority from a Faulkner scholar. The book had never held my interest. "They have loads of mosquitoes in New Orleans, so I understand his inspiration."

"How was he regarded by the townsfolk of Oxford?" I ask.

"Now he's well respected, but during his lifetime it was a *typical* relationship between talent and town. Neither of them paid each other much credit or mind. That's how it was then."

Griffith knows a lot about Faulkner, but he's pretty well versed in Bob Dylan too. Hibbing ought to put me on retainer for all the nice stuff I've said about it on the trip. Griffith's eyes light when I tell him about Dylan's boyhood home.

"It's not open to the public, is it?"

"No, but there might be a job opening for you there someday."

We walk around the grounds, which includes a fishpond and several out buildings. Kudzu smothers the trees.

"That where he kept the hot tub?" Graham asks, and I think about William Faulkner, sucking on a pipe, soaking in a Jacuzzi.

Turns out it's the detached kitchen, which Faulkner used as a smokehouse.

"Check it out," Graham says, bending over. He shows me a couple of brick fragments near the foundation. "Here you go, here's your William Faulkner souvenir."

"We can't take this," I tell him. "This stuff belongs here. Your vandalism is out of control."

"I didn't cause the bricks to break," he says. "I merely found the fragments." He puts the larger, slightly moldy, piece in my hand. I hold it there a moment, then stick it in my pocket.

We head south of Oxford on Highway 7, over hills we see through a Jackson Pollock–like spray of butterflies and insects on the windshield. The road cuts across central Mississippi, back toward Highway 61. The corn, eyebrow high, already has tassels. Graham stocks the CD changer with appropriate music: Muddy Waters, *The Real Folk Blues*; Sunnyland Slim, *Sunnyland Train*; B. B. King, *King of the Blues*, Disc 1; Son House, *Delta Blues and Spirituals*; Robert Johnson, *King of the Delta Blues Singers* (gold disc) and Charley Patton, *Founder of the Delta Blues*.

Save Poor Bob If You Please

My son has also pulled out reams of computer printouts from his Internet research and his notes. While he drives, he asks me to mark key sites on our new Mississippi map. There are three Robert Johnson graves—two marked, one unmarked—and Graham doesn't want to take any chances.

"We're going to all three," he announces. "One way or another, I want to be standing over him." He's marked a few other graves to visit.

These days have been long and I'm grateful, because I want to lux-uriate in them.

"I think that unmarked grave is outside of Greenwood," he says.

Rows of neatly planted beans and tomatoes. The Tote-a-Bag con-venience store, Crazy Charlie's Gun and Pawn, the Blue Room, a night club outside of Greenwood . . . *I want to remember it all.*

On July 6, 1963, at a rally on Silas Magee's Farm outside Green-wood, Bob Dylan first performed "Only a Pawn in Their Game," his long ballad about the murder of civil rights leader Medgar Evers, shot in the back on the steps of his home in Jackson the month before. Bob blamed society for Evers's death, portraying the killer as just another byproduct of a community that bred hate. You see this performance in the documentary *Don't Look Back*, as he's surrounded by a small group of black farm workers, some sitting on the backs of flatbeds. If the camera had panned across the road, it would have shown white-robed Klansmen. No wonder Bob looks so nervous. A few years later, when Bob began playing rock 'n' roll, he sang, "I ain't gonna work on Maggie's Farm" no more, everyone seemed to take that as a reference to President Johnson, but I'm more literal. I thought he meant *Magee's* Farm.

Greenwood's got that postnuclear look to it, largely void of peo-ple. We park downtown, but there are few signs of life. After a cou-ple of blocks we come to Spooney's Bar-Be-Que, where two young black men sit on the stoop and the CLOSED sign is prominent in the glass of the door behind them. They don't work there; they're just copping some shade.

"Doin' some bowlin', buddy?" One of the men, the one in the porkpie hat, points to my shoes.

"Actually, we're just looking for directions. Do you know where Little Zion Church is?"

His face clouds and he turns to his buddy. "Little Zion?"

"Down this street right here," his friend points. "Not too far down, you'll see it, if it's the one I'm thinking about."

"All right, we'll go looking for it. Hey," I motion toward the door. "This place open later?"

The first guy shakes his head. "No, Spooney's not open on Sunday. Not much is. You looking for a place to eat?"

He gives us directions to a place he says we'll love not far away, but we go looking for the church first. We find it, but it's in the middle of town, and the place we want is in the country.

"Look at the sign," Graham says. "'New' Zion. The place we want is Little Zion. They got mixed up."

So we drive back to the Spooney's neighborhood and easily find the place they recommended. When we step into the Crystal Grill, we're not disappointed so much by the place but that the guy would recommend it for us.

The paper placemat in front of us reads "Let Us Give Thanks," and offers Catholic, Orthodox, Jewish and Protestant prayers with the advice, "You may wish to say 'grace' before your meal. The prayers of your faith are shown to assist you." We order turkey and dressing, gravy, green beans, turnip greens, sweet tea and something called pineapple-cheese cake. The restaurant refers to its lunch menu as "mind-boggling," and perhaps it is.

It's like stepping into an Indiana diner. We're back in the white-bread world of ham loaf and persimmon pudding. All the customers are white.

"He probably thought this is where we'd be most comfortable," I say.

"I would have been comfortable at Spooney's."

All afternoon, on the way down from Oxford and in our few sightings of humans around Greenwood, we'd seen only black people. Now we were in the strongest concentration of white people we'd seen in the state.

"Kind of surprised to find this place in this town," Graham says, "especially when they're bumping country." His eyebrows indicate the P.A. system.

The food is good, the sweetness of the pie tingles at my jawbones. Eventually, a church-dressed black family shows up in the entrance of the restaurant and the hostess takes them behind the rope into the "section closed" area.

As we're paying, the hostess asks how we liked everything.

"Real good," I say. "Just like home."

"And where is that?" *We're so obviously strangers. Should I give her the long version or the short version?*

"Indiana. Say, would you mind if I looked at your phone book? We're trying to find something, a church called Little Zion."

She thumbs through the pages for me. "White church?" she asks, knitting her brow. At first I think she means the exterior color.

"I don't think so."

"Oh, I know the one you mean," she says. "The one where that blues guy is supposedly buried." She takes out a Crystal Grill card with a map on one side showing directions. She augments it with an extension of Grand Boulevard, which turns into a county road north of town. We'll find the church there.

This is also the road to Money, the little town where black teenager Emmett Till whistled at a white woman in 1955, and was murdered. Till was visiting from Chicago and didn't know the Mississippi rules. One of his killers said after his acquittal, "What could I do? He thought he was as good as any white man . . . I'm no bully, I never hurt a niggah in my life. . . . And when a niggah even gets close to mentioning sex with a white woman, he's tired o' livin' . . . I'm gonna kill him." Till's mother insisted on an open casket at the funeral, so people could see the brutality her fifteen-year-old son suffered. Maybe those killers used to eat at the Crystal Grill, "a dining tradition in the Delta for more than 50 years."

In the car, heading out of town, Graham howls, he's so happy. "We're on the trail of the hellhound," he yells. In his research he came across a National Park Service website devoted to the Delta blues that took its name from Robert Johnson's haunting "Hell Hound on My Trail."

Greenwood, like Clarksdale, seems to exist at the extremes of poverty and wealth without much in between. Leaning homes on blocks on one street, grand columned mansions on the next.

"Maybe they ought to make the state slogan 'Land of the Haves and the Have-Nots,' " I tell Graham.

"I want to see black people come out of those big-ass homes," he says. "We didn't see it in Clarksdale. Things are still not equal, or even close."

Greenwood ends and we're on a blacktop, cutting through cotton fields to the site of the church. A few miles north of town, we find it off on the west side of the road. We pull in the gravel drive and up to the church door, padlocked on a Sunday afternoon.

We're working from a magazine clipping that gives the approximate location of the unmarked grave and has a picture of Rosie Eskridge, an eighty-five-year-old woman, pointing at it with her walking cane. She says her husband buried Robert Johnson under a spreading pecan tree.

There's a small scattering of graves in the trees on the south side of the churchyard, the headstones tilting as if shaken by the wind, names washed off by time. It's hard to walk through the graveyard without feeling that we're disturbing the peace. Graham looks up, carefully examining the trees, holding the magazine clipping for reference.

Finally, he finds the tree and a large depression underneath. "It's probably in here," he says. "You can see where the ground goes down. It looks like that's the place."

Are you really there, Bob? He's our new Bob now. We've been listening to him in the car and for the first time, I've been struck by all of the references he makes to himself. There are the obvious "*Me* and the Devil" and "Hell Hound on *My* Trail." But we'd been playing the music really loud, and I kept hearing things I'd never heard before. I'd just bought a gold disc of *King of the Delta Blues Singers* and couldn't believe the clarity. Apparently, they'd mastered these discs from pristine old 78 rpm's found since *The Complete Recordings* came out in 1990, making Robert Johnson a star all over again. Listening to these newly discovered recordings in the car, it was like he was in the back seat. For the first time I hear his plea to God: "Have mercy," he begs, "Save poor Bob if you please."

I didn't hear his version of that song first. Like millions of others, I came to Robert Johnson through Eric Clapton and the Rolling Stones. But when I finally did come to Robert Johnson, I think I felt some of the pain that tortured him.

"I haven't thought about this in years," I say to Graham. "You know when I got that album, *King of the Delta Blues Singers*?" He shakes his head. "The day your mom left and went back to Indiana. We'd decided to separate. She needed to go away and clear her head and she wanted me to do the same. So she took you guys away early on a Saturday morning. By the middle of the afternoon, I was going crazy, I was so lonely. I went shopping, and of course that means the record store. And I found *King of the Delta Blues Singers*, and I thought, 'Man I've always heard about this record.' Bob . . . Eric Clapton . . . all these people I loved always talked about Robert Johnson, so I figured it was time. I got it and took it home and I listened to it probably six times all the way through that weekend, and I never talked to another human being those few days. I didn't call my mother . . . I didn't call anybody, didn't talk to anybody. Maybe I said thanks to the record clerk, but that was it. I don't think I'd ever been so lonely and depressed in all my life, just me and this dead man." I look down at the depression under the pecan tree. "If that *is* you, Bob."

Graham doesn't say anything; maybe he feels uncomfortable. Maybe it's something he hasn't wanted to think about either.

"It's an odd compliment, I guess. He made something so good—art, I think we can safely call it—something so good that we can't listen to it. I know I don't listen to it often. *I can't*. It's almost too painful to hear."

"I think because it's unmarked, this must be the place," Graham says. "He's here somewhere, I bet."

"Maybe he *belongs* in an unmarked grave." I turn to Graham, trying to smile. "Would you like to say a few words?"

He straightens up, looks around over to the churchyard and the cotton fields, then back down at the ground. "Thanks for rock 'n' roll, Dude." He picks up a pecan as a souvenir. "It's odd that the grave is unmarked," he says. "I mean, a man of his stature. . . ."

"Not sure he had any 'stature' at that point," I say. "He'd put out some records, but he was just another bluesman of his time, and there were so many of them they must've been bumping into each other on the sidewalk. ' 'Scuse me, Blind Grapefruit. Didn't mean to bump you there.'"

He laughs. "Nice place to be buried, though." Graham looks again over to the cotton fields across the little road. "He's found peace. I'd want to be buried in a place like this."

We find a silk carnation blown off another grave into the gravel drive and put it at the depression under the tree. "It's the best we can do for you, Bob."

See That My Grave Is Kept Clean

Graham's back behind the wheel, heading toward the second grave site. He's asking me for directions to Quito, a little village south of Greenwood. Johnson's last performance was at Three Forks store. The store was moved to a place within a half mile of this *other* burial site. Graham's turned up the music, and that haunting voice booms out of the speakers and over the cotton fields as he guides the War Wagon to grave number two.

Had I heard Robert Johnson before that weekend, or had I just heard *of* him? Since high school, Eric Clapton's "Crossroads" had been one of my favorite songs, with its glorious chaos and pain. When I finally heard Robert Johnson that horrible weekend years later, I was struck by the spare sound of "Cross Road Blues." Everyone has a crossroads. I was lucky to have Robert Johnson provide a soundtrack for mine.

We'd found evidence of a campfire behind the Little Zion Church. No doubt legions of blues enthusiasts had put that place on their tour maps after the story broke about the unmarked grave. The next place, down in Quito, was more well known. There was a headstone for Johnson there. Still, finding these places isn't easy.

"Mississippi is just fucked when it comes to road signs," I say. "And they name one of the biggest lakes in the state after the governor who tried to keep James Meredith out of Ole Miss."

"It's weird," Graham says, "because it's so beautiful and I like so many of the people."

"It's a 'terrible beauty,' like Ireland. Look at the cotton, the trees along the road."

We negotiate through Greenwood and an industrial park south of town, and we're back out in the sparse countryside. Glancing over the map with all of Graham's notes, I tell him America needs a national cemetery for bluesmen, like Arlington for the military. I get my desired effect—a laugh from my son—but I'm not joking. The visit to Little Zion Church shook me. For a moment, the Billy Pilgrim in me was a thousand miles and fifteen years away, listening to Robert Johnson in a dark house, all alone. No pictures of Robert Johnson had been published back then, and I had no idea what he looked like. He was just that mysterious, hard-edged voice.

"Do you feel close to Robert Johnson, driving down these little roads?" I ask. "This little road was here when he was alive. And it's obvious it hasn't even been repaved."

"And these railroad tracks," he points. "They were here then. Maybe he walked them."

We're turned around, trying to find Quito. Part of the problem is the roads we want are too small to be numbered on the map. As if understanding our problem, Robert stops singing "Me and the Devil Blues" and offers a spoken aside: "Baby, I don't care where you bury my body when I'm dead and gone." It makes me laugh, and I rewind the disc to hear the line again.

"That's Three Forks," Graham says. It's a little, unmarked store and roadhouse at the corner of a country lane. "It wasn't here when he played here his last night. They moved it here. But the church ought to be over here." He turns down a dirt road.

"You ought to be a reporter," I tell him. "I always thought I had a good memory for details, but you kick my ass."

A quarter mile down the road, up on a small knoll we find Payne's Chapel. But for the cross, the building could be a rural auto-parts store. There are several cars parked in the churchyard already, and a group of young black men gather on the steps. Maybe they're waiting for someone with the keys.

I introduce myself to a guy in a formfitting burnt-orange T-shirt. He tells me his name is Xavier Manning.

"I bet you get tired of people like us," I say, and I'm about to tell him why we've come to his church on this Sunday afternoon.

"No problem," he says, smiling. He turns and points. "He's right over there."

It's a simple flat marker: "Robert Johnson. May 8, 1911–August 16, 1938. Resting in the Blues." Flowers, guitar picks and quarters—for the tip cup, of course—rest on the marker. The grave, like the rest of the cemetery, is well tended. Birds sing from the trees at the edge of the graveyard. No signs indicate "Robert Johnson Over

Here," though this is probably the most-visited of his grave sites.

"This is pretty and all," Graham says. "But I don't feel him here. I think he was at the other place."

"But this is closest to where he died, right?"

A couple more guys have gathered on the church step, and we introduce ourselves and thank them for letting us visit. One of the new guys, Sean Ward, seems puzzled by our presence.

Xavier explains. "They're here to see Robert Johnson's grave."

"Who?" Sean asks.

"Robert Johnson," Xavier says.

"He's buried *here*?"

"Right over there," says another guy, Mark Ramsay. "Go find it."

"Thanks for letting us look," I tell them. "Is it disruptive, people coming around looking for his grave all the time?"

Xavier dismisses it. "Oh, we get it, but it doesn't disrupt anything."

"Did you know your church is on the Internet?" Xavier and his friends seem startled, so we tell them about the pictures of the church and the grave and the directions, which turned out to be pretty accurate. "So you guys having a meeting here? You the church board or something?"

"Masons' Lodge," Xavier says. "Just our weekly meeting."

The sign is gone from Three Forks country roadhouse. It's got that tan fake-brick shingle on the side, and my vandal finds a small, torn piece in the dirt in front of the porch, dusts it off and announces he's keeping it for a souvenir. The windows are boarded up, but the place has obviously been visited by blues scavengers. We look through a small opening in the boards covering the windows and imagine Robert Johnson standing on the sagging wooden floor inside, playing his guitar.

There are a lot of stories of Robert Johnson's death, but they all focus on this place. He'd been in Greenwood for a while, playing at

The Masons' Lodge of Itta Bena, Mississippi, was meeting at Payne's Chapel when we showed up to find Robert Johnson's grave site.

house parties and juke joints like Three Forks. He'd been seeing a married woman in the area, and her husband owned Three Forks. By all accounts, Johnson wouldn't have cared about that. If he wanted a woman, it didn't matter if she was married.

The last night he played here, other musicians performed as well—Honeyboy Edwards, Houston Stackhouse and Sonny Boy Williamson. Williamson remembered that during a break someone offered Johnson a drink from an open bottle. Williamson grabbed it from him and warned him never to drink from an open bottle. Johnson was furious and when offered another drink, he took it.

There was strychnine in the whiskey. He was taken to the home of a friend and survived the night, but he contracted pneumonia and died three days later. The death certificate lists "no doctor" as the cause of death. As part of the legend—the same legend about selling his soul to the devil—it's said that in his dying hours, Johnson crawled on all fours and barked like a dog in his agony.

Two miles farther down the road, another churchyard, another marker. We pull off the road in respectful silence, slowing so our tires don't spit any gravel into the yard. It's another nondescript church, like Payne's Chapel, with two bolted doors and a modest steeple. There's a miniature Washington Monument with a quote from "Me and the Devil Blues" near the top: "You may bury my body down by the highway side." His instructions were followed to the letter. The part of the monument facing the church has the photo-booth portrait of Robert Johnson, lips dripping a cigarette, and underneath his name is carved: "His music struck a chord that continues to resonate. His blues addressed generations he would never know and made poetry of his visions and fears."

There are other graves nearby. There's been a funeral earlier today—dirt still mounded, no time yet for rain to smooth the clods into mud. Silk and plastic flowers rise from the ground.

This monument in the Mount Zion churchyard was erected by Columbia Records after *The Complete Recordings of Robert Johnson* became a certified gold record in the early 1990s.

As with the Payne's Chapel site, visitors have left guitar picks and quarters on Johnson's marker. We pick up some obvious litter. I remember a song from Bob Dylan's first album, the one made when he was twenty but trying to sound older: "See That My Grave Is Kept Clean."

Across the road is a small creek and we see some fishermen on the bank about a quarter of a mile down. Highway 7 is a few feet away, but no cars pass while we wander the grave site. We don't talk, both probably listening to internal music. I'm hearing Robert Johnson murmur, "Can't you hear that wind howl?"

Again we whisper. I put my arm around Graham. "What do you think, Boy?"

He smiles. "It's beautiful, Dad. '. . . bury my body down by the highway side . . .' If he isn't here, he *should* be."

"And the creek right across the road, right out here in the middle of nowhere. Wherever he is, I hope he's resting."

Wherever he is. As a young man, he lost a wife and infant in childbirth. It was then that he lashed out at God, and the stories of deals with the devil followed. I'd visited three places today, and if he hasn't found peace, then maybe no peace is to be found.

Minority Report

Mississippi smells like barbecue everywhere we go. We stop in Belzoni for vending-machine snacks, again aware we are in the minority—no white people in the city limits other than ourselves and a police officer. People walk through the streets as if cars are merely gnatlike nuisances, incapable of causing any real harm. We're listening to Charley Patton now, whose recordings predate Robert Johnson's by a decade. It's hard, either because of technology or enunciation, to ever be truly sure of Patton's words, but just as we pull into Belzoni, we're pretty certain we've heard him sing "Belzoni" in one of his songs.

We pick up Highway 49 and head north toward Indianola. As we slow into town, it becomes Dr. Martin Luther King Jr. Drive. It's similar to Belzoni with its all-black population and the street-festival atmosphere.

"This must be some cultural thing," I tell Graham. "If this was an all-white neighborhood, I don't think we'd be seeing this. The kids would all be inside watching TV."

"Definitely, they wouldn't be into just hanging out in the street."

The area is thick wih bodies and Graham drives slowly, anticipating someone running in front of the car.

"It just seems real social, all the kids hanging out," he says.

"And the old people are sitting in chairs on porches, some of them in the street. . . ."

It's so different from what we know. As we turn down Hannah Street in Indianola, on the hunt for a club Graham wants me to see, we hear one kid yell, "Hey, look at these white boys." We suddenly feel on display.

"They're probably wondering, 'What in the hell are you doing here?'" Graham says.

It isn't just a tight community, it's a thick community. The older people sit around folding card tables in the dirt front yards, and they smile as we pass. Some of them wave. I imagine their thoughts: "So, y'all come to see some *poverty*? We *got* some poverty for your ass."

Two young couples play cards on milk crates at the curb. A kid practices his high jump, using a phone cord tied between two trees.

"It's such an odd feeling to be outnumbered," Graham says. "It makes me think how much it would suck to be black in an all-white town."

We stop to ask some kids directions to Club Ebony. They're too young to have been there, but they want to act like they know all about it. Turns out we're on the opposite end of Indianola from the club, so they have to give us pretty complicated directions, which turn out to be right on the money.

"They were pretty nice," Graham says, when we pull away.

"You didn't expect them to be?"

"No, I've just . . . I don't know, I've felt uneasy in that last town and here. I mean, thinking about what one of my ancestors must've done to one of their ancestors."

"I know, but in Mississippi, I'd be more worried about the white people than the black people."

"Nobody's messed with us wherever we've been," he says. "Everybody's been nice. Most people when they look at us, they don't give us the evil eye. They just recognize that we're out of place.

Finally we find Club Ebony and since it's Sunday, it's closed. It's a red barn with handbills taped to the walls, and a small hole in a front window. Graham wants to walk around and look at the old night spot mostly because it's where B. B. King plays his homecoming concert each year here in his hometown. As a child Riley B. King lived in Indianola before moving off to Memphis. Downtown, we find a wall-sized B. B. painted on an empty building's brick wall.

One more grave for the night. The sun's going down and it's hard to read the printout by flashlight, but Graham's pretty sure where he's going. We head west from Indianola toward Greenville, where we decide to spend the night. Just to the north of the highway is Holly Ridge. Down a county-line road we see a large, tan-colored cotton gin. Families live along this road, so we park past the homes and walk through the graveyard in the shadow of the gin. We look at the graves as we pass, reading the handmade memorials. One says, "From your kids, we love you," at a gravestone marked "L. Humphrey." The graveyard has no fence and is nearly devoured by cotton. On the east side of the cemetery, near the railroad tracks, we find the head-

Artist Lawrence Quinn created this mural for the 2000 B. B. King Homecoming in Indianola, Mississippi. It's at the corner of Front and Second streets.

stone for Charley Patton. In the middle of the cotton bolls, with the more modest graves surrounding it, the impressive monument reflects the last light of the day. It's sunset and the cotton glows in the fading light; it does not look real. Ten feet away from Patton is a recent grave.

There's money left on Patton's grave too, more for the tip cup. Wildflowers grow nearby.

"This trip's taking an odd turn," I say to Graham. "Seems that all we're doing is looking up dead people."

"No shortage of them," he says.

Robert Johnson's grandparents were slaves. Charley Patton was the son of slaves. Here we are in a field of cotton. *Is this what it was all about?* I think about a line from *Slaughterhouse-Five*, though Vonnegut was writing about a different war: *"There must be tons of human bone meal in the ground."* The year after the Civil War ended, Mississippi spent a fifth of the state's revenue on artificial limbs. Under my

We found Charley Patton's grave just before sunset. He rests in a cotton field near Holly Ridge, Mississippi.

feet is a man who was a link to that, whose voice was little more than a growl and one step removed from a field holler. From him came Robert Johnson and the others. And he's resting there in a cotton field under a sky more beautiful than any I'd ever seen. Standing there, with my son, I felt as if all of our history had converged in that place.

"It's a beautiful marker," Graham says, softly. "Did you know that John Fogerty paid for it?"

Fogerty was the leader of one of my favorite rock 'n' roll bands, Creedence Clearwater Revival. Though he was infatuated with the music of the Mississippi Delta and imitated it on his records, he had never been here until a few years before. I'd read that in *Rolling Stone*. I did not remember anything about his buying a headstone for Charley Patton's grave, but I know to never doubt my son.

"Then I guess I have another reason to like him," I say.

"He respects the people that inspire him," Graham says.

"The more you know, the more you realize you need to know," I say. "You hear Muddy Waters, then you have to go back and hear Robert Johnson. What did Clapton say? Johnson was the 'most soulful cry of the human voice'? Then you hear Robert Johnson and you have to hear Charley Patton. And before him, you had slaves singing in fields. There wasn't recorded sound." I point down at the grave. "Maybe this is where it all started, all of the music we love so much."

It's dark as we head west toward Greenville to find a place to stay.

"It sounds corny," I tell Graham, "but I feel kind of holy after being to these graves. Don't you? Do you feel sanctified?"

"I feel like I know what it's all about."

We know we sound ridiculous, so we're doing our best Indiana white-boy imitation of a gospel preacher.

But then Graham's voice is back to normal. "Wish I would have brought my guitar," he says wistfully. "I would have liked to have sat there and played a song. It probably would have gotten all warped in the heat, though."

We cross Highway 61 near Leland, finally making it to Greenville, where we cruise the streets looking for a motel. Everything Graham's read about Greenville scares him—warnings to not be on the streets at night. But as we drive around, it looks no different from any other town until we stop at a light and look down the cross street and see the fire of a crack pipe at the corner. The momentary light shows a hard face, intent on the drug.

"I don't think we're in Kansas anymore, Toto," I say.

"I don't think we ever were." He pulls away when the traffic light turns green.

Delta Morning

I wake disoriented in the Greenville Comfort Inn. *Where am I? Who am I?* Then I remember I'm on vacation and look over to see my sleeping son beside me. For a moment, I think, *I* can't *have a son. I'm too young to be a father.* Then I remember: I'm closer to fifty than forty. I have three children. This big, snoring man next to me is indeed my son.

It's almost nine, late for me to wake, but the trip has worn me out and I'm sleeping later than usual. Out the window, Greenville looks good in the sun, business day beginning and traffic heading toward downtown. One of my heroes used to walk these streets.

Hodding Carter is always a hit when I talk about him in my journalism history class. He was an Associated Press reporter back in the early 1930s when he bought a newspaper in Louisiana and crusaded against the corrupt governor, Huey Long. When a radio news bulletin flashed that a man in a white suit had shot Governor Long on the capitol steps, Betty Carter went to the closet and was relieved to find her husband's white suit still there. Assassin he was not.

Long had the last laugh. Before his death he mandated that only newspapers he approved could get the lucrative business of printing city and county government legal advertising. There was only one newspaper in Louisiana he didn't approve—Hodding Carter's.

And that's when Hodding Carter folded his newspaper and moved his family to Greenville. There was already a newspaper here, but it didn't believe in hurting people's feelings or publishing the names of young white men who committed mischief. Carter operated under different rules, and his newspaper succeeded in part because of novelty. The people wanted a newspaper that wasn't afraid to step on toes. Eventually, Carter bought out the long-standing newspaper and merged it with his own to create the *Delta Democrat Times*.

During the 1950s and 1960s, it was probably easy to write editorials for the *New York Times* decrying the evils of segregation. It was another thing to do that in the *Delta Democrat Times*. Hodding Carter's desk was in his newspaper's storefront, and opponents hurled bricks through the front window. Carter used a pistol as a paperweight. His children grew up listening to death threats on the upstairs extension phone and crawling around in the shrubs outside the house when calls about bombs seemed too real. It was hard to be a man of principle when you looked the enemy in the face every day on the streets, but Hodding Carter managed.

He campaigned for Senator Robert Kennedy in the 1968 presidential race, to show that Kennedy spoke for people everywhere. He was flying back from the California primary when the pilot announced that Kennedy had been shot, that the wound was probably fatal. In the row behind him, Carter heard a man say something like *two-down-one-to-go*. Carter, who was seventy-two and legally blind, pulled himself up from his seat on the airplane, grabbed the man by his lapels and beat the shit out of him. Four years later, Hodding Carter died.

The newspaper left the Carter family's hands years ago, no doubt another symbol of change in the New South. It was a small, family-run newspaper, but time turned it into a hot property. Now it's part of a chain and, like so many newspapers, it has lost its personality.

Driving around Greenville, stoked with coffee, we're reading signs aloud again. It's the home of Uncle Ben's rice. Chief's Sports Parlor. A sign tells us that after cotton, catfish farming is the biggest industry.

We turn off Highway 82 to Washington Street, to Main Street, trying to get to the river. Bostick Brothers advertises "Cold Beer—Restrooms—Ice."

"It doesn't get any better than that," I say. "What else would you want?"

"They could advertise women," Graham says.

We drive down toward the levee, where the Mississippi River

winds through this part of the country like interlocked fingers. You can stand on the bank in Mississippi, look across a small sliver of Arkansas and into another part of Mississippi. Peaceful now, this is where the fury of the 1927 flood was felt worst. Memphis Minnie wrote "When the Levee Breaks" about that flood, and Charley Patton, in his nearly wordless cry sang, "High Water Everywhere," in which he adopts a variety of characters and voices to tell the story of the flood. In Faulkner's "Old Man," a convict tries to save a pregnant woman from the river's fury. The high water of 1927 lingered in Mississippi's culture. Greenville was under water for seventy days.

The river started rising in late summer 1926 and was considered *in flood* for more than 150 days. Nine inches of rain fell during April 1927 and with the hard rain and melting snow feeding the Ohio and the Missouri, the water couldn't be held. The levees, which had allowed black sharecroppers to farm the reclaimed land and make a life for themselves, were strained, breaking in more than 120 places. For my generation, "When the Levee Breaks" is merely a sonic assault by Led Zeppelin. But to the people who lived here, Memphis Minnie's original warned that a way of life was ending. The flood waters covered an area larger than New England.

In the end, the flood spawned legislation to bring levees under federal control and turned management of the river over to the U.S. Army Corps of Engineers.

These levees go back further than the sharecroppers' needs. Mound-building Indians lived here in the prehistoric era. What became Greenville was the highest point of land between Memphis and Vicksburg. During the Civil War, Union troops tried to capture the town. When the townspeople put up too much of a fight, the city was burned to the ground. But as any good realtor will tell you, location is everything, so the city was rebuilt.

On Silky Sullivan's advice, we're looking for Doe's Eat Place. It's near where we saw the fire of the crack pipe the night before, and the kind of neighborhood you want to avoid after dark. But the morning is still blindingly bright, and Nelson Street isn't frightening, just some broken glass, boarded-up windows, an occasional strolling wino.

In the morning sun, the brilliance of the colors is surreal: Two girls, the oldest probably thirteen, both smoking and wearing extremely tight clothing, one of them in a hot-pink spaghetti-strap ensemble, glowing against her dark brown skin. I've been awake for hours, had three cups of coffee, but still the sunlight leaves me blinking.

There's a club Graham wanted to see and he's disappointed to find it boarded up. We're standing there when a man walks up, breaking his stride to say hello.

"That ain't open," he says. "That's 'Annie Mae's Café.' " He's talking about the old song by Little Milton. Lots of places claim to be inspiration for that song. "Outta bidness."

Graham kicks at a stone in the parking lot.

"Usually, unless they have the blues festival, don't nobody come back here." He says it without intimidation, as a gentle warning.

White blues fans used to make pilgrimages to this place, the Flowering Fountain, knowing that owner Perry Payton would look out for them, no matter how rough the neighborhood got after a few beers.

"Yeah, Perry died, passed away about a year ago."

"At least we got to see it," Graham says. The Ike and Tina Turner Revue used to play here, fifty cents at the door.

The man's name is Johnnie White and he's on his way to work. We introduce ourselves and he shakes Graham's hand with both of his. "How are you, young man?" He starts to walk off but stops and turns around. "It's for sale, if you're interested."

Doe's Eat Place is a merger of concrete block and wood frame. Part of it used to be a grocery store, part of it used to be a honky-tonk. It was started by Domenick "Doe" Signa and his wife, Mamie, and it's been the family business since 1941 with the same menu—*meat*—

though Mamie did add hot tamales in the 1950s. Although Doe and Mamie were white, the restaurant served only black diners until two decades back, when whites were finally allowed in.

The front door is open, so we walk in, marking ourselves as newbies. Regular customers enter through the kitchen.

Doe II is about my age and has been working steadily at Doe's for twenty-four years, "off and on for thirty." He had a baseball scholarship to Delta State University up the road in Cleveland. When the Major Leagues didn't require his services, he returned home to the family business. "I got a little business degree and I came back here." He nods at his uncle. "Charles's been here all his life."

He and Charles run the place with a handful of employees. "We serve big steaks and tamales," Doe says in understatement. The steaks are as big as my belly. "Our smallest steak is two pounds and they get up to four pounds. That's a T-bone." He shows me a monstrous cut of meat.

"That's your smallest steak?"

"We don't serve ribeyes or filets or anything. Daddy never has done anything like that. We tried to do it, but people just seem to know what we serve, and me and Charles end up takin' home all the damn ribeyes and eatin' them ourselves. Then we make our own tamales." He leads us through the kitchen. "That's our tamale machine right there." The kitchen has a huge oven full of spitting steaks, and seating for some special guests. The dining room seats twenty. The steaks are as thick as the Memphis phone book. The tamales are cooked in grease. Shrimp dance in a whirlpool of butter.

Walking through the kitchen, we tilt to the side. "We got to get the floor leveled off a bit," Doe says, as if it's another one of those things they've been meaning to get to for the last forty years. "We had some guys from Gallo wine here the other night. They're the ones who put on that B. B. King Blues Festival up in Indianola." He starts reeling off the list of people who come from all over the country to dine at Doe's.

At Doe's Eat Place in Greenville, Mississippi, Charles (left) and Doe Signa serve steaks as big as your head.

It hasn't exactly been franchised, but an Arkansas restaurateur who used to fly his friends over to Greenville for dinner at Doe's got the rights to the name and menu and set up shop in Little Rock back in the 1980s. It soon became a favorite hangout for Governor Bill Clinton, and for a while in the 1990s it was *the* place for the Clinton clerisy to be seen. Hunter Thompson and Jann Wenner did the *Rolling Stone* interview with Clinton at the kitchen in that other Doe's.

That's upscale Doe's. This is the original, still in a rundown part of town, and this is the real Doe.

"We got second- and third-generation diners," Doe brags. "Some of their daddies were coming here fifty years ago."

Driving into Clarksdale

The morning is still too bright on Mississippi 1 north from Greenville. We're following the river back up to Clarksdale. There are a few more things we want to see there before we get back on Highway 61 for New Orleans.

The sun casts long shadows in the rows, enhancing the symmetry of the cotton fields. We've got Robert Johnson playing again, heading toward Rosedale. Nothing's there, so far as we know, except that Robert wanted to go there to "barrelhouse on the riverside." I'd never hear his songs again with their mentions of Rosedale and Friar's Point and not feel a little more affinity for him, at least for his time and place.

The windows are down and Graham taps his hand on the car window frame in time to Johnson's knifelike guitar runs on "Up Jumped the Devil." Odd that we like this music so much—music that came from slavery, from cotton fields like this, from the poverty blurring by the windows of our Explorer. That's a world we've never known. The comedian Robert Klein used to do a routine back in the 1960s, during the so-called blues revival, about whether he, a white man, had the right to sing the blues—funny, but also a good question.

There's a difference between the blues—born from real, heart-breaking experience—and whining. There seems to be a lot of that. A credit card maxed out, an unreasonable boss, an annoying colleague—that's whining. I listen to Robert Johnson and think about the wife and child lost together. Was he nineteen then? He took an oath against God. *That's the blues.*

"Bear crossing" signs are right outside of Rosedale, along with a dozen graves by the railroad that runs by the river. We drive up on the levee, but a gate blocks our path. People wave at passersby here, and men on tractors call hello.

"I think this looks the same way it did when Robert Johnson walked through here," Graham says. "Except maybe for that Double Quick over there."

We cut over to Shelby to pick up 61 north again, so we'll drive into Clarksdale on the main road. Past the Blues City Plaza strip malls (Radio Shack, Dollar Tree, Wal-Mart), convenience stores and fast food, we come up again to the crossroads. As we idle at the light, we look over and see an Asian man in a white Ford. He's got a Guayabera shirt and a dragon tattoo on his forearm. It's eighty-five degrees, but seems much hotter.

The Blueseum, as Graham calls it, is in the old Yazoo and Mississippi Valley Railroad Depot. The restored area by the tracks has been renamed Blues Alley by the town fathers, and the address of the Delta Blues Museum is on John Lee Hooker Drive. Hooker's just one of the great musicians born here. Must be something in the water, since so much talent came from this town: Sam Cooke, Junior Parker, Ike Turner, Jackie Brenston, Son House and Sir Mack Rice (composer of "Mustang Sally").

There's an older couple visiting the museum, the only traffic on this Monday. I ask the young black girl working behind the counter if I can talk to the curator, and she makes a call and takes us upstairs to see Tony Czech. He's dressed in a Henley T-shirt and has a neatly cropped beard and a methodical Missouri twang. His office is a tribute to everything cool—Graham and I covet an autographed picture from his late friend Stevie Ray Vaughan.

Tony gets a phone call, and while he softly chats with the person on the other end, Graham whispers in my ear: "You cause a distraction for me, will you?"

"You mean, like start a fire or kill someone?"

"Exactly. I'm going to score that Stevie Ray Vaughan autographed picture."

Tony's leafing through some recent donations when we come into his office—crates of 78 rpm's. There are a lot of blues discs, but some of the recordings are by Mae West, Marilyn Monroe and Bill Haley and His Comets. There's also the whole "Who's on First?" routine by Abbott and Costello.

Tony insists on giving us a personal tour, leading us through the main exhibit hall downstairs—it used to be the waiting room of the train station—and the walls are filled with memorabilia, blown-up pictures of Muddy Waters, Robert Johnson and Charley Patton, with long, explanatory blocks of text with mini-essays on the artists. It's a lovingly crafted museum. In the middle of the room is a reconstructed log cabin.

" . . . And this is Muddy Waters's cabin," Tony says.

"We've been looking all over for that," I say. "We went down around Stovall the other night."

"The House of Blues had it out on tour for a while, raising money for the museum, but now it's here and it's gonna stay here."

Graham's on his own, wandering around looking at exhibits, but Tony and I go a little slower, lingering over artifacts. There's a case of battered guitars Graham studies while Tony and I admire the life-size wax figure of Muddy Waters. The Robert Johnson display is weathered, the signboard stained with the touch of many hands.

"Who's your typical visitor?" I ask. "I mean, it seems like the blues audience is a bunch of middle-aged white guys like us."

"My impression is that it is mainly a white population, baby boomers who know Clapton and the Stones. And now everybody has finally come to a point where they are now able to come out and see the original."

"You go to a blues concert and you don't see any black people in the audience."

Tony shrugs. "I think it's part of their heritage that they don't want to remember. It might also be that as whites accept their music, they want a separate identity. So rap is their new music."

"But even that's been appropriated by all those thirteen-year-old white kids who listen to it."

Tony gives me a *what-can-you-do* look. Whatever the case, "blues *does* sell," he says, noting that the museum brought in forty-five hundred dollars over the Memorial Day weekend. He leafs through the guest book and reads off some of the comments from the visitors. "These are the people I work for," he says.

Tony doesn't want to be stuck in the past, so he seems proudest of the museum's arts and education program. Kids from Coahoma County attend classes to learn how to sing, play guitar or harmonica, or write music. He taps on the picture of a girl in the display by the door. "This kid is great," he says. "You should've heard her when we had the kids play last week."

Tony suggests we try the place next door if we're hungry. It's a short walk down Blues Alley, but I can tell Graham is agitated about something.

"Check it out," he says, pulling a wad of tissue from his jeans pocket.

"Oh, you finally learned to blow your nose? It took me until I was twenty-six."

"No, I got the tissue in the bathroom to protect what's inside." He unfolds the wad to show me two-inch-long splinters.

"So, what the hell is that?"

"Muddy Waters's cabin," he says proudly. "One for you and one for me. I thought you'd like to have this."

Part of me is touched, but part of me is worried about being banned from Clarksdale.

Ground Zero is a restaurant and juke joint whose grand opening the week before made it into *People* magazine. One of the owners is actor Morgan Freeman, and his frequent costar Ashley Judd showed up for the first night.

"That's the story of my life," I tell Graham. "No matter where I go, I manage to just miss Ashley Judd."

Inside, the place looks like it's been in business for forty years. None of the chairs match, there are several varieties of worn table-cloths and the floor is uneven. The front door is carved and graffitied with messages like "Mothers, lock up your daughters," and both the ceiling and floor inside need tiles.

The lunch plate is meat loaf, butter beans, fried grits, cornbread and cobbler. Graham substitutes mashed potatoes for grits and says they are the best he's ever eaten. The beer, nearly frozen, lasts two gulps. A high-school-aged kid brings me another one almost imme-diately. The cook comes by the table as we're finishing the meat loaf.

"You full yet?"

"Not yet. We're still waiting on the cobbler."

He scowls, as if he has failed to satisfy us. When the cobbler comes out, there are flecks of vanilla bean in the ice cream.

Morgan Freeman lives nearby. Here's this millionaire, Oscar-nominated actor and he's living in northern Mississippi. When peo-ple ask why, he says, "Because I can live anywhere."

He has two partners—Howard Stovall, of *the* Stovalls as in Sto-vall's Plantation—and a local attorney named Bill Luckett.

Luckett, tall, near-lanky, with gray hair, is one of those guys with his hands in everything. Start talking to him and you'll realize how much he's done to bring Clarksdale back from the brink of extinction.

It's Luckett who made sure a sign went up at the crossroads—the interlocking guitars—when a PBS documentary noted that there was no monument there. It's Luckett who works on broadening the base of the blues festival and who invests in economic development.

He went to college at the University of Virginia in the 1960s, working as a house painter during the summers to pay tuition. He assumed he would stay on the East Coast after graduation and attend law school there. He probably would have spent his life and career on the East Coast, but the Vietnam War was in all of its fury, and Luckett decided a posting to a Mississippi National Guard unit was the best way to deal with his military obligation.

He's never forgotten his homecoming. "I have a vivid memory of coming down out of Memphis after my graduation from Virginia. It was different then. There were none of the casinos you see now. Highway 61 was shrouded, with an old railroad trestle bridge and dark, overhanging trees. It was gloomy, and then I hit the flatland north of Clarksdale and it was like I was coming down, out of that dark tunnel, blasting out in the sunlit Delta."

Much to his surprise, he stayed in his home state, getting a law degree at Ole Miss and returning to his hometown for private practice and, eventually, investment in a blues club. "When I grew up here, blues music was just painful wailing," he says. "You couldn't dance to it and I just didn't like it. I remember the 'other side of the tracks,' where the blues clubs used to be, it'd be wall-to-wall people on Saturday nights. Looked like Disney World to me. But my conversion took place when Howard Stovall came back to town, about ten or eleven years ago. He was the featured speaker on one of the library programs, and I went to learn for myself. He awakened me to the fact that this is truly American music, it and jazz are the only true music America has produced. Now I love it."

He also loves being part of change. Schools were segregated when he went to Clarksdale High. "I remember one particular black girl, back in tenth or eleventh grade, right when we integrated. I remember her walking up the stairwell and people spitting down on her."

Some of the racial anger is still there, he says, but it's no longer

approved. "Tolerance is the biggest change in Clarksdale." Nothing
seems to piss him off more than white northerners coming to town
and making pronouncements about the racial conditions. I'm thinking, *This dude's a mind reader.* "I can detect it with some of my son's
friends when they visit," he says. "They see our nice house and they
act like, 'Well, you're over here on this part of the town . . . and in
that other part of town. . . . So I said, 'Look, I'm going to drive you
around Clarksdale and I'll show you some nice houses, and you tell
me if a black person or a white person lives there.' When they left,
they went away thinking it isn't as bad as it was."

When Freeman, Stovall and Luckett decided they wanted to start
a blues club, they looked all around town before settling on the place
next to the Delta Blues Museum. The building had been abandoned
for thirty years. A few doors down, Freeman and Luckett have
started a gourmet restaurant named Madidi. I look over the menu
and see it's way out of our league. The Ground Zero meat loaf plate
is just fine.

It's a long process to rebuild a town and give it back its character.
Luckett's just one of several businessmen who have invested in
Clarksdale, banking on the blues-tourist dollars. "We want the
tourists to get what they come for. We're kind of saving the town."

Morgan Freeman had hired Luckett as an attorney to help him on
a home restoration project. They became friends because they have
shared interests: "Fine dining, helping people, and flat-out raising
hell," Luckett laughs.

Stayed in Mississippi a Day Too Long

Graham wants to make another stop on the Dead Bluesman Tour.
South of Clarksdale on Highway 49 is Tutweiler. In 1903, at the
railroad station there, W. C. Handy was waiting for a train when he

first heard the sound of a young man playing a bottleneck guitar and singing. The sound seduced him and he began composing blues music. More fanciful music historians suggest the guitar player at the station was Charley Patton.

The station was demolished long ago, but the foundation has been kept as a ground-level mural. When we get there, it's baking in the sun, presided over by a young kid in blue jeans, a backward Baltimore Ravens baseball cap and a nuclear-yellow T-shirt. The only picture of Charley Patton shows him glowering, wearing a suit. Maybe he would affect hip-hop style today. Our presence in town seems to interest almost everyone but this kid, who's obviously waiting at the station, but not for a train. Everywhere else we walk through the small town, we draw stares. Little children, seeing the camera around Graham's neck, want to know if he works for a newspaper.

Across from the station is a set of murals depicting blues history and offering a wall-sized map to Sonny Boy Williamson's grave, right outside of town. Sonny Boy's grave was in the cemetery next to Whitfield Church, a dilapidated, leaning structure near the highway. We've seen pictures of the church, but like the train station, only the foundation remains. We walk through the weeds and waist-high grass, amid the forgotten graves, one for a five-year-old, one family plot with headstones tipped over. Overgrown with weeds, we find the stone for Lachary Lynn Taylor, dead after one year, "our little darling" under an engraving of baby booties.

In the small, tended part of the cemetery, we find Aleck Miller, "better known as Willie 'Sonny Boy' Williamson." He grins lasciviously from the photo at the top of the marker, and rows of harmonicas, rocks and coins are lined up neatly at the base. There was another Sonny Boy Williamson before Aleck Miller, but Miller appropriated the name and made it famous. Williamson could be a mean prick and an opportunist but he was, along with Little Walter, one of the great harmonica players. In his last years, he was popular

This is all that's left of the Tutweiler train station—the floor. At this station in 1903, W. C. Handy heard a young musician playing guitar flat, scraping it with a knife blade. He said that's what inspired him to write blues music. Some people like to think the guitarist was Charley Patton.

in Great Britain, recording with Eric Clapton, Jimmy Page and other disciples. He left them with an insult. "They wanted to play the blues so bad," he said, "and they played them *so bad*." After returning from one of his European tours in 1965, he died at his home across the river in Helena, Arkansas.

Graham wants to see the Mississippi State Penitentiary, the infamous Parchman Farm. Seems you couldn't be a real Mississippi blues man without doing time in Parchman. When folklorist Alan Lomax visited the prison in 1939 for his Library of Congress project, he recorded Bukka White. Son House also served time. Lots of blues songs talk about Parchman, but the signs tell us not to stop, not to take pictures. Graham nevertheless squeezes off a few shots surreptitiously.

The cotton fields look like they've been carved by huge moles. We stop in Drew, where Charley Patton, Tommy Johnson and Willie Brown used to play on the town square for tips from farmers. Howlin' Wolf, part of a later generation, did the same. It's a flat, open, empty square—lots of space to open up the guitar case and set down the tip cup.

Next stop is Ruleville, home of Fannie Lou Hamer, the civil rights activist who shook up the 1964 Democratic convention with her efforts to unseat the all-white Mississippi delegation. It was also a hopping music town back in the 1920s and 1930s, when Howlin' Wolf used to play the streets for tips. There's no action today, other than a slim woman in a flowered print dress walking down the street, her head covered in a towel.

We turn on State Road 8 toward Highway 61 and soon come to Dockery Plantation. This is where Charley Patton lived and where scores of blues men—Willie Brown, Son House, Tommy Johnson—all played at house parties in the tenant homes. Roebuck "Pops" Staples, leader of the Staple Singers, remembers as a child growing up on Dockery, hearing Patton and Robert Johnson play at Saturday-night fish fries. Where the plantation road crosses State Highway 8, Graham tells me that's another possible site of Robert Johnson's crossroads.

We pull off on a little dirt road to take a picture of the barn with the sign on the side: DOCKERY FARMS, EST. 1895 BY WILL DOCKERY, 1865–1936, JOE RICE DOCKERY, 1906–1982. This plantation was regarded as one of the friendlier places for black people to work, since the Dockerys treated their workers with respect. The plantation fostered a blues culture that nurtured Patton and his contemporaries. Since this is where Patton played and partied and where so

Dockery Farms, near Ruleville, Mississippi, might be the birthplace of the blues. A veritable Who's Who of music worked here as farmhands by day, musicians by night.

many people learned from him, it's sometimes called the birthplace of the blues.

There's what looks like a market building right by the highway—probably a place where they used to sell produce. A hunter green Volvo is parked in front. When we get out of the car, an elderly woman—skin nearly translucent but her eyes still penetrating—emerges from the building with a watering can.

"Oh, hello," she says, surprised but polite. She's apparently used to visitors taking pictures.

We introduce ourselves and she tells us she's "the last of the Dockerys." She says, "I have three daughters, but they've all moved away." I glance at the names on the side of the barn and figure she was probably of the age to be Joe Rice Dockery's widow.

"Just trying to pretty the place up a bit," she says, watering flowers in front of the building. We ask to take her picture but she says, "Oh no, not today," adjusting her hair.

Back in the car, Graham can't believe he met a *Dockery*. Right before we get to Cleveland, we see a church sign: "Walk softly, speak tenderly, pray fervently."

"You know the song I can't get out of my mind?" I ask him. It's amazing any other song can be in my head, with the way he's blasting Led Zeppelin's "Traveling Riverside Blues." "There's this Bob Dylan song he hasn't recorded—at least he hasn't released—called 'Mississippi.' He gave it to Sheryl Crow and it goes: 'There's only one thing that I did wrong, I stayed in Mississippi a day too long.' I wish to hell I could hear him sing it."

"Do you think we've stayed too long?"

"Oh no. I think that's a line he pinched from some old prison work songs they used to sing at Parchman Farm. It's one of those recurring themes, like 'I got a bird that whistles, I got a bird that sings.' Bob takes elements of blues songs into his music. He's like a distillation of everything American, when you think about it." I sing the refrain, the only part of "Mississippi" I know. "I sure like that song."

"You think Clapton's made this trip?" Graham asks.

"I doubt it. He's a rich rock star. Can you imagine him driving around in a limo, rooting through the weeds to find Sonny Boy's grave?"

"He might. I mean, these were his heroes."

"I hate to disappoint, but I just don't see it. I'm not sure a limo could negotiate some of the corners in these small towns." I picture it for a moment. "It would be cool if he did that, though."

At Cleveland, we pick up Highway 61 again and resume our free fall to New Orleans. It's a two-lane, faded blacktop, dirt shoulders, cutting through rich, flat farmland, punctuated by small shacks.

"Jesus, Boy," I say. "There's history everywhere through here. I know it's depressing, but at the same time there's kind of a dignity. Jesus was poor. Look what that boy did. You want something done, ask a poor person."

"You think the people around here resent us . . . resent people driving through their towns, looking at them?"

"'Poverty tourists' you mean?" I watch the cotton fields blurring by. "There's something about all of this that seems a little strange. A blues museum. The Shack Up Inn—sharecropper shacks relocated and turned into a motel so middle-aged white guys can have that quintessential Depression-era Negro experience. No wonder I only see white people at blues concerts. You go to the 'blues' section of Best Buy, and they're all white guys. We've mummified the blues. It's like we've *embalmed* them."

"They haven't made it *too* touristy."

"I know it's sort of hypocritical to say that, but I can't help feeling kind of *guilty*. Think of all these white middle-aged guys springing chubbies for these blues guys. I mean, think about where the music *comes from*. It comes from oppression. And now we've enshrined poverty, charging eighty bucks a night to sleep in a sharecropper's shack. To people who grew up in poverty, isn't this some kind of insult?"

He drives silently for a while. Muddy Waters is on the CD, singing "I Can't Be Satisfied." Finally Graham says, "Maybe that's why it's so popular with us, I mean, with the white guys and all. It's an experience we never had, but it's something that made these people strong. Maybe we just envy it is all."

"I like all these people. That museum dude and all," I sigh. "I'm happy that there *is* a museum of Delta Blues but it makes me feel weird. Maybe black people turned away from the blues because it was 'music of oppression.' Maybe rap or hip-hop is music of empowerment. I hope to God that if they put me on some shrink's couch, I don't like blues because it represents oppression and *I like it*."

Town Square

Huge old plantation homes dominate the stands of trees that interrupt the massive cotton fields. When we get to Rolling Fork, we want to look around. This is where Muddy Waters was born. It's a pretty town, with a footbridge spanning a small creek.

We park on the town square in front of the Washateria and walk to a gazebo on the square. A middle-aged black man sits inside, wearing an American-flag baseball cap backward and strumming an acoustic guitar. His name is J. C. Moore and this is his hangout. He's drinking a Bud from a paper bag with a woman named Willie Mae Johnson and a white dude who introduces himself as Hotshot Jones. Hotshot has gray and dirty-blond hair, wears a black Ford racing shirt and shorts, and looks like he's gone a few weeks without bathing.

Good way to spend an afternoon—sipping on a Bud tallboy, listening to this guy play the blues.

"This is Muddy Waters's hometown, right?" I ask after we sit down. "Is there anything around here, like a memorial or something?"

"I'll play you a Muddy Waters song," J. C. says as an answer. *I'll* comes out *Awl*. He thumbs the strings and sings "Hoochie Coochie Man." Hotshot and Willie Mae sip their beers, and Graham sits next to J. C. He loves to watch musicians.

I'm the hoochie coochie man, everybody knows my name

"Everybody!" Hotshot shouts suddenly, lifting his brown bag in toast. It doesn't seem like much of a brag. It's too hot for there to be a lot of foot traffic, but everyone who passes waves hello to J. C.

A cop car cruises by, and the cop smiles at us. Brown bags don't seem to bother him.

Willie Mae teases me about how much Graham resembles me. "He got your chin," she says.

J. C. Moore holds court in the gazebo on the town square in Rolling Fork, Mississippi, birthplace of his famous brother-in-law, Muddy Waters.

"Poor kid," I say.

"He got your eyes too," J. C. says, interrupting his singing. He's moved on to another song.

"How long you been playing?" Graham asks.

"Ever since I was about seven years old," he says. "But I quit when I was fifteen. I got religion. I started back in 1980, when I was fifty-eight."

He doesn't just know Muddy Waters songs—he knew Muddy. J. C.'s sister is Muddy's widow. He begins singing "Rollin' Stone," the Muddy Waters song that inspired the name of the band and the magazine. When he finishes, he sings "Baby, Please Don't Go." He's a blues jukebox.

"You use standard tuning?" Graham asks him.

"Naw, I just tune it by ear." He takes off his guitar and hands it over. "You want to play some, young man?"

"Sure." Other than at Dave's Guitar Shop, Graham hasn't gotten to play in weeks. "I'll give you some time to drink."

"He's been dying to play," I tell J. C. "He's been driving for weeks, and he's doing the air-guitar thing the whole time."

Willie Mae giggles, still looking back and forth between Graham and me. I think she wants to pinch Graham's cheeks, she likes him so much. Graham thumbs a chord.

"That's the first lick I learned on the *git-tar* right there," Hotshot says.

Hotshot served in Vietnam ("got shot in the ass") and says the cops in another town are after him because he threw a guy through the front window of a billiard hall. The benevolent eyes of the Rolling Fork cops make him nervous.

It's steamy-hot in the world outside the gazebo, but the shade and the beer keep us cool.

J. C. and Graham talk music, and Hotshot tells me about his jail stays. He's avoiding a girlfriend today. He raided her wallet, and she didn't find it a bit damn funny. Willie Mae finds this—and just about everything else—hilarious. Graham starts to give the guitar back and J. C. protests, "Go *on*, you got some good chords. Keep playing." Graham's face glows.

When it's time to get back on the road, Graham passes the guitar back, and J. C. tells him, "You play real good," and they shake hands. I shake Willie Mae's hand and tell Hotshot, "Good luck with your legal troubles."

J. C. stands to see us out of the gazebo. "And when y'all come back through here, look for me."

Back on 61, we skirt the edge of the Delta National Forest. Around Egremont, the wire sculptures of dinosaurs by Wesley Bobo still stand, although he's moved up to Tunica. I'd like to introduce him to Gerry Loh, that Minnesota roadside sculptor. Farther south in Onward is the site of Theodore Roosevelt's famous 1902 bear hunt. Members of the presidential hunting party tracked a black bear and tied it to a tree, then summoned the president so that he could shoot it. Roosevelt refused and asked the bear be let go. A Brooklyn shopkeeper read the story of the bear's reprieve, and his wife made two stuffed bears. They were sold as "Teddy's Bears," with the president's permission.

We find the river again at Vicksburg, site of the horrific 1863 siege, during which Union General Ulysses Grant starved the Confederate garrison—and the town—into submission.

Sixty-one crosses the Natchez Trace Parkway, a self-consciously pretty highway lovingly maintained and free of the rusting cars, gutted shacks and dilapidated billboards on our route. That road doesn't have businesses hawking "live nude girls" next to a place for "spiritual advising."

The sun is going down when we reach Natchez, the farthest west we've been. We pull off to the side of the road, just to watch the sun glide into the horizon, turning leaves ahead of us into yellow spectacles, and the ones beside the highway a deeper, more majestic green. It's so beautiful, Graham nearly hyperventilates.

"My God," he says. "Look at how the sun draws stripes across the sky." The rays arch above us.

"You know in Key West, it's a big social thing," I say. "Everyone gathers, all the tourists and locals, to watch the sunset. But I don't think they get a better one than this."

It's dark and we hurry to New Orleans. We're staying at a friend's, and we don't want our hostess to stay up too late.

The sunset is beautiful, but also grandly depressing. Our trip is ending.

We cross into Louisiana and the road is desolate. I have the feeling it's sloping down, as if we're coming out of the mountains.

A Door in the Heart

The Sonic Drive-In in Baton Rouge is generous: eight cherries in a cherry limeade. Over burgers, we decide to cheat and take the interstate into New Orleans and then come back to Baton Rouge in a day to enjoy Highway 61 in the sunshine. The last leg of the trip goes fast, but it's still nearly midnight when we find our bed for the night in New Orleans.

Sherry Alexander was one of the women who looked after me when I moved to Florida as a newly divorced "orphan." Sherry was my age, a Ph.D. student and a single mother of two children. She made sure I was fed and that I had a place to do laundry. I hadn't lost touch with Sherry, but we wrote e-mails or talked rarely. She was hired at Loyola University and loved to play hostess in New Orleans. Still, it seemed kind of a stretch for me to call her and ask if she could put us up, but she graciously offered her couches.

It's late and Sherry has to teach a class tomorrow, but she wants to show us as much of New Orleans as we can manage. She sets us up in the living room and warns us that her daughter, Alexandra, is out on

a date—I marvel at the fact that when I last saw her she was four—
and Graham and I soon fall asleep. We wake when a young woman
lets herself in. You see time passing faster when it's through encounters a decade apart. I smile, murmur hello to the little girl who
doesn't remember me, and fall back asleep.

Almost home. New Orleans is close enough to Gainesville for a long
weekend. It's a seven-hour drive, no challenge for a road warrior such
as myself. I brought the kids here on that long-way-around trip back
to Indiana one summer. We'd stayed with friends in Pensacola, spent
the day in New Orleans and got far enough north in Mississippi to
visit McComb, birthplace of Bo Diddley. The kids loved Jackson
Square, with the artists and the mimes, the shrimp po' boys sold on
the street and the old-world mystique.

I'd brought Graham and Mary with me two summers before when
I went there for a convention. There was a mixup with the reserva-
tions, so we ended up in the penthouse at Le Meridien, with a 180-
degree view of the city and thirty-foot ceilings. We invited more
former graduate students, now professors elsewhere, to our room for
a party, mostly to show it off. We stocked the bathtub upstairs (the
bed and bath were in a loft) with beer. Mary disapproves of drinking,
but she enjoyed playing host, running up to the guests as soon as they
came in the room, her hands clasped: "Would you like import or
domestic?"

I'd been to New Orleans just six months before. This is the place
where I asked Nicole to marry me. Florida was playing in the Sugar
Bowl, so I booked us a place—a romantic bed-and-breakfast—over
the Internet. But when we saw the hotel, it was horrifyingly dirty.
Nicole said she couldn't spend the night in a place like that. So
there we were, New Year's Eve in New Orleans, nowhere to stay. I
figured I'd have to wait to pull the engagement ring out of my
pocket. But then we lucked into a suite at a good hotel and spent
New Year's Eve in the French Quarter. At midnight, I slipped the

diamond ring on her finger and demanded, "Marry me. That's not a question." For a moment, Nicole stared at the ring on her finger as she was jostled and pushed by the French Quarter crowd. "Yes, I will marry you," she said. After we kissed, she thrust her finger into the air and screamed, "I just got engaged!" Standing in front of Preservation Hall, we were hugged and congratulated by drunken strangers. That is the essence of New Orleans—in the right mood, you'll accept a hug from people you normally wouldn't let touch you.

Graham's exhausted and it's hard to wake him. Sherry's gone, but she's left a note saying she wants to show us some of the town in the afternoon. When she finally returns from work, she and Alexandra walk us to Frankie and Johnny's for some crawfish, shrimp étouffée and beer. She's determined to show us a good time, but with our general fatigue and the filling meal, we're on the verge of a food coma. Afterward, Sherry wants us to see more of the neighborhood. She even tracks down a mule-drawn taffy wagon.

"Is there that much demand for taffy?" I ask.

"Well, no," Sherry says, "but isn't it cool that we have a taffy wagon?"

Since she's lived here for a decade and I've only been a visitor, she insists we pile into her Honda for a quick tour of Uptown and the Garden District. The big meal and her driving (she favors the lurching approach) fatigue us. We drive by Commander's Palace, one of my favorite restaurants in the world. Nicole and I had our post-engagement dinner there a few months before. I promise Graham to take him there sometime, when the ship comes in. He's more interested in the above-ground cemetery across the street.

"The story is," tour-guide Sherry begins, "that after one rainy season, some of the bodies came through the outside wall of the cemetery, where they were interred. And the people eating in the restaurant saw it happening."

"I guess the dead have no privacy in New Orleans," I say.

We go by Loyola and Tulane and Harry Connick Jr.'s home and Anne Rice's home, but when we show little enthusiasm, Sherry decides to take us back to her place.

"We must be grave disappointments to you," I say. "I think we have that end-of-the-trip lethargy."

"There's *so much* to see here, though," she says. "You really need to see a lot of *stuff* here."

Back at Sherry's, Graham looks a little sick, so he lies down for a while, and Sherry and I talk about old friends and our families and how watching children grow up—especially other people's children—makes us feel old. I tell her about what Tom Wolfe had said during his week on campus the year before. We went out to dinner his last night and talked about our kids. His are roughly the same age as mine. He waited until he was nearly fifty to marry, and fatherhood followed soon after.

"So we're getting sentimental," I say, "and I say something like how I didn't really know what love *is*, didn't understand its profound *depth*, until I had children. And he said—there were nearly tears in his eyes—he said that he had gotten married late and so had come late to fatherhood. He said, 'And I think, "My God, I could have *missed this*." They opened up a door in my heart that I didn't even know was there.' "

I hear Graham, his back to us, softly breathing on the couch across the room.

Miss Iler

Sherry tries to rile us to action again so I offer to buy her dinner in the French Quarter ("You know, locals never come here," she says). We have ribs at Silky O'Sullivan's and they're good but missing the wallop of the Memphis counterpart. This place is morguelike compared to Memphis, but maybe it's the absence of goats and the metabolically challenged proprietor. I ask Graham the best meal he's had on the trip.

He wipes off barbecue sauce and says, "They were all good. I can't think of a bad one. The ribs at Silky's, the other one, they were probably best. Then there's Blueberry Hill."

"Best place we stayed? Motels, I mean, not friends' houses, because Sherry's would win that competition."

She smiles and rolls her eyes, "Yeah, right."

"Maybe that funky place in Minnesota. It was sketchy, but that was part of the charm. My overall favorite might be the place in Canada."

"OK, best day?"

He smiles. "They were all good. If I had to choose, maybe that day in Mississippi when we stood over Robert Johnson and Charley Patton."

We walk around the Quarter, but it's surprisingly quiet and we're so exhausted, we just want to go home—all the way home.

The next morning we're ready to leave but Sherry insists we wait around until after her class. She wants to take us to a good-bye lunch at the Café Atchafalaya, run by her friend Iler Pope. When we find out she grew up in Drew, Mississippi, we're interested.

The café is a block south of Magazine Street in the Garden District. Miss Iler is what you might call a Southern whiskey woman, eyes in a fixed squint from fifty years of cigarette smoke, voice mellowed in aging barrels. She has a full house for lunch, but she sits with us when she isn't tending other tables.

"You went through *Drew*?" she asks, her eyes widening. "Well, honey, you *did* tour Mississippi."

"Yes, we took a lot of sidetrips off 61."

"Parchman, the state penitentiary, is about three miles." She's doing inventory in her head. "Did you go to Clarksdale?" Her eyes grow larger until I answer. "See, when I was a young woman growing up in the Delta, you could go down these bumpy roads to these old houses and they would be having alcohol and *muuusic* . . . the best music you've ever heard. And it was just there, down that country road. You'd turn to the left and turn to the right and all of a sudden it was sitting there, all the lights turned on—they always had *lights*—and we'd hear some music, *my God*, we'd hear some music."

"We went down some beautiful roads in Mississippi," I say.

"Mississippi? Don't get me started."

"They welcomed you? At those house parties?"

"They were as nice as they could possibly be. I never even thought that they wouldn't be. Conversely, it would not happen in reverse. Had they come to one of our clubs, they would not have been let in. That's just the way it was. I wouldn't likely do it today because they'd likely take me out and beat my ass."

For a moment, she's lost in memories of growing up. "And then we used to go up to Memphis? To a place called the Plantation Inn?"

I'd heard of it, of course. "They would have Bo Diddley and Little Richard. And they would play all night, and I mean *all night*. Then we had to drive back to make it to Sunday School. When we were in summer school, we'd sit there wearing our sunglasses, sleeping, after a night up in Memphis."

She looks around the restaurant. "Mercy, we're gettin' *buuuusy*. Let me check on things."

Our fried green tomato BLTs arrive, and when she gets back, they're half gone. "Glad you like the food," she says dryly. "I came up with that idea in the grocery store the other day. I got in line, about four buggies, five buggies back, and I hate to wait and my *muuther* always said when you have to wait, you should use your time productively. And I thought the café needed some special, and this come in my head. And we have sold the living *hell* out of them."

"How long ago did you move from Mississippi?" I ask.

"This year, in August, it'll be thirty-five years," she says, slowly, then her face slips into mock horror. "My chile's going to be forty in August! God sakes America, I don't know how that happened. I just turned around and he's forty years old."

I point at Graham. "He was four years old last time I saw him."

"My chile's come home for a *viiisit,*" she says, "and I go in to get him up this morning . . . and there's this *man* in his bed. I just love him though. You know, he's so seldom home, and I'm mad at him right now because I called him not long ago at *work?* And he has his own damn office, his own *firm.* And I'm just chatting away and he says, 'Mother, my bill time is between two hundred and fifty and three hundred dollars an hour. What is it that I can do for you?' And I said, 'You can kiss my *ass!*' He knows he's really bad, because I am the only mother he's ever likely to have."

Where the Highway Ends

When Graham's ready, we hit the road, to get back to Baton Rouge and take Highway 61 down into New Orleans. We pick up some convenience-store coffee and take the interstate north. It's a dull drive and we're tired, and I'm struck by the artificial nature of this exercise—it's not organic free-spirit just-let-it-happen traveling. It's like reality-TV recreating the experience.

Still, we're enjoying the time together, and when the coffee kicks in and we start the drive back on 61, we begin to see that the road has lost some of its flavor here, near the end. It's just an ordinary road.

"I used to think that when I died I wanted my ashes scattered over the Ohio River," I tell him when we cross the Mississippi. "But Indiana doesn't feel like home anymore. It's just a place I visit."

"Scatter them at the Temperance River," he says.

"That's a beautiful spot. Maybe we'll scatter my ashes in the Keys."

"Bahia Honda," he says. "That's the most beautiful place I've ever seen. Scatter me there too."

———

Leaving Baton Rouge, heading south toward New Orleans, Highway 61 is called Airline Highway and it's a lifeless road, bumper-to- bumper. For the first time, we hate Highway 61. It takes us four light changes to get through the intersection of 61 and Siegen Lane. This is a horrible, boring drive and Highway 61, with its grand trajectory through the country and history, deserves better. We're indignant until we see Southpoint Volkswagen alongside the road, and fists start flying. Not many slugbugs in Mississippi, but when they're lined up like M&M candies in the parking lot, they're hard to resist. Graham slugs me fourteen times, winning this match.

South of town, Highway 61 runs through swampland between the cities. Big bags of garbage float in standing water on the shoulder. Graham stops to take pictures of rusting, decaying cars on the side of the road. He walks along the banks of a mucky pond, looking for turtles. When he was four, he and Sarah caught a couple of turtles at the creek near our house in Oklahoma. "I'm going to call my turtle 'Speedy,'" Sarah announced. "I will call mine 'Fasty,'" Graham replied.

It's humid and sticky through here, and the suffocating air makes me miss the chill of northern Minnesota.

We stop at Stump's Shell near Gramercy, home of a mutt named Spot. He used to run the highway, so Sherry Brown, one of the clerks, adopted him for the station. He sleeps in the garage overnight.

Graham takes Spot's picture, and when the shutter clicks, the dog flinches and runs back into the darkness of the garage.

"Kind of a strange reaction," Graham says.

"Makes me wonder what happened to him in an earlier life," I say.

Back on the road, we're nearing the sprawl of New Orleans.

"I'm getting kind of depressed," I tell Graham. "The highway is dying, and it deserves a grand death. I'm afraid we're going to come up to a T-Bone and there will be a sign that says 61 END."

The road has turned into a stop-and-go string of convenience stores and bars, faded-cranberry-colored motels and odd combination businesses—one place advertises 'seafood and haircuts.' To restore some majesty, we put on *Highway 61 Revisited*. Like a gunshot, "Like a Rolling Stone" begins, and despite ninety-five-degree heat we roll down the windows to share the song with the New Orleans suburb of Kenner. People on the streets don't seem to care. The last miles of the highway are the hardest. We plod through Metairie, through warehouses and abandoned buildings; a partly pink adobe grocery, looking like a miniature Alamo; the Tulane University Medical Center. Finally, the road crosses Interstate 10 near the Superdome and turns toward the French Quarter.

Highway 61 ends without fanfare. There's no sign. The road slips anonymously into the city near Rampart Street. A few blocks away is a night club called the Funky Butt. Standing in front of that place nearly a century ago, Louis Armstrong first heard the sound of a cornet and decided he wanted to make that sound too.

"It ended the way it began," I say. "Out of nowhere we saw that Highway 61 sign in Canada. All of a sudden we *don't* see one here."

"It whimpers away," Graham says. As if on cue, Bob begins singing "Highway 61 Revisited."

We walk around the French Quarter before leaving town. It's early afternoon, and the discarded cups and smells of the night before are still on the street. We get a coffee at Café Du Monde and sit on a bench on Jackson Square. When we walk to Preservation Hall, I ask Graham to take a picture.

"This is where I asked Nicole to marry me."

"Let's preserve it for all time," he says. "You getting excited?"

"Yes. Falling in love with her is the smartest thing I've ever done."

A bald black man with a beard comes up and says, "May I borrow seventy-two cents?"

Graham gives him a dollar and I give him seventy-five cents, and

Through the bug-spattered windshield, we saw Highway 61 reach its ignoble end. It disappears anonymously into the French Quarter.

the man becomes agitated. "Help me out," he says, "help me out now," and he hops on one foot, coaxing us to find more change in our pockets. Suddenly, he yells, "I'm gay! Marvin Gaye!" and walks off singing "What's Going On."

It's early afternoon, and the characters of New Orleans are starting to show up for work. At the corner of St. Ann and Decatur, we find a couple of tap-dancing kids in large, economy-size running shoes. *Keep on working, kids*, I think, *this is how Louis Armstrong got started.* I doubt he wore Reeboks, though.

This corner is where we saw the mime when Graham and Mary and I were here two years ago.

Mimes don't talk, but rules are different in New Orleans. He was a middle-aged black man painted gold, and at first he did the usual routine of sneaking up on Mary, an easy mark for being surprised. He continued with his act, but then suddenly spoke.

"Do you belong to him?" he asked Mary, cocking his head toward me.

"You're not supposed to talk," I said.

"Get over it," the mime said.

"He's my dad," Mary said.

"Mine, too," said Graham.

"Well, take care of him," the mime said. "I had a father too but he died. You never know when you might lose your father. You should cherish him."

"We will," Graham said.

"Now, a tip would be nice," the mime said to me, sticking out his hand. I pulled some crumpled bills from my pocket. When I gave them to the mime, I saw that he was crying.

It's a long, boring interstate drive back to Gainesville. Lots of things await—packing and moving to a new house, marriage and a merger of families. After six thousand miles on the road, going home seems like the greatest adventure.

High Water Everywhere

The Key West wedding was spectacular, and Nicole was a beautiful bride. The new family was photographed at sunset on the Casa Marina beach. My new daughter Savannah was flower girl, Sarah and Mary were bridesmaids and Graham, of course, was best man. The summer ended and Graham went back to school at Indiana University.

Bob Dylan released his album *Love and Theft* on September 11. I planned to buy it the day it came out, but like millions of people that night, I reached out to family. Nicole, Savannah and Sarah and I watched the horrible news together and called Mary back in Indiana. But I couldn't find Graham. When I finally got him the next day, he told me he'd spent the night at a friend's house, watching the news like the rest of us.

I turned forty-seven that weekend but did not want to celebrate. Then Nicole gave me a present: I was going to be a father again. It was a *life-goes-on* moment.

Love and Theft is Bob Dylan's history of American music, all sung in that broken-speaker voice of his, ragged and magnificent. It's a mixture of styles—country blues, rock 'n' roll, even something that sounds like a show tune. There's a song based on Charley Patton's "High Water Everywhere," and Dylan finally recorded "Mississippi," the tune that had haunted me. Bob's version is mournful and melancholy, and whenever I hear the opening rippling of the guitar strings, I remember Mississippi, with Graham beside me in the car. The music and the trip and the tragedy all merged in my mind, and it was impossible to separate them.

A few months later, we found out our baby was a boy, due on Bob Dylan's birthday, May 24. Graham was finally going to have a brother.

When we talked, Graham and I always went back to the trip, laughing at some small moment—about Silky or the weird guy at the Broadway Oyster Bar—or remembering the beautiful Temperance River or the limitless cotton fields. We'd seen so much of the ridiculous and glorious country together that we were still overwhelmed. I asked him to write something about our trip, so he'd never forget. A few days later, he sent me this note:

Wanting to leave my draining, cumbersome town. Fourteen years had been enough. The second we left the city limits I could breathe a little deeper.

Moose, bear, the bucolic country-side—movement, serenity . . . Canada.

The northlands—10,000 lakes, my favorite time of year and the best time to be here. The strange feeling of standing in the front yard of the greatest songwriter ever, feeling his words seeping into me.

The idea of not knowing where we were going to be the next day felt strangely comforting. Exploration: my god, the Temperance River is breathtaking and to think we would have missed it if we didn't have to take a piss, thanks to our inherited small bladders.

Hours of talking and recording conversations with my father—how strange to find out things about each other for the first time while speaking into a tape recorder, now being able to preserve those memories.

Going from the white northern 'eh's *and* what are you talking a-boots? *to the undecipherable southern slang of David Bill Bird the First and the drawl of the enormous and enormously cool Silky Sullivan. Two days before my birthday in a bar in St. Louis, meeting and watching the king of surf guitar wail as he walks through a White Castle drive-thru. By chance, being in Memphis on my birthday (again serendipity), walking on Beale Street. Mmmm . . . the Gibson factory. . . .*

Completely shocked at how segregated this country still is. Going through Minnesota, Iowa, and Wisconsin one week and rural Mississippi the next. My god, doesn't Mississippi give any money to these communities?

The only white people in miles, one of them me, the other my dad, strange to be a minority. . . .

Blake, rural Mississippi, brown bagged 40's and stealing road signs, going down a dirt highway blasting Son House and Muddy Waters—does it get any better?

Haunting to see the endless cotton fields. If you squint you can still see the souls of the oppressed people in the fields against the rust colored sky, and hear the bottleneck slide against the nickel strings of a guitar as a man's soul is played out on a six-string Stella. If it weren't for the telephone lines you would think that we had entered a time warp.

An indescribable, eerie, yet wonderful feeling standing six feet above the greatest bluesman and the forefathers of rock and roll. It was humbling.

Exhausted and weary we rode into one of the greatest cities in the world, New Orleans, the end of the line. I had aged a year in those 6,000 miles, learning much about this mysterious country, myself and my father.

Maria Roling, our bartender at Paul's Tavern in Dubuque, gave birth to a baby boy in August 2001. She named him Jake.

Hibbing High School held its annual all-class reunion in July 2001. The oldest graduates to attend were from the class of 1937. Bob Dylan, class of 1959, did not attend; he was on tour in Scandinavia.

In May 2002, after a decade of hosting "Bob's Birthday Bash" every May 24, Zimmy's restaurant in Hibbing was able to rally enough community support from the Hibbing town fathers to stage the first of what supporters hope will be an annual week-long celebration called "Dylan Days."

The Soulsville U.S.A. project was completed, and the Stax Museum of American Soul Music opened to the public.

Silky Sullivan ran for the United States Congress in Louisiana's Second Congressional District. "There's no backbone in Washington, so I'll bring the ribs," he said in announcing his bid. He had no quibble with the incumbent, a Democrat. "If people are happy with what he's doing, vote for him," Silky said. "But if you want change, give me one year. I'll go up there with empty suitcases, but when I come back they'll be full of money for people in the French Quarter." Silky finished third in a field of five on Election Day 2002, winning 11 percent of the vote.

Robert Johnson's grave in the Little Zion churchyard is no longer unmarked. A monument was erected, but the inscription makes no reference to the blues.

Nicole didn't last until Bob Dylan's birthday. Graham's little brother, Jackson Daniel Dylan McKeen, was born May 21, 2002.